Rock Your World

A 365-Day Christian Devotional for
Young People

by

Bill and Debbie Scott

New Canaan Publishing Company Inc.
New Canaan, Connecticut, U.S.A.

10 9 8 7 6 5 4 3 2

ISBN 1-889658-20-0

Library of Congress Cataloging-in-Publication Data

Scott, Bill, 1963-
    Rock your world : a 365-day Christian devotional for young people / by Bill and Debbie Scott.
        p.cm.
    ISBN 1-889658-20-0 (trade paper)
        1. Young people--Prayer-books and devotions--English.
    2. Devotional calendars. I. Scott, Debbie, 1958- II. Title.

BV4850 .S34 2000
242'.63--dc21   00-030511

Printed in the United States of America by New Canaan Publishing Company Inc. (www. newcanaanpublishing.com)

Rock Your World

January 1

This book of the law shall not depart from your mouth, but you shall meditate on it day and night, so that you may be careful to do according to all that is written in it; for then you will make your way prosperous, and then you will have success. (Joshua 1:8)

Have you ever watched TV late at night? I mean *really* late, after midnight, in the early hours of the morning? If so, you've seen shows and infomercials featuring people who are trying to sell you success through their books, videos, or seminars.

It amazes me that thousands of people, including Christians, will buy this information and spend good money to do so, but won't take time to read what the Bible has to say about success—for free. I'm sure there are a lot of good and helpful books out there, but *nothing* tops the Bible. Everything you need to know about success in life is right there, but far too seldom do we turn to it for advice. If you will take time to read God's Word on a daily basis, really study it and memorize it, you *will* be successful in the things that really matter.

I encourage you during this next year to have regular devotions and make it a habit to study God's Word. If you are pressed for time, take this book with you each day and read it on the bus, in the car, at lunch—but make the time to hang with God.

Dear God,

In Your Word is life. Give me the desire more and more to read and study the Bible. Grant me understanding as I read it, and help me to apply all that I read to my life. In Jesus' Name,
Amen.

January 2

Come now, you who say, "Today or tomorrow we will go to such and such a city, and spend a year there and engage in business and make a profit." Yet you do not know what your life will be like tomorrow. You are just a vapor that appears for a little while and then vanishes away. Instead, you ought to say, "If the Lord wills, we will live and also do this or that." (James 4:13-15)

This time of year makes people think about New Year's resolutions: new habits, new relationships, new beginnings. Setting goals for ourselves is a good thing, but first we need to go to God in prayer, and ask that we might act according to His will. Remember, His will is done no matter what; if we keep this in mind and rejoice in it instead of struggling against it, we will save ourselves a lot of frustration.

This year, make your resolutions Christ-centered, prayerful ones, and you're bound to succeed.

Heavenly Father,
I come to this New Year believing that You will stay and guide me. Help me in the coming days to see the new opportunities You have for my faith and my life. Change my old futile habits into new ones that please Your will. In Jesus' Name,
Amen.

January 3

Consider it all joy, my brethren, when you encounter various trials, knowing that the testing of your faith produces endurance. And let endurance have its perfect result, so that you may be perfect and complete, lacking in nothing. (James 1:2-4)

As Christians, we are going to face many tests in our life. What separates us from others is that we can use the strength of God to face these tests. During times of challenge in our life, we are forced to see what kind of faith we really have in God. God can even use the challenges to increase our faith in Him. When we see God come to our aid, it gives us confidence in Him; it increases our level of faith.

We have a saying in our home, and it is simply this...*we don't do panic!* The reason we don't do panic is because we believe God will meet our needs, even when tests and challenges come at us from all sides. I would encourage you not to panic at whatever you are going through; instead, believe that God is big enough to meet your needs, even if your problems seem overwhelming. Remember, when you're under pressure, God is on your side, and you don't do panic!

Extra time in the Word
If you're looking for a really cool book to read in the Bible and one that is very practical, try reading the book of James.

Dear Lord,
Thank You for meeting all my needs, even those I don't know about. Help me not to panic in times of trouble, but to put my faith entirely in You. In Jesus' Name,
Amen.

January 4

Therefore there is now no condemnation for those who are in Christ Jesus. (Romans 8:1)

Have you ever been plagued by guilt? Haunted by memories of something you did that now you're ashamed of? I believe Satan puts these thoughts in our heads to make us feel rotten, unworthy of God's love. Next time Satan reminds you of your past, remind him of his future, and stand confidently on this powerful promise from God's Word.

Isn't it good to be free in Jesus? Make sure you share this

verse with at least one person today. It could make a big difference in someone's life!

Dear Redeemer,
Thank You for setting me free from sin and releasing me from the power of death and the devil. Help me to look not at my past or my sinful self, but only to You. In Jesus' Name, **Amen.**

January 5

and in Him you have been made complete, and He is the head over all rule and authority... (Colossians 2:10)

This short but very powerful verse is something we all need to be reminded of. So often we think, "If I could just get that special car, dress, shoes, CD, game...then everything would be great and everybody would think that I'm cool." People look for their completeness in things or achievements or relationships, but this verse says it all. Maybe you should take an honest inventory of where you're looking for completeness. Remember—true fulness is in Christ alone.

Dear Lord, Giver of all things,
Please help me not to be greedy or materialistic, mistaking my "wants" for my "needs." Thank You for the fulness I have in You. In Jesus' Name,
Amen.

January 6

Therefore, confess your sins to one another, and pray for one another so that you may be healed. The effective prayer of a righteous man can accomplish much. (James 5:16)

Everyone, including me, has struggles from time to time, and we all need our brothers and sisters in Christ to pray for us. We may think, "I can't tell anyone I'm struggling with *this* in my life; what would they think of me?" And so we carry around these heavy problems alone.

God gave us Christian friends so we can share our burdens with one another. We are each others' support group! The next time you find yourself with a problem, reach out to your Christian friends, and ask them to pray for you. There is strength in numbers.

Almighty God,
Thank you for the fellowship of the Christian brothers and sisters you have placed all around me. Help me to confess my need of others, and to receive their support and prayers with gratitude. In Jesus' Name,
Amen.

January 7

I will give thanks to You, for I am fearfully and wonderfully made; wonderful are Your works, And my soul knows it very well. (Psalms 139:14)

Ever think, *if only I were just a little taller, better at sports, had brown hair, a smaller nose, bigger muscles*...the list goes on. I'm sure most of us have had such thoughts. If you've ever judged someone else by the way they look, then you'd better read and re-read this scripture. And you'd better plan on taking up your complaints with God! After all, we were all made in His image.

Next time you are tempted to find fault with looks—yours or someone else's—do what the Word says. Praise God for being fearfully and wonderfully made.

Dear Lord God,
Please help me not to be judgmental about appearances; we are all Your glorious and wonderful creation. Thank you for all that You have made, including me. In Jesus' Name,
Amen.

January 8

...His divine power has granted to us everything pertaining to life and godliness, through the true knowledge of Him who called us by His own glory and excellence. For by these He has granted to us His precious and magnificent promises, so that by them you may become partakers of the divine nature, having escaped the corruption that is in the world by lust. (2 Peter 1:3-4)

Temptation is something we all face, and sometimes it seems so hard to stay on the right track. When you're tempted to do something wrong, study this passage of scripture. It tells us that we have everything we need to live a life that pleases God. All the other things we think we need in our lives pale in comparison to what we already have in Christ. Pray for strength to overcome temptation, and offer thanks to God for "His very great and precious promises."

Eternal God,
Help me to defeat temptation and obey Your divine will. Thank You for the victory wrought for us at the Cross. Through Jesus' victory, change us more and more into Your likeness, to share in Your divine nature. In Jesus' Name,
Amen.

January 9

For the eyes of the LORD move to and fro throughout the earth that He may strongly support those whose heart is completely His. (2 Chronicles 16:9)

God wants to help His children. The Bible says, "The eyes of the LORD range throughout the earth," and He's looking for people who are loyal to Him. That doesn't mean perfect people who don't make mistakes. Being loyal means praying and seeking Him daily. You might say, "I'm so busy; I don't have time to spend with God," but how badly do you want God's power in your life? Do you want to come out of the troubles you're facing? Remember, God wants to give you His strength and wisdom. Take time today to see what answers God has for your life.

Lord Almighty, *Strong to Save,*
Grant that I might show my love to You whom I truly love. Thank You for all that you provide me. Help me to love You above everyone and everything else. In Jesus' Name,
Amen.

January 10

For the LORD gives wisdom; from His mouth come knowledge and understanding. (Proverbs 2:6)

In our search for wisdom, we go to seminars, read self-help books, maybe even watch daytime talk shows. But the Bible is where the answers are! Wisdom comes from God; God speaks to us through the Bible. It isn't a big mystery at all.

Don't waste time looking in other places; go to the real source: God, and His Word!

Dear Lord,
Amidst all the words that I will hear today, I give You thanks for Your Holy Scripture. Help me to hear and learn gladly of that Word, which is alone Truth and Life. In Jesus' Name,
Amen.

January 11

For sin shall not be master over you, for you are not under law but under grace. (Romans 6:14)

"You are not under law, but under grace" does not mean that you can sin as much as you want and depend on "grace" to get you out of trouble! Rather, it means that when we do fall, we can have forgiveness through Christ. All you have to do is repent, confess your sin to God (even though He already knows about it), ask for forgiveness, and turn away from the sin.

God promises a way of escape so that sin is not our master. Though Satan will lie to you, cheat you, trick you, and deceive you, remember this: God always tells you the truth, and the truth will set you free. Satan cannot *make* you do anything. He doesn't have the power. You make the choice whether to fall for his lies or to command him to leave you! Sin always pays off with death, but God's gift is eternal life. Next time you are tempted, ask God to show you the way of escape. It works every time.

Gracious God,

Deliver me from all things in this life that will keep me from You, and from whatever will imprison me and lie to me. Forgive the sins that I have committed this day. Set me free in the name of Your beloved Son Jesus Christ, that I may truly be free. In Jesus' Name,
Amen.

January 12

Answer me when I call, O God of my righteousness! You have relieved me in my distress; Be gracious to me and hear my prayer. (Psalms 4:1)

Have you ever found yourself in some kind of trouble, where everything you try to correct it only seems to make it worse? If only we would go to God first, and talk to Him about our troubles. He is waiting patiently for us to come to Him, and He has all the answers for life's situations.

Did you know that God even cares about the small things? While getting ready for church one day, I found myself missing one shoe. I looked and looked. I ended up tearing the house apart, but I still couldn't find that shoe! Exasperated, I finally called out, "Lord, show me where the shoe is!" Within a couple of minutes, I found it. This may be an amusing example, but it helps to make the point. Slow down, think, talk to Him *first*, rather than as a last resort. You'll find you'll save yourself a lot of time and frustration. When in need, small or big, take it to God!

Lord of all creation, even of all the small things,
You care enough even to know the number of hairs on my head. Grant that I may talk with you daily just as if I am talking to a friend, face to face. In Jesus' Name,
Amen.

January 13

But I say to you, love your enemies and pray for those who persecute you...(Matthew 5:44)

OK, this is some cruel joke, right? I'm supposed not only to love my enemies, but to pray for them as well!? No, you didn't find the first mistake in the Bible. This verse is probably one of the most difficult ones to fulfill, because we have the natural desire to lash out and get even with a person or people causing us pain. We want to knock them back to next week!

This kind of response is the way the world acts, but to do what God commands requires the Holy Spirit. To react in the way of the world would be so easy, so tempting...and so against God's command. If you really want people to see that you're different, and to let your light shine for Jesus, try this Scripture. Can you think of someone who has hurt you? Do something nice for them today, and pray that God would do a great work in his or her life. God will give you the strength to apply this verse in your life.

Almighty Lord,
Save me from my enemies, from all those who would try to harm me. Save me also from myself, and give me a spirit of love and forgiveness, rather than bitterness and anger. Help me to forgive even as I have been forgiven. In Jesus' Name.
Amen.

January 14

Wait for the LORD; Be strong and let your heart take courage; Yes, wait for the LORD. (Psalms 27:14)

Our society says everything should be instant. We have microwaves for instant ready food, and credit cards for instant purchases. Why save up? JUST CHARGE IT! Often we don't "wait for the Lord," because we just won't give Him the time to work anything out in our life. We think that if we don't see the answer instantly, then God doesn't care and He isn't going to answer our prayer. We get into a lot of binds through taking matters into our own hands rather than going to God in prayer. We should wait for God to move on our behalf. Remember, the Lord always shows up in time!

Heavenly Father,
You know all of my needs, even my impatient wants. Thank You for all that You provide me with. Help me to wait for my prayers to be answered, even when they are answered contrary to what I want or demand. In Jesus' Name,
Amen.

January 15

Do not be deceived: "Bad company corrupts good morals." (1 Corinthians 15:33)

This is a *very* important verse to abide in! So many people believe they are strong enough Christians that they can hang around people without the same values, with no effect on their own life. The truth is, it's always easier to pull someone down than to pull someone up. It is impossible for you to spend *all* your time with non-Christians and not be affected in terms of how you think, how you may react to temptation, and so on. It's fine to be friendly with non-Christians, and God would not wish otherwise. But if your closest circle of friends - those you know you can really count on - share your faith, you will have so much to gain. You should consider the same in dating. If all of your friends are non-Christians, then make a point of getting to know some Christians who will be your friends, support system, and prayer partners. You will find that there's a bond between Christians that no one else, even the nicest people, can share. God gave us that bond, just as He gave us this verse because He loves us and doesn't want to see us get hurt.

Righteous Lord,
In turning to You I have found the smoke of my own deception and wrongdoing graciously dispersed. Help me to show my faith and especially Your eternal light, in all people I encounter each day. In Jesus' Name,
Amen.

January 16

The wicked flee when no one is pursuing, but the righteous are bold as a lion. (Proverbs 28:1)

Fear is just the opposite of faith. Fear is doubt and unbelief; faith is trust and belief in God, and the knowledge that God will do what His Word says. Remember, Satan is the author of fear. To act on tear is to act as if Satan is bigger than God.

Stay hooked on faith. Stand on God's promises for your life—He never changes and neither do His promises. He is the same yesterday, today, and forever. And remember, everything is possible for those who believe.

My Lord and Master,
By Your eternal, divine power please help keep my faith strong. Help me to trust in Your mercy, Your choosing of me, and Your unfailing love. In Jesus' Name,
Amen.

January 17

"No weapon that is formed against you will prosper; and every tongue that accuses you in judgment you will condemn. This is the heritage of the servants of the LORD, And their vindication is from Me," declares the LORD. (Isaiah 54:17)

Have you ever had someone speak badly of you, or make fun of you, or make things up about you to spread gossip? This verse is very comforting at those times. I know our flesh wants to retaliate, but we don't have to. God's already got everything under control! Because God instilled His love into our hearts through the Holy Spirit ("the love of God has been poured out within our hearts" (Romans 5:5)), we have the power to respond in love. What we need to do is pray for those who hurt us, so that the spiritual blinders will fall from their eyes. If we act by His Word, God will bless us for it.

Lord,
Your Word is a lamp that lights up the way I should walk. Give me the right words to respond to people whose own words can hurt me. Allow me to respond with the Holy Spirit, not from my embittered heart. In Jesus' Name,
Amen.

January 18

If you abide in me, and my words abide in you, ask whatever you wish, and it will be done for you. (John 15:7)

God's Word is powerful. If you keep it in your heart, your life will reflect its holiness. Stay in God's Word and make your choices to be His choices, your will to be His will. Doing this is not only pleasing to God; it can also save you a lot of heartache. This is because what may not seem like a very major decision to you may turn out to make important differences in your future.

God knows all and sees all. He knows the future, and when you are walking in His knowledge, the puzzle pieces of your life will come together, even if they don't make sense to you at first. God may not speak to you from a cloud or appear to you in a vision, but He *does* answer prayer. Pray for guidance and trust in the Lord. If you let Him, He will help you with every choice you make.

Almighty God,
I can't see all like You can. Often I can't even see where I am going. But I trust in You. Please guide me to where I should go; give me a sure future and an inspiring hope. In Jesus' Name,
Amen.

January 19

For you have made the LORD, my refuge, even the Most High, your dwelling place. No evil will befall you, nor will any plague come near your tent. For He will give His angels charge concerning you, to guard you in all your ways. (Psalms 91:9-11)

Without a doubt, there is danger all around. Some people are afraid to step outside their homes or even allow their children to go to school, for fear of someone bringing a gun or drugs. This scripture gives comfort.

However, receiving God's protection is conditional: you first have to make God your "dwelling." This means several things: keeping what Christ called 'the greatest command-ment': "You shall love the LORD your God with all your heart and with all your soul and with all your might" (Deuteronomy 6:5); trusting in the Lord for all things; believing He knows what is best for us; and listening to Him through His Word. Doing these things will keep us from all manners of peril and temptation.

God Most High,
Please keep me safe from all harm. Help me to put my trust in You and to love You with all my heart and soul and strength. I know You are with me always. In Jesus' Name, **Amen.**

January 20

Death and life are in the power of the tongue, and those who love it will eat its fruit. (Proverbs 18:21)

I once read that for every negative thing said to you, it takes seven positive things to make up for it. Have you ever had an idea that you thought was really good, but when you shared it with someone else, they shot it down? You know how it makes you feel: like someone knocked the wind out of you. Maybe even ashamed or belittled.

We need to be *encouragers* of our brothers and sisters, uplifting and supporting each other. Remember to watch what you say!

Loving Lord,
I want to be loved and appreciated, and not thought of by others as someone who tears down everyone around me. Help me to see the positive things about persons I know and meet; help me to speak well of them, and to use well the gift

of encouragement, inspired by Your Holy Spirit. In Jesus'
Name,
Amen.

January 21

*For if you forgive others for their transgressions, your heavenly
Father will also forgive you. (Matthew 6:14)*

Freedom is something everyone wants desperately, but
true freedom only comes through Jesus Christ. Forgiving
others for wrongs done to you sets you free. Forgiving
someone doesn't necessarily mean *forgetting,* as if the wrong
done to you never happened. You may still feel hurt or even
angry, but you have given the situation to the Lord, and
started down the path to healing. If you feel like you cannot
forgive, then pray for help: "Father, help me to forgive and
be obedient to your Word." If you do that, then God can start
to change your heart.

Remember, God first forgave you, and removed your sins
as far from you as the east is from the west.

Dear Lord,
I can think of a lot of times when I was hurt. It's hard to let
go of some of those hurts, but even when I don't feel like
forgiving someone, remind me to forgive them, and take
away the burdens of hurt that I would rather live without.
Thank You for Your great, eternal forgiveness, given in Your
eternal Son's death and resurrection. In Jesus' Name,
Amen.

January 22

*Blessed are the peacemakers, for they shall be called sons of
God. (Matthew 5:9)*

It's a great feeling when we're at worship or at a church
function, when most everyone is happy and it's easy to have

a Christ-like attitude toward those around us. But how do you handle it when you call a friend on the phone and he or she is short with you? Or when you go to pick up the CD you ordered and it's not in yet, or they ordered the wrong one? These are times when it can be easy to lose your cool.

Just because someone is acting toward you with rudeness or carelessness doesn't mean you have to *react* with the same. Instead, work at being a peacemaker. Two wrongs don't make a right. If it is possible, as far as it depends on you, live at peace with everyone.

God of Peace,
You are slow to anger, and abound in steadfast love. Help me to live at peace with others, to keep my temper in check. Let me rise above petty disputes and offenses and be strong in You. In Jesus' Name,
Amen.

January 23

For since He Himself was tempted in that which He has suffered, He is able to come to the aid of those who are tempted. (Hebrews 2:18)

People get addicted to different things for different reasons. However, all addiction, whether it be to drugs or alcohol, TV or video games, keeps us dependent on physical things to satisfy us, taking our focus away from God.

If you give God your addiction, He will give you freedom and new life. The devil will test you, but you have a choice. Satan cannot cross God's will, and God's will is that you be free of your addiction. Pray for deliverance, and if you need help, get it. And above all, trust in the Lord.

Dear Lord God,
You are stronger than the most powerful addiction. Strengthen me, and help me to turn away from temptation

and toward You. Thank You for Your deliverance. In Jesus'
Name,
Amen.

January 24

*...for you are still fleshly. For since there is jealousy and strife
among you, are you not fleshly, and are you not walking like
mere men? (1 Corinthians 3:3)*

Satan was the first victim of pride, cast out of heaven
because of his prideful striving for power. Pride trips you up
by making you compare yourself with others, criticizing
them to make yourself look better. Don't fall into this pattern
of behavior. Instead of seeking worldly things like beauty or
popularity, try to be more like Jesus. Make Him your standard
of perfection.

My Lord and Master,
Thank you for all that you give me, all my inspiration,
gifts and abilities, but remind me always where my treasure
lies: with You and Your Kingdom. In Jesus' Name,
Amen.

January 25

Every good thing given and every perfect gift is from above,
coming down from the Father of lights, with whom there is no
variation or shifting shadow. (James 1:17)

Do you have an image of God as standing in heaven with
a baseball bat, just waiting for you to mess up so He can let
you have it? Well, if that's your image of God, I've got good
news for you. God is good, and He never changes. He has
our best interests at heart. He doesn't delight in our failings.
He wants us only to love and serve Him.
God has given His Word to mankind, which we can either

reject or accept. If we accept, we trust God and are obedient to His Word. If we reject His Word, we are in trouble. You see, God doesn't just drop His blessings on us. We have the same covenant of blessings as Abraham, but He only brings forth the blessings if we believe and obey His Word.

The scriptures cited below are just a few that show God's loving kindness toward His children, and how He fulfills the desires of those who love Him. Check them out.

1. Proverbs 10:24
2. Psalm 37:4
3. Psalm 145:19

Father of All Mercies,
Everything changes in this world, and there is nothing eternal to trust in apart from You. I trust in You, and have made You my hope forever. In Jesus' Name,
Amen.

January 26

"... For I know the plans that I have for you," declares the LORD, "plans for welfare and not for calamity to give you a future and a hope..." (Jeremiah 29:11)

The youth of today have been labeled "Generation X," because they are perceived to lack direction. Some say unkindly that they seem to wander aimlessly, wondering why they are here on earth. Some have parents who seem not to care. Some kids join gangs for their sense of belonging and purpose. I've even heard kids call gang members their "family," and say that they would die for one another. If their eyes could be opened to this scripture, they would see that God does have a plan for their life—and that someone already died for them, over 2000 years ago. They would realize that they do have a real family, a purpose, and a destiny in Christ. I believe Jesus has called "Generation X" not just to survive, but to thrive!

God of Abraham, Isaac and Jacob,

You have welcomed me, in Christ, into Your eternal family, the Church, the Body of Christ. Thank You for the sweet fellowship and presence of Christian brothers and sisters here in my life —Thank You that I now belong to the congregation of those whom You have called by name. In Jesus' Name,

Amen.

January 27

...for God is not a God of confusion but of peace... (1 Corinthians 14:33)

When we're facing a tough situation, we're supposed to pray for guidance. So why does this sometimes seem to make us even more confused than we were to begin with? This scripture tells us the confusion is not coming from God. It is likely coming the struggle between the loud voice of our own selfish will and the still, small voice that is God.

God's Holy Spirit is gentle; He leads and guides, He isn't pushy, and He never, never causes confusion. So if you're seeking and praying for wisdom and you feel confused, keep praying, quiet your own voice, and *listen*. God, the Author of peace, will make His presence known.

Gracious Lord,

Thank You that Your Spirit is always with me to lead and guide, inspire and comfort. Thanks most of all that through the Spirit You have led me to a living faith in Your Son. In Jesus' Name,

Amen.

January 28

Beloved, if our heart does not condemn us, we have confidence before God; and whatever we ask we receive from Him, because we keep His commandments and do the things that are pleasing in His sight. (1 John 3:21-22)

If you want your prayers to be answered, start by living a life that is pleasing to God by keeping His commandments—and *keep praying*. Remember, what's important is not how long we pray, or what words we choose, or whether we're kneeling, standing, or sitting. It's believing and praying in the name of Jesus. Praying in His name is basing your prayers on what He has done, not what *you* have done.

If you haven't been keeping His commandments or living a life that is pleasing to Him, don't try running from Him or pretending it didn't happen. Just confess your sins and receive His forgiveness. Don't allow sin and condemnation to keep God from moving in your life. He is faithful and just and will forgive you your sins and cleanse you from all unrighteousness. He wants to answer your prayers!

Lord Jesus Christ!
Son of God! Have mercy on me, a sinner.
Amen.

January 29

But I say, walk by the Spirit, and you will not carry out the desire of the flesh. (Galatians 5:16)

Far too many believers allow their bodies to determine their choices in life. We persist in harmful and inappropriate behaviors like smoking, overeating, drinking, and promiscuity, with the excuse, "I've tried to quit, but it's just too hard!"

It *is* discouraging when we fall. But we need to get back up again as many times as it takes. We must not allow condemnation to keep us down with the attitude of, "Well, I messed up again, so I might as well sin some more." Don't get discouraged. Don't allow yourself or anyone else to tell you that you're bad, insignificant, or unworthy. The Bible says that you are "His workmanship, created in Christ Jesus" (Ephesians 2:10). What could be more valuable and worthy than that?

Instead of talking about what a mess you are, remember these words: "by His doing you are in Christ Jesus, who became to us wisdom from God, and righteousness and sanctification, and redemption" (1 Corinthians 1:30). Don't focus on the problem; get focused on the answer!

Heavenly Father,

For Jesus' sake take away my sin and failings this day, and in exchange, out of Your divine mercy and grace, grant me forgiveness, joy and new life. In Jesus' Name,
Amen.

January 30

God is faithful, through whom you were called into fellowship with His Son, Jesus Christ our Lord. (1 Corinthians 1:9)

Did you know that God wants us to keep fellowship with Him on a daily basis? And that doesn't mean just having a "relationship." I have relationships with people who are nothing more than acquaintances. A lot of people think they're having fellowship with God, when in reality what they're having is a lot of emergency meetings. Waiting for a crisis to happen, then running to God for help.

If you really care about someone, the chances are that you can't wait to talk to them, be with them. How would you feel if someone you loved dearly only came to you in times of crisis, never calling you just to say hello, or spending time with you? It would probably get a little old. Now, I'm *not* saying that God doesn't want to hear about our problems— He does! But He wants and desires much more than that. The more time you spend with God, the more you realize how reliable His Word is. You will also discover what joy there is in His presence.

Also remember, it is not enough to be out there doing God's work and not giving Him any personal time. It would be as if all your parents did was work to meet financial needs, but they never spent any time with you. There would be quite a void in your life.

So if you're not already in fellowship with God, start now. Spend time with Him today.

God my Creator and Redeemer,
Help me to pray unceasingly, talking with You throughout each day face to face. Thank You that You have promised never to leave me. In Jesus' Name,
Amen.

January 31

Iron sharpens iron, so one man sharpens another. (Proverbs 27:17)

I believe one of the greatest needs of God's people today is accountability. We all need a special friend, someone strong in the Lord to whom we can be accountable. I know a few Christian artists who have put together a board of people they can turn to for advice and counsel. These people will give their honest opinion about the art; for example, whether the artist is staying true to the Christian message through his or her work.

There is power and wisdom in being accountable. If you had someone you had to answer to every few weeks or so, wouldn't you feel stronger during those times of temptation? If you don't have anyone to whom you can be accountable, pray and ask God to send someone your way. Don't think that you're above temptation. Remember, you may think you are strong, but you could fall at any moment.

Dear Lord,

I give You thanks for the community of believers in You, and for the fellowship I find among them. Please help me to find Christian friends from whom I can learn, and with whom I can grow in knowledge of You and Your will. In Jesus' Name,
Amen.

February 1

Now the word of the LORD came to Jonah the second time...
(Jonah 3:1)

Can you imagine being Jonah, ignoring God's commands and getting swallowed by a whale? I bet that got his attention! A lot of people get things wrong the first time, like Jonah did by not listening to God, but that doesn't mean that they're failures. Making a single mistake isn't failure; failure is making the same mistake continually—not falling down, but allowing yourself to stay down. So learn from your mistakes, and listen to God the first time around!

Almighty Lord,

When Your Word comes to me, let me not fail to hear it and act on it. Thank You for the Holy Scriptures, Your Word to us, and most of all for Your only-begotten, Incarnate Word, crucified and risen for our salvation. In Jesus' Name,
Amen.

February 2

A gentle answer turns away wrath, but a harsh word stirs up anger. (Proverbs 15:1)

This is only one of many verses God gives us to guide us toward a happy, successful life. We live in a world that often solves its problems through anger. Anger can become a habit in handling uncomfortable situations, but it's a cheap substitute for handling situations God's way. Anger is a tool of the devil. It is a failing method and never, never solves a problem successfully.

The Bible gives better alternatives, and Proverbs 15:1 is one of them. Have you ever tried to be gentle and kind when someone is angry with you? Nothing melts someone else's anger more quickly than a calm attitude. I am encouraging you to do it three times before you decide it doesn't work. Give it a try!

Gracious Lord,

In Christ You have given me a new heart and mind. Whenever anger threatens to take control of me, quiet me in Your presence, so that I may have the peace which only You can give. In Jesus' Name,

Amen.

February 3

But each one is tempted when he is carried away and enticed by his own lust. Then when lust has conceived, it gives birth to sin; and when sin is accomplished, it brings forth death. (James 1:14-15)

We need to remember these things about temptation:

There will always be temptation.

God never does the tempting.

Temptation flourishes on thinking that is not grounded in the Word of God.

Don't allow your situation to make you vulnerable to sin.

Don't give in to persuasion or peer pressure.

Don't be ruled by your emotions.

Some things we are to stand and resist, except for lust, from which we are told to flee.

Each time we give into temptation, it makes it that much harder to say no the next time.

God my Savior,
When temptation comes and places me in the time of trial, help me to resist it, and deliver me from evil. Set Your holy angels over me, and lead me in Your way of righteousness. In Jesus' Name,
Amen.

February 4

But if any of you lacks wisdom, let him ask of God, who gives to all generously and without reproach, and it will be given to him. (James 1:5)

This isn't a very long verse, but it can make a world of difference in our lives. God is telling us that if we lack wisdom in a relationship, job, friendship, with parents, or whatever, He will give it to us. All we have to do is ask.

Isn't it cool to know that God has all the answers to our problems? He doesn't have to go away and think about your problem and try to come up with an answer. He already knows. God loves you and really cares about what you are going through, and the good news is that He wants to share His wisdom with us. When you've had a really rough day, or week, or month, maybe it's because you don't have the answers for certain questions in your life. *Cheer up!* God has them. Take time today and ask Him for the wisdom you need!

Heavenly Father,
It's hard to admit that I often am not even close to the answers and wisdom I need, but I know that You know all things. Remind me by Your Spirit to ask for Your eternal

wisdom. In Jesus' Name,
Amen.

February 5

Your word is a lamp to my feet and a light for my path. (Psalms 119:105)

The Bible tells us, "You are the light of the world...let your light shine before men in such a way that they may see your good works, and glorify your Father who is in heaven" (Matthew 5:14,16).

There are a lot of things in the world that can threaten and dim that light, but you can overcome them by focusing on Jesus and His Word. We need to be different, to be a light to the world and show people that there is a better way. We need to have an answer for people who ask us why we are filled with hope and peace when our circumstances might suggest something different. Let God's Word light your own path, and you can bring hope to those who are in darkness.

My God, who dwells in heavenly light,

Can people see Your light in me and my life? In Christ I have found that kingdom of light where there is no darkness. Help me to shine Your light, so that others may see it and come to know You also. In Jesus' Name,
Amen.

February 6

Trust in the LORD with all your heart and do not lean on your own understanding. In all your ways acknowledge Him, and He will make your paths straight. (Proverbs 3:5-6)

I don't know about you, but I get pretty freaked out when I don't understand what is happening to me. Perhaps you are experiencing something in your life that leaves you clueless as to what is going on. God gave us this verse to give us hope. We don't have to understand everything going on around us. If we will just have the faith to believe that God has everything under control and stop trying to lean on our own understanding (or lack of understanding), He will lead us in the right direction.

Back when I was looking for my first full-time job at a Christian radio station, I told the Lord I would take the first one offered to me, no matter what. I was going to let Him choose the station. Now, I had really been hoping for a station that played some great jams. Imagine my disappointment with my first job just outside Tampa, Florida—I accepted the job sight unseen, and when I got there I found out that the station was in an old house trailer. The music was old hymns of the faith, which of course isn't bad, but a little "slower" than what I had been looking for. I wanted to quit my first week there, but I decided (as my mother had always advised me) to trust in God. Two weeks after beginning that job, I received a phone call from a Christian station on the other side of Tampa that played great Christian jams, had wonderful studios...and yes, I got the job. This cool station would only do in-person interviews, which I would have been unable to do had I not just moved to Tampa. The Lord knew that, of course, and I believe that's why He brought me to the first station for a short period. Imagine what I would have missed if I had leaned on my own understanding.

God always knows what is best for us and how to meet our heart's desires. He just wants us to trust Him. Are you willing to trust Him today?

Lord,
You know what's best for me, even though I often think that only I know what's best. Help me to accept what You have given me, and where You lead me. In Jesus' Name,
Amen.

February 7

Why are you in despair, O my soul? And why are you disturbed within me? Hope in God, for I shall again praise Him, the help of my countenance and my God. (Psalms 43:5)

When you ask most people about hope, many would tell you their hopes have often turned into disappointments. For others, hope is little different than uncertainty, like "maybe it will happen and maybe it won't; all we can do is hope." In reacting this way, they are speaking of worldly hope, not Godly hope. Godly hope never disappoints us. When God told Abraham he would be the father of many nations, Abraham was 100 years old, and his wife, Sarah, was 90. From a worldly perspective it would appear pretty hopeless to have a child at that age. But Abraham had God's word that it would happen. He had to ignore his natural circumstances and stand on what he knew God had told him. "[H]e did not waver in unbelief but grew strong in faith, giving glory to God..." (Romans 4:20).

Almighty God,
My hope is in You, knowing that You will continue to guide and bless those who place their trust in You. In Jesus' Name,
Amen.

February 8

"With people this is impossible, but with God all things are possible." (Matthew 19:26)

Just when you thought that you couldn't hold on any longer, here comes this verse. I'm sure you can think of difficulties you're facing right now which you know you don't have enough strength to keep facing day after day.

Well, you don't have to do it alone. God is a personal god

and He loves us very much, so much that He is willing to give us the strength to do something that we can't do on our own. When I try to use my own strength to get things done, I often find out that it isn't nearly enough to get me through. I know I couldn't face life's challenges if not for the supernatural strength I receive from the Lord. God never meant for us to live our lives on our own strength; He means for us to use His strength so we can face whatever is before us. I encourage you today to ask God for His strength in whatever difficulties may be present in your life.

Mighty Lord,
I find that I fail to ask for Your strength and guidance when things are easy for me, but then when things get tough, that's when I remember to look to You. Whether good days or bad, help me to ask for Your loving, powerful presence to be my refuge and inspiration. In Jesus' Name,
Amen.

February 9

But now faith, hope, love, abide these three; but the greatest of these is love. (1 Corinthians 13:13)

The Bible tells us that God is love. But what kind of love? The supernatural love in 1 Corinthians 13 is the kind that isn't selfish. It doesn't keep records of when someone does wrong, and it loves even when that love is not returned. Can you imagine what would happen to people's stomach ulcers and tension headaches if everyone lived according to 1 Corinthians 13? When we walk in love, we step into the supernatural; selfishness and unforgiveness have to go.

If you need freedom from anger that has you bound, declare that you are going to walk in the love God intended, then let the hostility go. Dare to release it, and experience what God has intended for you all along, to live the life He has called you to live.

Give yourself to love—the supernatural love of God—and see what a difference it can make in your life.

Loving Lord,

I confess that I often fail to love others as I love myself, and especially that I fail to love You above everything else. In spite of that, You show Your love to me in amazing ways, for which I can barely begin to give thanks. Teach me all that I should know about love, and how to express Your love to others. In Jesus' Name,
Amen.

February 10

The Spirit of the Lord is upon me, because He anointed me to preach the Gospel to the poor. He has sent me to proclaim release to the captives, and recovery of sight to the blind, to set free those who are oppressed, to proclaim the favorable year of our Lord. (Luke 4:18-19)

Sharing our faith can make us nervous. We think, "Oh, I'll say the wrong thing and sound stupid." In fact, most of us would rather clean bathrooms than share our faith! But the Holy Spirit will give us the words and the boldness to share with others if we just open our mouth and try.

There are a lot of hurting people out there who need someone like you to do exactly what Luke 4:18-19 says. Don't allow fear to stop you. Depend on God's Word and God's strength. Give it a try today.

Gracious Lord,

Inspire my mind and my mouth, so that I may speak Your praises to all those I encounter. Inspire me, Lord, for Jesus' sake. In Jesus' Name,
Amen.

February 11

Therefore do not let sin reign in your mortal body so that you obey its lusts... (Romans 6:12)

One very dangerous sin is the habitual sin. You know, the kind that you do repeatedly, even though you know it's wrong. People may think, "I'm under grace, so I'll go ahead and sin and ask for forgiveness later," or perhaps we rationalize it by saying to ourselves, "Well, it's just a small sin." But the Bible says if you are born again, you are dead to sin. Satan would try to keep you thinking you can't stop on your own. Well, the Spirit of Jesus that lives in us can help you! That doesn't mean that we won't be tempted from time to time, but the Bible does declare that if we submit ourselves to God and resist the devil, he will flee. You may feel that your life is so messed up that there is no way you can learn to walk with God, but you can. It may take practice—after all, most habits, both good and bad, take time to make. Just start reading the Word, and praying, and spending more time with the Lord. The more you do these things, the more you will experience the new life promised us in Romans 6:4.

Stop riding the fence, get "hooked" on God's Word, and start walking in the victory He promises us!

Almighty Creator,
I often find sinful habits are hard, almost impossible, to break free from. What shall I do? Thanks be to You and the victory Your Son won upon the Cross, so that I might be forgiven and freed from my sin! Lead me in the way of Jesus' Cross, and teach me to look to him whenever I am tempted by old habits. In Jesus' Name,
Amen.

February 12

Do not be grieved, for the joy of the LORD is your strength.
(Nehemiah 8:10)

You know how it is when you're joyful about something—you beam. Sometimes you smile so hard you think you could burst! Well, that's how we should feel about our relationship with God. It's easy to feel discouraged and full of complaints, but what we need to do is be full of joy! After all, what do others think when they see Christians walking around grumbling and complaining? It sure doesn't offer them much hope. Why should they want to know the Lord, when they can grumble just fine on their own!

Once when I was going through a particularly difficult time, I felt like my joy was being zapped right out of me. I was so focused on my problem that I couldn't enjoy the wonderful things God was doing at the time. I actually found myself not wanting to call my dad (who isn't a Christian), because I didn't want him to see me like that. After all, I was trying to be a good witness. That's when I realized that something was definitely wrong. I started praying and asking God to restore my joy, and stopped focusing on the problem rather than the Problem Solver (God). Once I did this, and really got into the Word, the problem became smaller and smaller. Keep in mind that joy and praise together release strength and power in you, and God does inhabit the praises of His people!

Lord of Heavenly Glory,
Teach me to feel Your joy as part of my faith. You created the heavens and the earth, and together all creation sings Your praises. Make me mindful of all that You have done throughout history, including the glorious things You have done for me. In Jesus' Name,
Amen.

February 13

PRAISE the LORD! How blessed is the man who fears the LORD, who greatly delights in His commandments...He will not fear evil tidings; his heart is steadfast, trusting in the LORD. His heart is upheld, he will not fear, until he looks with satisfaction on his adversaries. (Psalms 112:1,7-8)

It doesn't matter what you are facing, God is strong enough for you to handle it. When you face a hardship, things might look pretty bad, and it may be tempting to give up. This is why it is so important to be in the Word every day. Strengthened by God's promises, you can face whatever comes your way. You can be settled in your mind that He will take care of you, and that you don't have to be afraid, for we are God's children and we have His favor with us. As Psalms 5:12 says, "For it is You who blesses the righteous man, O LORD, You surround him with favor as with a shield."

So when your next dilemma comes and you wonder, "How will I ever get out of this disaster?" claim God's promises of His favor and grace in your life. That way you can face things with confidence and unwavering faith, and know God will take care of you.

Whom can you share this with today?

Almighty, Blessed Father,

I come to You as a helpless child, but I believe that You will protect me in every time of danger, and guard me from every evil, out of Your pure divine mercy and grace. Therefore I thank and praise, serve and obey You. In Jesus' Name, **Amen.**

February 14

"For the mountains may be removed and the hills may shake, but my lovingkindness will not be removed from you, And my covenant of peace will not be shaken," Says the LORD who has compassion on you. (Isaiah 54:10)

Happy Valentines Day! Isn't it good to know, on this day that celebrates love, that we have a love which will not be shaken and will never fail?

Everyone is looking for someone special, hoping to find that one "sure" thing…and so often they are disappointed. God, Who out of perfect love for us sent His only Son to die for our sins, is the only "sure thing" in this life; only He can totally fill the void in our lives.

Instead of searching for the "perfect" boyfriend or girlfriend, seek God's love first. And take heart—God doesn't want you to be lonely. You do your job, which is to love and serve Him, and He will make sure that at the right time, you run right into that special someone.

Loving Father,

Help me to look for the right kind of love in my life; not love as the world knows it, but Christian love, which transcends human feelings. Thank You for Your perfect love, and grant that I may love You better. In Jesus' Name,
Amen.

February 15

Set a guard, O LORD, over my mouth; Keep watch over the door of my lips. (Psalms 141:3)

People speak of having a problem with controlling their tongues, but the tongue only reveals what we are really thinking. If we want to change our words, we must first change our hearts. Words can bruise the hearts of our friends and parents. Words can hurt just as much as a blow in the stomach or a slap across the face. Once said, those words can't be taken back. Ask yourself before you speak, "Is this kind, necessary or true?"

Take the challenge today, and think about what you are going to say. If you find yourself biting back harsh or unkind words, ask God to make a change in your heart. Soon your words will reflect that change.

Merciful Lord,
Only You and Your powerful grace can change the condition of my heart. Cleanse me from my sin; make me pure in heart, so that I may one day see You face to face. In Jesus' Name,
Amen.

February 16

...let us cleanse ourselves from all defilement of flesh and spirit, perfecting holiness in the fear of God. (2 Corinthians 7:1)

A lot of people are not very comfortable with the word "holy"—they think of it as a "religious" word. It may sound a little "judgmental," a word that puts people on the spot about how they live their lives. But sometimes "on the spot" is just where we need to be.

What if one Sunday morning, instead of preaching a sermon, your pastor brought in a movie to show during worship, a movie with maybe some nudity and some swearing? Everyone would be appalled, and would probably leave the church. But do you ever bring that kind of movie into your home? Or go to the theater and see an "R" rated movie? If so, exactly what is the difference? We are the body of Christ, and the Bible tells us to seek to be perfect, just as God is perfect.

Once a friend and I went out for pizza with a group from her church. To our surprise, after we ordered the pizza, most of the guys at the table ordered beer. We were quite disappointed.

As a fairly new Christian and a child of alcoholics, I thought to myself, "God delivered me out of this—why would I want to get back into it, especially now that I'm a Christian?" I also felt it to be a bad witness to other people; the Bible says we shouldn't do anything that could cause our brothers and sisters to stumble (see 1 Corinthians 10:32). Something that might not seem like a big deal to you could indeed cause your brothers and sisters in the Lord to stumble, and could even contaminate your body or spirit.

Think it over. Choose holiness—it's not a dirty word!

Heavenly Father,
You have redeemed me from my former life, and now I have crossed over to eternal life with You in Your Son. Remind me that people will watch the example of my words and deeds. In Jesus' Name,
Amen.

February 17

He said, "Do not stretch out your hand against the lad, and do nothing to him; for now I know that you fear God, since you have not withheld your son, your only son, from me." (Genesis 22:12)

Imagine being told to sacrifice your own child. What must have been going through Abraham's mind? God wanted to see if Abraham was willing to be obedient, and the amazing thing is, however grief-stricken, angry, or confused Abraham was, he didn't question God's command. What obedience!

We all have things that we hold dear to us. If God asked us to give them up for Him, how hard would it be? Would we be willing to do just as Abraham did, and be ready to give our most prized possession to God? Genesis 22:14-19 tells of how pleased God was with Abraham's trust and obedience, for which God told him he would be greatly blessed. We need to remember that what we release to God, He will replace with something even better, and that He rewards us for faithfulness and obedience.

Are there things in your life God has been asking you to surrender to Him? Follow Abraham's example and obey.

Lord of Hosts,

When my faith feels weak, help me still to obey Your holy word. Strengthen me for my daily journey with You as I live my life, and enable me to hear Your call to whatever I should do. In Jesus' Name,

Amen.

February 18

Cease striving and know that I am God... (Psalms 46:10)

This sounds so easy, but I believe it can be one of the hardest things to do. When you are praying, do you ever sit still and listen for God to answer? Or do you just tell Him all that's going on and what you need from Him, and then go on your merry way?

We need to learn to be still and wait on the Lord, which sometimes will take more than just five or ten minutes of our time. God is always close at hand; He has given us His Holy Spirit to comfort, guide and strengthen us no matter what we are facing. He never intends for you to face any problem alone, no matter how big or small, and He will never leave us or forsake us. The Bible says He is "a friend who sticks closer than a brother" (Proverbs 18:24).

So even if we have nothing else, we have the One who is most important—God and His Holy Spirit. He will guide us through life, if we are willing to be still and wait on Him.

Dear Lord,

Often in my life I can't find much quiet, let alone enter Your divine, still presence. Give me, I pray, a thirst for simply sitting and praying in Your stillness. Then I will find the peace and quiet I so desperately need. In Jesus' Name, **Amen.**

February 19

The thief comes only to steal and kill and destroy; I came that they may have life, and have it abundantly. (John 10:10)

Many teenagers have had thoughts of suicide. If this includes you, you are not alone. This scripture tells us who the culprit is behind these thoughts...the "thief," or the devil, who is always looking for a way to destroy lives.

You may be facing some incredibly tough things in your life right now, but you need to remember that God has a plan for your life, and that your hardships have not caught Him by surprise. Your problem is temporary; suicide is forever. If you have a friend who is suicidal, tell someone *NOW.* Yes, your friend may be very upset with you temporarily, but which is worse—an angry friend, or a dead one? If you are struggling with thoughts of suicide yourself, pray, and talk to someone *NOW*—your parents, your pastor, a teacher or counselor at school. This is too big for you to handle on your own.

Look again at today's verse—God has given us *life*. He doesn't just want one you can put up with, but one you can live to the full. Your life is precious...and God really does care!

Dear God, the Source of all life,

I give you great thanks this day for my life: You have given and preserve my body and soul, so that I may live life to the fullest. In Jesus' Name,
Amen.

February 20

But God demonstrates His own love toward us, in that while we were yet sinners, Christ died for us. (Romans 5:8)

Loving your friends doesn't depend on how likeable they are. It's easy to do the right thing when our friends deserve it, isn't it?

In my hometown of a thousand people, there was only one shoe repair shop. The old man who ran it was very rude and unkind to his customers, and for some reason seemed to enjoy humiliating them. I complained to God in prayer about his attitude, expecting Him to sympathize with me. Against my will, however, I felt moved by the Holy Spirit to show this man the love of Christ. I knew that meant doing acts of kindness, even though I didn't feel the man deserved it.

I have to admit it was very hard to do, but that Christmas I bought him a present, which he accepted without even thanking me. Then at Easter I gave him an Easter gift with a tract of the Easter story inside. Then I brought him cookies with stories of God's love tucked in them. He never did thank me, but after several months he stopped being mean to me, and once, when I brought in my dog's leash to be repaired, he fixed it for nothing—and smiled. He began saying hello to me when I saw him at the general store.

The following year, he died of cancer. I am so thankful now that I responded to the situation God's way, instead of my way.

Let me give you a challenge. Is there a difficult friend or classmate whom you need to handle with the love of Christ? It won't be easy, but it wasn't easy for Christ to go to the cross for us when we didn't deserve it. The Good News is...*He did*!

Dear Lord,
You show Your love to all of us in spite of not everyone

responding to You. Help me to remember that Your Son died for all sinners, even the most unlovable ones. In Jesus' Name,

Amen.

February 21

The LORD is near to the brokenhearted and saves those who are crushed in spirit. (Psalms 34:18)

Wouldn't it would be wonderful if we all grew up in a two-parent home with lots of love? Unfortunately, we live in a sinful world, where the shortcomings of those around us, including our parents, affect us.

God has said that He will be a Father to the fatherless (see Psalm 68:5) and will fill the emptiness in our hearts. As we walk through life, many circumstances grieve us, and it doesn't seem possible that God can heal the ache in our hearts. Too often, we look to other people or things to solve the problems and hurts in our lives, but *no one* loves and cares for you like Jesus. He can carry you through your difficulties and pain. So if you've been dumped by your boyfriend or girlfriend, or if you don't feel like you have a friend in the whole world, take heart. Jesus died for every hurt and problem that you suffer, and He wants you to lean on Him and give Him your troubles, not carry them yourself. All you have to do is ask.

Heavenly Father,
You have promised in Your Holy Scripture that You are not simply like a father to us, but like a loving father. Thank You for the wondrous love shown to Your beloved children. In Jesus' Name,

Amen.

February 22

There is one who speaks rashly like the thrusts of a sword, but the tongue of the wise brings healing. (Proverbs 12:18)

This is true, but we don't consider it carefully enough. Have you have ever been tormented by someone's "reckless" words? Maybe it was some kids at school who made fun of you or made nasty remarks about your appearance. Words can be very damaging; they can keep us in bondage, making us feel "different," or like we "don't measure up." On the other hand, they can bring encouragement and life.

Read your Bible and find out who you are in Christ. Start renewing your mind in the Word of God, and then when someone says something negative about you, you will not be shaken, because your feet will be planted in the true Word of God.

Almighty Lord,
You have redeemed me and call me by name. Let me never be ashamed of belonging to You. In Jesus' Name,
Amen.

February 23

Watch yourselves, that you do not lose what we have accomplished, but that you may receive a full reward. (2 John 8)

I don't know about you, but I know quite a few people who are in church on Sunday, and living like the devil the rest of the week. They have one foot in the church and the rest of their body in the world.

A guy I used to work with is a prime example. He would go to church each Sunday with a joint in his pocket ready to smoke on the way home. When he got married, he and his wife had a lot of problems, and he always wondered why God didn't heal his marriage. He felt like God had let him down! He was always ready to call on God when he needed to get out of a jam, but then when things were going well, he would continue in his old ways and hang with the old crowd. He was never willing to give it all up for God.

The Bible says that a double-minded man is unstable in all of his ways (see James 1:8) and should not to expect to receive anything from the Lord. Let's make sure that we're on fire for God, and give up all the things that could make us double-minded and unstable, so we aren't lukewarm for Him.

Dear Lord,
I believe in and entrust myself to You. Let me obey you, and serve no other gods, no false idols. In Jesus' Name, **Amen.**

February 24

Nehemiah 9:17

But You are a God of forgiveness, gracious and compassionate, slow to anger and abounding in lovingkindness. (Nehemiah 9:17)

The devil would have us believe that God is just waiting for us to mess up so He can punish us, but this scripture tells us just the opposite. God is compassionate, slow to anger, and abounding in love.

A lot of people feel there is no way God could forgive their sins, that what they did is beyond forgiveness. But no sin is unforgivable, except never coming to God to ask for forgiveness. God is always waiting for us to come to Him, always willing to give us a second, third, or hundredth chance. So once you have asked Him to forgive you, don't let the devil keep bringing up your past to you to keep you in turmoil. God puts our sins in the sea of forgetfulness. Don't allow the devil to go fishing for them!

Gracious Lord God,

You are always a compassionate, forgiving God to all of those who repent of their sins. Let me not hide all the wrongs I commit; help me to confess them before You, so that I may receive Your forgiveness, and Your righteousness. In Jesus' Name,

Amen.

February 25

So then let us pursue the things which make for peace and the building up of one another. (Romans 14:19)

Hurricanes can leave a path of destruction as they go through a city. Homes can take on a similar nature. Through divorce, death, or abuse, our lives can be torn apart. Often we are so deep in our own hurt that we don't realize other members in our family are hurting too. The key words in this verse are "make every effort." Growing up means becoming part of the solution, not part of the problem. We need to do our part in restoring peace in our home, for the good of our entire family.

When the hurricane in our home is at its peak, maybe it's time to throw a "rope of love" to someone, rather than a rock of criticism.

Dear Lord,

Show me what I can do to reach out in love to those close to me. Many people have shown me just such love and caring; inspire me to do the same for others. In Jesus' Name,

Amen.

February 26

Therefore you have no excuse, everyone of you who passes judgment, for in that which you judge another, you condemn yourself; for you who judge practice the same things. (Romans 2:1)

It is so easy to judge others isn't it? But do you remember when you first became a Christian? You didn't have it all together as soon as you asked the Lord into your heart; you had to grow. Learning to walk the Christian walk is a life-long task. It's so easy to look at those who are just beginning their walk with the Lord, and judge their every move. Sometimes we don't give them a chance to grow and mature in the Lord; we expect them to be where we already are in our relationship with Jesus. Maybe you're reading three chapters of the Bible for your daily devotions, and jump on their case because they're only reading five verses.

Relax. Let those new to the faith have room to grow. No one on this earth is perfect; we all have areas in our life we need help with, and my hope is that other Christians will show me the same grace that I try to show my friends. This doesn't mean you approve of someone committing sin; it means you don't beat them over the head and make them feel like a loser for blowing it.

The bottom line is, there is a difference between helping someone grow in Christ and judging them. Try this: put your arm around someone, and help that person in his or her Christian walk. Let them know you care and want to help. If they are sinning, maybe they don't realize it, and you could point it out to them in a non-judgmental way. Give them room to grow, but be there to help them as well. Pray that the Holy Spirit would begin working in his or her life, and never forget to pray for your own continued Christian growth as well.

Almighty Lord,
Show me my sins, and help me to speak the truth in love

about sins I see outside of myself. In Jesus' Name,
Amen.

February 27

But Jonah rose up to flee to Tarshish from the presence of the LORD. (Jonah 1:3)

God told Jonah to go to the city of Nineveh and tell the people there about God. Jonah made the decision to say no, and fled by ship in the opposite direction, toward the city of Tarshish. After Jonah got on the ship, a huge storm came. Frightened, the sailors asked Jonah what they should do. Jonah, realizing the storm was the result of his disobedience, told them to throw him over the edge of the ship into the water. They did so, and Jonah was immediately swallowed by the "great fish" waiting there for him. Jonah cried out his repentance to God from the depths of the whale's belly, and God commanded the whale to spit him out. Jonah then obeyed God (finally!) and went to Nineveh as he had been told.

We probably won't ever get swallowed by a whale for our disobedience, but this story clearly shows the consequences of sin. God always wants to better us and those around us through our obedience to Him.

Is Satan offering you an opportunity to run from God? If so, say NO!!!

Loving Lord,
Direct and show me the way I should go in my life, even when it seems like I try to go the very opposite way! In Jesus' Name,
Amen.

February 28

Let no one look down on your youthfulness, but rather in speech, conduct, love, faith and purity, show yourself an example of those who believe. (1 Timothy 4:12)

I really believe that teenagers are the church of *today*, not tomorrow. I also believe that God is going to use the youth to begin the next revival that our country really needs.

All throughout the Bible, God raised up young people to turn the tide. David was only a boy when he faced and killed Goliath. Mary, the mother of Jesus, was just a teenager when she was told that she would become the mother of the Messiah. And when Jeremiah was sixteen years old, God told him, "Before I formed you in the womb I knew you, and before you were born I consecrated you; I have appointed you a prophet to the nations." (Jeremiah 1:5). Doesn't that blow you away? Jeremiah sure was taken back—remember, he was only sixteen! He protested that he didn't know how to respond as he was only a child. But God wouldn't have any excuses: "Do not say, 'I am a youth,' because everywhere I send you, you shall go, and all that I command you, you shall speak. Do not be afraid of them, for I am with you to deliver you" (Jeremiah 1:7-8).

Don't wait to start your ministry until you become an adult; God wants to use you today! Start a Bible study on campus, be a witness for Christ to your friends, neighbors, and teachers. Even before you were born, God had a plan for your life. Don't let anyone look down on you because you're young—show them by example that you're a real man or woman of God!

Lord,

I want to serve You in Your Kingdom. Inspire me by Your Spirit to witness to the Good News about Your beloved Son. Tell me what my calling and ministry are, within the fellowship of all who follow Your way. In Jesus' Name,
Amen.

March 1

Therefore, accept one another, just as Christ also accepted us to the glory of God. (Romans 15:7)

Accepting a friendly person who treats you with respect is easy. But accepting the mean, unkind person? That's another story.

This kind of acceptance doesn't mean you are to accept the sins of others, to put your stamp of approval on their behavior. But you are to accept them as other human beings designed by our Heavenly Father. Jesus talked with the Samaritan woman at the well when no one else would...and she responded by accepting Him. Jesus had dinner with Zaccheaus, a hated tax collector...and Zaccheaus accepted Him. Do you see a pattern here? You don't know what's going on behind the doors of others' hearts, what pain has been inflicted upon them to cause them to appear rude and uncaring. Loving the unlovely is not easy, but Jesus set the example when He first loved us.

Who needs you to accept him or her in Christ's love today?

Loving God,
Even though it's hard to accept the fact that You accept me, I confess and believe in Your love. When I feel like not accepting someone, remind me how Jesus accepted people. In Jesus' Name,
Amen.

March 2

for all have sinned and fall short of the glory of God... (Romans 3:23)

The first step in your Christian walk is to realize that you are a sinner and that you are not perfect—no one is but Jesus. Because we have all sinned, it is necessary to come to God, ask for His forgiveness, and receive Him into our hearts. God knew that we would make mistakes and continue to sin, which is why He sent Jesus to die for us on the cross.

It's important to realize that you cannot *earn* your salvation; it's only through confessing your sins and accepting Jesus into your heart that the hope of eternal life is possible. We could never be good enough to pass through the gates of heaven on our own merit; we need the blood of Jesus to wipe out our sins and give us a new life in Him. If you have never confessed that you are a sinner, and have never asked Jesus to be the Lord of your life, then you have not yet taken that necessary step. Here is a simple prayer to get you on track.

Dear Lord,

I realize that I am a sinner, and I ask You to forgive me of my wrongdoings. I believe You died on the cross for my sins, rose from the dead three days later, and are alive today. I want You to be the Lord of my life; I want to have a personal relationship with You, and I want You to take my life and do whatever You will with it. Thank You for coming into my heart and receiving me as Your child. In Jesus' name I pray,
Amen.

March 3

Therefore, do not throw away your confidence, which has a great reward. For you have need of endurance, so that when you have done the will of God, you may receive what was promised. (Hebrews 10:35-36)

What verses! This sounds quite easy to do, but it can be surprisingly hard when it comes right down to it. How many of us start out a new project full of enthusiasm—until one little hardship or obstacle comes along, and then boy, do we whine! We start doubting and complaining, and we become very discouraged.

We need to use the faith God gave us, and start trusting Him. Psalms 37:7 says "Rest in the LORD and wait patiently for Him." Now, I know our definition of "patiently" might not be the same as God's. We think being patient is waiting a week, where God may require our patience for a month, or a year. Remember—our patience develops strength of character, and helps us trust God more each time, until our faith is finally strong and steady and ready for anything!

So how long do you have to wait? You wait until you see results. Keep your confidence in God—He will keep His promises if you persevere and do His will.

Lord,

I want to follow You all the days of my life. Show me where I should go, what I should do. I want to do Your will, so I will cling to Your Holy Word and the fellowship of Your faithful. In Jesus' Name,
Amen.

March 4

But when He, the Spirit of truth, comes, He will guide you into all the truth; for He will not speak on His own initiative, but whatever He hears, He will speak; and He will disclose to you what is to come. (John 16:13)

Listening to God is something that gives a lot of us trouble. Is it God we're hearing, or just ourselves? Well, you don't have to wait for a voice from heaven, or a burning bush. If you really need to know what God wants from you, there are several ways God speaks to us and gives us wisdom:

Through His Word.

Through prayer and openness to the voice of God.

Through Christian fellowship.

Through the church, by counseling or preaching.

Keep in mind that God is never hiding from us, nor is He far away. He is always ready to help and give us wisdom

(James 1:5).

Next time you feel you really need to hear from God, claim this verse and spend some time in prayer. And remember to spend some quiet time *after* you pray, so you may hear from the Holy Spirit.

Gracious Lord,
Sometimes understanding Your Holy Spirit is like trying to grab a fish! But You have assured us of the Spirit's comfort and counsel. Whenever Your Son Jesus is preached and witnessed to, then I will know that the Spirit is present, and I will give thanks. In Jesus' Name,
Amen.

March 5

Behold, I am the LORD, the God of all flesh; is anything too difficult for me? (Jeremiah 32:27)

If we really believe this verse, then why do we worry about anything? How many times have you hung on to your problems, worried about them, looked for your own solution, instead of taking the problem to God *immediately* when it first enters your life? Too often we don't turn over our problems to God until we've done everything we can in our own power to solve the problem. Then we give God the leftovers.

You might be thinking, "You don't even know me—there's no way you can understand what I'm facing right now!" You know what? You're right! But that's not what's important. Read the last part of the verse: "Is anything too hard for me?" God is not up in heaven muttering, "I've never had to solve a problem like this! I thought I could do anything, but I never knew something like *this* would come up." God is able and willing to solve the problems in your life, if you will let Him.

Almighty God,

Your First Commandment is often the hardest to keep. By Your Spirit You have worked faith in me to see that You alone are God eternal and almighty, and I trust in you. In Jesus' Name,

Amen.

March 6

"Peace I leave with you; my peace I give to you; not as the world gives do I give to you. Do not let your heart be troubled, nor let it be fearful..." (John 14:27)

People desperately want peace in their lives. The world tries to get it through things like meditation, therapy, New Age, alcohol, drugs, or sex. Christians know these don't bring true peace, but provide only temporary escapes. They may hide problems for a while, but the problems always come back. The only true peace comes from the Holy Spirit; that's why He is called the Comforter.

The Bible tells us where to turn when we need help. "Come to Me, all who are weary and heavy-laden, and I will give you rest" (Matthew 11:28). I usually find that when I get upset over something, it's a sure sign that I'm trying to carry it on my own. That's when I have to go to God, lay it at His feet, and tell Him I'm sorry and that I'm giving the problem to Him.

And try not to worry. Worry is a sin, just like a lot of other things. Worry is saying that God isn't big enough to handle your problem. Keep the communication lines with God open about everything. Remember, He already knows, so it's not like you're keeping anything a secret from Him. Confess your fears to God and accept His peace. And be worry-free!

Loving Lord,

The peace that I have found in You is completely different than what I knew before as peace. Sometimes I forget that, but when I find myself harried by all of life's troubles, grant me the peace that only You can give. In Jesus' Name, **Amen.**

March 7

O GOD, You are my God; I shall seek You earnestly; my soul thirsts for You, my flesh yearns for You, in a dry and weary land where there is no water. (Psalms 63:1)

We often take God for granted. Do you "earnestly seek" Him, or do you only give Him time when it's convenient?

For any relationship to mature and develop, you have to invest in it. Look at dating, or marriage, or any other type of relationship. You have to spend time with the person to get to know him or her. If you don't, the relationship will quickly go stagnant. How long would a marriage last if the two people involved never spent any time together, aside from a few minutes here and there? Take a look at someone you know who has a happy marriage. Most happily married people could tell you how their partner would react in any particular situation. Why? Because they spend time together and know each other intimately. It is the same with our relationship with God. The more time we spend in His Word and in prayer, the easier it is to know what God is pleased with, and what He is not pleased with.

If you've neglected your relationship with God, it's not too late to get back on the right track. Ask for His forgiveness and His help in making time with Him. So what if, to do so, you need to learn to turn the television off, or stay off the phone, or go to bed a little earlier, or get up a little sooner? Whatever the case may be, make a conscious decision that you are going to do it, and start today!

Dear Lord,

I don't always realize that simply talking to you is prayer; there are so many things about prayer I should understand

but I don't, not yet. The first disciples asked Your Son to teach them to pray: I also need to learn how to pray, so please teach me. In Jesus' Name,
Amen.

March 8

"Yet even now," declares the LORD, "Return to me with all your heart, and with fasting, weeping and mourning; and rend your heart and not your garments." Now return to the LORD your God, for He is gracious and compassionate, slow to anger, abounding in lovingkindness and relenting of evil. (Joel 2:12-13)

When chosen Israel was retold the Covenant with God, it was given the choice of two ways: a way of life, obeying God and keeping to the blessings of the Covenant; and one of death, rejecting the gracious choosing of God. As one who is called by God, you are now invited to make the same choice. One way involves rejection of God, the indulgence in sin, and the limitless graspings of the fallen, selfish human heart. The other way is one of life, because it is eternal life with God, who forgives your sins in His eternal, only-begotten Son, Jesus Christ. Choose life!

Most Blessed God,
Despite walking in my own selfish way, I have heard the call to follow Your Son Jesus Christ in His divine path. Grant me strength in the Spirit to follow in His death and in His resurrection. In Jesus' Name,
Amen

March 9

choose for yourselves today whom you will serve... (Joshua 24:15)

We must decide whom we are going to serve and get serious about it. The Bible warns of the consequences of not making that choice, of having had only a mediocre relationship with God: "So because you are lukewarm, and neither hot nor cold, I will spit you out of my mouth" (Revelation 3:16). Maybe you went to church when you woke up in time, or prayed before dinner, but still put almost everything else in your life before God. It's time we grew up spiritually, and made Jesus the Lord of our lives!

The Bible says that a double-minded person shouldn't expect to receive anything from the Lord (James 1:7-8). If you are wondering why you feel your prayers aren't getting answered, maybe it's time to take spiritual inventory. Pray for strength and God will help you. Choose to serve Him today.

Almighty God,
I give you thanks that You have chosen me in Your wondrous grace, for the sake of Your Son's saving work. Enable me to tell others of this life-giving, life-saving work. In Jesus' Name,
Amen.

March 10

But seek first His kingdom and His righteousness, and all these things will be added to you. (Matthew 6:33)

So many people are searching for the right person to marry, the right boyfriend or girlfriend, the perfect career, the right place to live, and so on. This scripture tells us that if we put God first, and seek after Him, He will show us the right path. In other words, keep God first in your life. Don't take your eyes off Him; just keep doing His will, and the next thing you know, that right person, right friend, right career, will be in your path.

Don't be distracted by fears or anxiety about the future. Just keep your eyes on the One who has your best interests at heart.

Dear Lord,
There are a lot of tasks and activities that I have to do where I have a hard time seeing how they are part of Your kingdom and righteousness. Help me to serve You even in the most ordinary things I do. Be present even in those tasks, just as You are present in my mind and heart. In Jesus' Name, **Amen.**

March 11

The spirit of a man can endure his sickness, but as for a broken spirit who can bear it? (Proverbs 18:14)

A person crushed in spirit usually has been so hurt and devastated that he feels there is no hope. He or she has been wounded so deeply or so often thathe (or she) thinks it is impossible to be whole again. But God can heal anyone willing to trust Him and give Him their hurts and frustrations. After all, He is the One who brought Lazarus back from the dead; He is the One who parted the Red Sea; He is the One who turned the water into wine; He is the One who cast demons out of people; He is the One who made the blind to see. If He can do all that, then He certainly can heal a broken spirit.

Don't continue to live in the past with all your pain. Allow God to take away all of the hurting. Be honest with Him, turn to Him and admit that you are devastated and that you need His help. If you do that, He will see you through your crisis. No matter what has happened, your life can be changed.

Merciful Lord,

It is Your eternal will and nature to have mercy. As You forgive my past sins, help me to believe that I am forgiven, and thereafter to rise to serve You as a new creation. In Jesus' Name,

Amen.

March 12

Where there is no vision, the people are unrestrained, but happy is he who keeps the law. (Proverbs 29:18)

When God gives you a vision, or lets you know of something He wants you to do (He might speak to you through prayer, Bible reading, preaching, and the advice of Christian brothers and sisters), you are to set goals and make plans that will guide you. When God plants that vision in your heart, you have to cultivate it so it can grow. Pursue your plan steadily, and don't waver. Stand firm no matter what comes along—or what doesn't come along (like money). Remember, we walk by faith and not by sight. Also, study the Word of God with regard to your goals. Find scriptures that support your God-given goal and confess them daily. This is a real faith builder, and will help you avoid discouragement.

A friend of mine once told me she believed God wanted her to go on a missions trip. I saw her a few months later, but when I asked her how her plans for the trip were coming along, she told me that she had informed God that she would know that the trip was His will if the money was there. In other words, she was waiting for God to do all the work. Where's the faith in that? At first, she had truly believed that God was calling her to go, so she should have had faith and worked as hard as she could to make it happen. Instead, she sat back and waited for the work to be done for her, and her plans quickly fell apart.

Be diligent and consistent; follow what God has given

you, and you will see it come to pass. Keep that vision alive!

Dear Lord,

Help me earnestly to seek Your will for my life. Let me not be misled by my own selfish will, and strengthen me for Your service. In Jesus' Name,
Amen.

March 13

You shall love your neighbor as yourself. (Matthew 22:39)

How many of us can actually say we love our neighbor as much as ourselves? Our "neighbor" can be anyone in our life, but for now let's think about our literal, next-door neighbors. They may be strangers to us. I know it can be difficult to get to know new people, especially with everyone's busy schedules and so many people working on the weekends. Even when you're at home, the last thing you want to do is to hang out with people you hardly know.

I'm ashamed to admit it, but the last two places I lived, I didn't even know who my neighbors were. I wouldn't have recognized them if they had walked right by me on the street. We get so busy with other things—even important things, like missions work at church—that we forget our own neighborhood can need missionaries just like a poor nation might need them. A family can look and act like the "all-American family;" a nice home, a couple of kids, a couple of pets; and yet their lives may be falling apart. It's time that we as Christians started looking around at those close by, and seeing how they need to be ministered to. Love is not an option, it's a command!

Loving Father,

"Welcoming the stranger" isn't always easy. Help me to reach out to my neighbors—those I know and those who are

strangers to me. Let Your love shine through me and so draw them closer to You. In Jesus' Name,
Amen.

March 14

...do you not know that your body is a temple of the Holy Spirit who is in you, whom you have from God, and that you are not your own? For you have been bought with a price: therefore glorify God in your body. (1 Corinthians 6:19-20)

According to this, our bodies serve as a home for the Holy Spirit. Our bodies were important enough for God to pay the ultimate price. That means they no longer belong to us. We should therefore honor God with our bodies. This means making sure we're eating right; not smoking; not swearing; not having sex before marriage. It means being mindful of the way we dress, the jokes we tell, the way we talk to our parents, the music we listen to, and more. In fact, everything we do with our bodies should bring honor to God.

If you're honest, you'll be able to think of some areas of your life that are not honoring God. This verse is a reminder that God wants you to bring honor to Him in all you do. Admit to the Lord today what areas you need to work on, and then start afresh and move forward.

Almighty God,
Everything I have and everything I am belongs to You. Forgive me for my carelessness with Your gifts; grant that I may honor You through all that I do, and that I shall never abuse the body You have given me. In Jesus' Name,
Amen.

March 15

Who will stand up for me against evildoers? Who will take his stand for me against those who do wickedness? (Psalms 94:16)

I know most of us think we would always stand up for Christ. Just like Peter, who said he would never deny Jesus. But when the pressure was on, he denied Christ not just once, but three different times.

School and work can be very difficult, especially if most everyone around you uses foul language and lives a lifestyle that doesn't honor God. Be very careful—this can be where "bad company corrupts good morals" (1 Corinthians 15:33).

I once worked for a finance company in a very small office with only five employees. Everyone there, including the boss, used disgustingly foul language. When I asked someone a question, they would answer, and then add a few obscenities. I usually replied, "A simple "yes" or "no" would have been sufficient." They would kind of laugh, but it got my point across. They knew I was different because I didn't talk like they did. I wasn't invited to staff parties, but it really didn't bother me, since I knew all they would do is drink and swear.

When we moved away, I gave everyone there a Christian rock CD as a gift. I don't know what they thought of that. Still, I felt I had done my part by witnessing and sharing the Gospel with them, without falling into their habits just to fit in. A lot of people fear that if they don't act like the rest of the group, they'll be looked upon as "different." Celebrate that difference! The surprising thing is, no matter how much grief they might give you, other people will respect your restraint, even if they don't show it.

Dear Heavenly Father,

How could I ever be ashamed of You, my Creator and Redeemer? Let me boldly acknowledge You at all times; let

my every word and action reflect Your love and mercy, for Your glory. In Jesus' Name,
Amen.

March 16

But now your kingdom shall not endure. The LORD has sought out for Himself a man after His own heart, and the LORD has appointed him as ruler over His people, because you have not kept what the LORD commanded you. (1 Samuel 13:14)

The new leader mentioned is King David. Notice that God described King David as "a man after His own heart." Wouldn't it be cool if God said that about you?

Let me tell you a little bit about King David. He may have been a man after God's own heart, but that didn't mean he didn't let God down at times. Did you know that David lusted after a married woman? Then, as if that weren't bad enough, he had sex with her. Then he killed her husband so he could marry her. Wow! Lust, adultery, murder—and this was a man after God's own heart?

But David made things right with God. He repented and experienced God's mercy. Doesn't that give you hope in your own life? Perhaps you're struggling with a sin, and you really mean it when you tell God you're sorry, but then you fall again. Sometimes it takes a number of times finally to be victorious over a sin in your life. Pray that God will give you a hate for that sin, so it no longer appeals to you.

Don't give up. Stand up, and keep going. Don't ever underestimate God's mercy. He will forgive you if you're truly repentant. When all is said and done, you too will be a man or woman after God's own heart.

Gracious God,
Your ability to forgive me is beyond imagination. Help me never to make the mistake of thinking my sin is beyond Your power to forgive, but let me always seek You with a

contrite and trusting heart. Thank You for Your love and mercy. In Jesus' Name,
Amen.

March 17

I have set the LORD continually before me... (Psalms 16:8)

We get so preoccupied with the things of this life that we sometimes let those things take precedence over God. We hold onto worldly things whether they are pleasing to God or not. Sometimes they rule our lives; it's almost like they become our gods. It's easy to put God on a shelf and only use Him when we get into a bind. We find excuses to try getting along without Him in everyday situations, even though we profess Him as Lord and Savior of our life. Maybe it's because we don't actually believe He is entirely capable of caring for all our needs without our interference.

Even people in the ministry can easily become so preoccupied with doing things *for* God that they actually stop spending time *with* God. It's very easy to allow things to creep into our lives and take up our time so that we unintentionally put God up on that shelf. If you find that you have not set the Lord always before you, you haven't put Him first, then be honest, acknowledge this, and ask God for the desire to spend more time with Him. It's time to take God off the shelf permanently, and do what this verse says: always set the Lord before you!

God of All,
You are above all things. Help me to put You first in my life. Let me always remember that the work of Your kingdom is for Your glory, not my own. In Jesus' Name,
Amen.

March 18

Romans 12:19

Never take your own revenge, beloved, but leave room for the wrath of God, for it is written, "Vengeance is mine, I will repay," says the Lord. (Romans 12:19)

God tells us that holding a grudge against someone isn't right, that it isn't our responsibility to seek revenge on a person. If you do this, you're taking on responsibility that isn't yours. Holding a grudge or trying to get even is wrong. God has forgiven us, and in the same way, He expects us to forgive others.

I know a woman who seems to keep a mental ledger of people who have hurt her, including how many times, the date, and what was done to her. She is absolutely miserable, not so much because of the wrongs done to her, but because she hasn't forgiven these people. It eats away at her. When we do something that hurts God, He doesn't hold a grudge or take revenge on us. He has compassion for us. That's why He sent His only Son to die on the cross for us. Instead of sending judgment on us, He gave us the gift of eternal life.

If there is someone you're bearing a grudge against, write down his or her name on a piece of paper. Admit to God that you're having a hard time with this, but that you're willing to let Him take over and deal with it. Then tear up that piece of paper, telling God that you will no longer hold the sin against the sinner, that you are turning it over to Him. If it seems too difficult, ask God for strength, and He will give it to you. This will set you free!

Dear Lord,

I don't want to be a prisoner of my anger or bitterness over a past wrong done to me. Let me sacrifice these things to You and Your wisdom, so that I may live in peace and reconciliation. In Jesus' Name,

Amen.

March 19

For what will it profit a man if he gains the whole world and forfeits his soul? Or what will a man give in exchange for his soul? (Matthew 16:26)

People look for all kinds of ways to gain financial security. They plot, plan, and put together financial charts, thinking, "Just one more deal, one more big bonus, or one more win at the races, and I'll have it *made*." They keep searching, trying to satisfy that inner desire they think will make them happy.

It is of the utmost importance to remember that money will *not* bring you eternal life. Only Christ can do that. *He alone* can fill the void in our lives, and fill it with abundance. Not only that, but the Bible says He will give us the desires of our hearts (Psalm 37:4).

Eternal God,

It horrifies me to imagine gaining everything in the world and yet being without You and eternal life with You. Whenever I get my priorities wrong, turn me around to see that You are my greatest love and ultimate treasure. In Jesus' Name,
Amen.

March 20

A good name is to be more desired than great wealth, favor is better than silver and gold. (Proverbs 22:1)

People who lie sooner or later get trapped in their own lies. I have known too many Christians who lied and dealt dishonestly in their businesses. And you know, it sure didn't take long for the word to spread around that they should be avoided. My mother-in-law works in real estate, purchasing older homes to repair and resell. On many occasions, she could have cut corners to save money or time. But she has always gone the extra mile to make things right. And it certainly has paid off for her, because other people in the real estate business know her to be honest and fair.

A good reputation is valuable. In fact, it's something all the money in the world can't buy. Proverbs 19:22 tells us that it's better to be poor than a liar. When people mention your name, what do you want them to say about you?

Gracious Lord,

You teach me Your will through the witness of Your faithful, and Your Holy Word. Allow me to hear and listen for what is right and true and good in life, so that people may see my good works, and glorify You. In Jesus' Name,
Amen.

March 21

For all that is in the world, the lust of the flesh and the lust of the eyes and the boastful pride of life, is not from the Father, but is from the world. (1 John 2:16)

One form of "lust of the eyes" is money. This particular kind of lust is seen in people who form cliques based on it, including in their social group only others who have money, or wear a certain brand of clothing, or drive fancy cars.

God condemns attitudes like this, for these attitudes or actions say loudly that ownership of material things is more important than knowing God. The Bible warns against loving the world and the things of the world more than we love God (see 1 John 2:15, "[d]o not love the world nor the things in the world. If anyone loves the world, the love of the Father is not in him.")

It can be easy to fall into traps like this. The message of materialism is everywhere we turn, self-centeredly proclaiming, "I deserve these things, and I deserve them now!

Look out for 'Number One,' and forget about everyone else, right?" Wrong! That attitude "comes not from the Father but from the world."

Put aside "the boastful pride of life" and look only to God.

Provident Lord,

It's hard not to be so material; everyone seems to put so much emphasis on owning things, as if those things make a person what they are. Whenever I want things I don't need or shouldn't have, please tell me, and make me aware of my selfish greed. I want to be satisfied with what I have, and all that I am given out of Your divine, generous goodness. In Jesus' Name,
Amen.

March 22

Love is patient, love is kind and is not jealous; love does not brag and is not arrogant, does not act unbecomingly; it does not seek its own, is not provoked, does not take into account a wrong suffered, does not rejoice in unrighteousness, but rejoices with the truth; bears all things, believes all things, hopes all things, endures all things. (1 Corinthians 13:4-7)

What an inventory! If you think you might be in love, or if someone tells you he or she loves you, and you're just not sure, then check out this scripture to see if things add up. If the person who claims to love you is pressuring you for premarital sex, or to go out drinking, or to do something else against God's Word, then that should make you think twice. That kind of pressure doesn't reflect the love described in this Bible verse. Nor does a jealous boyfriend or girlfriend who doesn't trust you, or one who often loses his or her temper with you, or one who is always bringing up past mistakes. If these things are happening to you, it may be a good idea to re-evaluate your relationship.

If everyone would handle relationships according to this verse, a lot of heartache would be spared. Keep in mind that God wants you to be happy, and if your relationship is in constant turmoil, maybe it's time to pray and ask God why, and what's going on, and what to do about it.

Lord of all Love,

You are the author of all love, and have shown the world the greatest example of love that is possible. Teach me, one of Your beloved children, how I shall love. There is so much about love that I hardly know or understand. I will listen and learn all You will reveal to me. In Jesus' Name,
Amen.

March 23

My brethren, do not hold your faith in our glorious Lord Jesus Christ with an attitude of personal favoritism. (James 2:1)

Prejudice is a sin; we all know that. When we hear the word "prejudice," we usually think of prejudice against someone of a different race. But there are other kinds, too, including prejudice against people of different denominations. Some people think their denomination is better, that it alone has the correct way to interpret the Bible.

Or how about financial prejudice? Do you think differently about people based on how they dress? James 2 warns against judging a person's value by their appearance, showing favoritism toward those dressed in fine clothes. Have you ever caught yourself doing this? We need to be very careful not to judge a person's worth by what he or she looks like on the outside. After all, God looks at the content of our hearts, not the contents of our closets.

Lord of All Nations,

You have created a vast human family of many nations, races and languages. Help me to appreciate all humanity, whom you have created in Your Image and redeemed and restored according to the Image of Your Son Jesus Christ. As

You love Your human creation, Lord, instill the same love in me for all human persons. In Jesus' Name,
Amen.

March 24

For if we believe that Jesus died and rose again, even so God will bring with Him those who have fallen asleep in Jesus. (1 Thessalonians 4:14)

Many of us have lost a loved one. Maybe a grandparent, maybe a close friend, maybe even a parent. This verse can bring us comfort. Loving others sets us up for sorrow, but we can find solace in the knowledge that Christians will see one another again in heaven.

My mom died in November 1981 of a sudden stroke. Of course, I was shocked and grieved, but she had given her heart to the Lord on her deathbed, and I know I will see her again someday. It's hard to think so far ahead, especially when a death has just occurred. But God has provided a way for us to be reunited with our loved ones and spend eternity with them and Him. This should make us want to be very sure that all of our friends and family have heard the Good News and are going to heaven.

Jesus Christ is the victor! He has "abolished death and brought life and immortality to light through the gospel" (2 Timothy 1:10). Through Him, "death is swallowed up in victory" (1 Corinthians 15:54). So take heart; because of the death and resurrection of Christ, the grief that strikes when we lose a loved one can melt away. We can take comfort in knowing we will see them again.

Dear Lord God,
Please help me to remember that Your Son conquered death, and that our loved ones who die believing in You are not lost to us, but born to eternal life. Guide me and comfort

me through those scary and painful times, until the day that we are all reunited in You. In Jesus' Name,
Amen.

March 25

All Scripture is inspired by God and profitable for teaching, for reproof, for correction, for training in righteousness; so that the man of God may be adequate, equipped for every good work. (2 Timothy 3:16-17)

All of us grow up with traditions, and in Christian families, with Christian traditions. For example, maybe you open up one present on Christmas Eve and save the rest for Christmas morning. Or maybe your family goes over to your grandparents' house on Christmas Day. Traditions are nice, but they should never be confused with or take precedence over the Gospel.

Sometimes it is hard to tell the difference between our cultural beliefs and the Biblical truth. As we grow, we must make sure our beliefs are based on the Bible, rather than just tradition. That's why it is so important to know the Word of God. Then we can check our traditions against it, be taught, corrected, and trained by it, and so stay on track.

Take heed of Christ's admonition to the Pharisees: "You are experts at setting aside the commandment of God in order to keep your tradition" (Mark 7:9). Don't make the same mistake. Faith in Christ and adherence to the Gospel, not tradition, will lead us to eternal life.

Gracious Lord,
You have given us Your holy and true words; what a precious gift! Let us not spurn such a treasure, but respect it, obey it, and gladly hear and learn of it. In Jesus' Name,
Amen.

March 26

Set your mind on the things above, not on the things that are on earth. (Colossians 3:2)

How many of us practice this on a daily basis? Not many, I'll bet. We so easily get caught up in small things, and allow life's struggles and difficulties to overwhelm us.

I recently saw a documentary on Christians in other countries who are being persecuted for their faith in God. It showed small children being sold as slaves for about $15 each, and the dead bodies of people who had been beaten to death for having a Bible study.

Can you imagine that? What if you had to live knowing that if someone found you reading this devotional, you could be killed? It sure was an eye-opener for me, and I felt rather ashamed of myself for the many times I've allowed my bad attitude to dictate my actions. I had to repent and ask God to forgive me for having my mind set on earthly things.

Seeing that footage of fellow Christians suffering made my small problems seem suddenly insignificant. I have started to pray for these persecuted Christians, and I challenge you to do the same. Even though we don't know them personally, they are our brothers and sisters in Christ, and we need to lift them up in prayer.

Lord of All Hopefulness,

I commit myself this day to Your assembly of believers, the Body of Christ, throughout all corners of the earth. Unite us all in one common purpose and mission, to serve You and our neighbor. We give You thanks that You have entrusted us with such an important task, to be about the work of Your Kingdom. In Jesus' Name,
Amen.

March 27

[God made an oath] so that by two unchangeable things in which it is impossible for God to lie, we who have taken refuge would have strong encouragement to take hold of the hope set before us. (Hebrews 6:18)

Have you ever been disappointed by someone who lied to you? Probably everyone has, including me. Falsehood, misrepresentation, fraud, dishonesty, deception...after you have experienced these, it's hard to trust again; we want everything in writing and proven to us in advance. It's sad that it has to be that way, that what used to be agreed upon by a handshake now often requires an attorney, witnesses, and a notary public.

Because we have been betrayed and lied to in the past, it's especially wonderful to know that God never lies, that His Word is truth. We can go anytime to God's Word, and depend upon any of His promises, and know beyond a shadow of a doubt that they will come to pass. Never let your trust in God falter—He will never lie to you nor let you down. Be "greatly encouraged" by that promise!

Heavenly Father,
I want to find the truth, and in finding You I have found the ultimate Truth. Give me Your Truth in every part of my life, and set me free from falsehoods that I formerly would cling to. In Jesus' Name,
Amen.

March 28

The world is passing away, and also its lusts; but the one who does the will of God lives forever. (1 John 2:17)

Keep this in mind when temptations come along that sway you to do something you shouldn't be doing. Whatever pleasure sin brings is only temporary. Sooner or later it will wear you out, because ultimately, sin brings only death and destruction. Yes, the temptation can be strong, and the sin can look very good (that's why it's called temptation!). But we need to remember that "the world and its desires pass away" whereas heaven is forever.

Do the right thing. Ask for God's help, and turn your back on sin. You will be rewarded.

Eternal God,

There are many things in this world to desire. While the temporary things of this world crumble to dust between my fingers, let me see the everlasting reality of Your heavenly kingdom. In Jesus' Name,
Amen.

March 29

Let us hold fast the confession of our hope without wavering, for He who promised is faithful... (Hebrews 10:23)

When I started a group called New Generation Ministries, a lot of people didn't believe we could do it. In spite of the doubt and negativity, we held onto what God had told us, and didn't allow that doubt to enter our minds. Still, it was hard at times. When people threw discouragement at us, we just had to resist it. We told God we didn't believe what other people said, but only what He had said.

When the ministry started, we had nothing. But within one month, we had a brand new computer and monitor that an individual had felt led to buy for the ministry. We also had someone donate money so we could purchase a printer and a desk. Someone else donated the printing of our letterhead and envelopes. All this happened within just a few weeks!

Are you wavering on something God has told you to do? We need to tell Him that we will not doubt. Put any thoughts like that at the feet of Jesus. "Hold unswervingly" to His faithfulness, and He will indeed be faithful.

Merciful Lord,
The earliest company of Your disciples did not shrink from speaking out in Your name. Inspire me and my brothers and sisters to do the same thing, in the boldness of Your Spirit. In Jesus' Name,
Amen.

March 30

But the fruit of the Spirit is love, joy, peace, patience, kindness, goodness, faithfulness, gentleness, self-control; against such things there is no law. (Galatians 5:22-23)

Self-control. How many people give the cop-out answer, "I just can't control myself"? According to the Bible, that answer just won't do!

Remember Philippians 4:13: "I can do all things through Him who strengthens me." No matter what the problem may be, whether it's drinking, drugs, stealing, sex, an eating disorder—God will help you if you keep the communication lines with Him constantly open. Tell Him your weakness, and then find someone to whom you can be accountable, someone with whom you can meet and pray periodically. Get together with your partner and lift each other up in prayer. This can make a big difference in your life. Matthew 26:41 says, "Keep watching and praying that you may not enter into temptation; the spirit is willing, but the flesh is weak." Hang in there; you can make it!

Gracious Lord,
How can I show forth the fruits of Your Spirit? I give You thanks for placing me in Christ. Continue that work, I pray, that the Spirit may produce good fruit in me! In Jesus' Name,
Amen.

March 31

When my spirit was overwhelmed within me, You knew my path. (Psalms 142:3)

In times of sorrow or discouragement, our spirit can grow faint, and anxiety can rob us of our peace of mind. But when that fearful, overwhelmed feeling tries to creep in, take it to God, and give that fear no place in your mind. Instead, "let us draw near with confidence to the throne of grace, so that we may receive mercy and find grace to help in time of need" (Hebrews 4:16).

Bring your cares to God, and don't be faint-hearted—He knows our path, even when we do not.

Almighty God,
When things get tough for me I often forget to ask for Your help. You know the way I should go — help me to remember that! In Jesus' Name,
Amen.

April 1

Brethren, even if anyone is caught in any trespass, you who are spiritual, restore such a one in a spirit of gentleness; each one looking to yourself, so that you too will not be tempted. Bear one another's burdens, and thereby fulfill the law of Christ. For if anyone thinks he is something when he is nothing, he deceives himself. (Galatians 6:1-3)

Do you have a friend who has strayed away from Christ? It's tempting to go and shake some sense into that person, to tell them to wake up and smell the coffee! It's true they need to be confronted, but at the same time—as we've talked about before—it must be done gently and lovingly. Remember that the purpose of anything we might say to them is to help them come to repentance, not to hurt them. If we attack them, and we are harsh and judgmental, it's an instant turnoff. Chances are they won't listen to us.

We have to be led by the Holy Spirit, and not act on our own, when trying to reach out to those who have gone astray. Pray that the Spirit will give you the right words to say. Try to stick to what God's word *is;* don't get caught up in your own interpretations. Try to affirm all the good points about the person; don't just knock them down. Pray that your friend will listen, awaken to the knowledge of his or her wrongdoing, and return to the Lord.

And never forget to pray for strength for yourself. As this scripture tells us, none of us is above temptation. If we're not careful, we too can go astray.

My Lord and God,

When I have sinned and somebody needs to tell me so, let me listen carefully to their concern. When I have to tell someone else that they have strayed, please give me the right words. In Jesus' Name,
Amen.

April 2

let us consider how to stimulate one another to love and good deeds, not forsaking our own assembling together, as is the habit of some, but encouraging one another; and all the more as you see the day drawing near. (Hebrews 10:24-25)

Why bother going to church? When your alarm goes off on Sunday morning, do you ever think, "I'm too tired—I'll just read my Bible instead." Or, "Why can't I just worship God from home?" before snuggling under the covers and going back to sleep?

We need the spiritual food and the encouragement we get from one another when we attend worship. What if you were a member of the football team, and you never showed up for practice? You sure wouldn't be a very effective member of the team.

In the end, it comes down to this: worship isn't optional—it's one of God's Commandments. If you feel you are too busy to go to church, then you simply need to adjust your schedule. It's a very important time; there's something special about being surrounded by your Christian brothers and sisters, with everyone around you singing and worshiping the Lord. It's also a time to get recharged, to be still and allow God to minister to you, and to unload all of your burdens. Worship can be quite a problem-solver, too. Many times, the very thing I'm going through is what the pastor talks about in the sermon, answering a lot of my questions.

So don't be "too busy" to attend worship. It's another of God's many ways of taking care of you.

Dear Lord God,

Thank You for the opportunity to worship with others. Help me to remember that worship is not just an obligation, but a duty, joy, and privilege. In Jesus' Name,
Amen.

April 3

"Is anything too difficult for the LORD? At the appointed time I will return to you, at this time next year, and Sarah will have a son."(Genesis 18:14)

Well? *Is* anything too hard for the Lord? Most of us would probably say no! However, when something comes up that requires us to be patient and wait on God, we often get impatient and take matters into our own hands. Sometimes we act as if God needs our assistance. So we start dabbling. The next thing you know, we've gotten ourselves into some kind of trouble. Then we have to humble ourselves before God and ask for His forgiveness and help getting us out of it.

Look at Sarah: God plainly told her that at the "appointed time" she would have a son. (The key here is the *appointed time*.) But Sarah got tired of waiting. She took matters into her own hands by using her servant Hagar as a surrogate mother. After Hagar became pregnant, however, Sarah got jealous and treated her so badly that Hagar ran away. You see, Ishmael (Hagar's son) was not the son God had planned for Sarah. His plan was for Sarah and Abraham to have Isaac—which eventually, at God's "appointed time," they did.

Whenever you get impatient and feel that maybe God needs your help in moving things along in your life, remember that our timetable is not necessarily God's. Save yourself a lot of trouble, and wait for His "appointed time."

Almighty God,
We praise Your eternal omnipotence and everlasting love. Whenever I place you in a box, thinking that something is too great for You to accomplish, remind me again of Your true Power and Wisdom. In Jesus' Name,
Amen.

April 4

And just as they did not see fit to acknowledge God any longer, God gave them over to a depraved mind, to do those things which are not proper, being filled with all unrighteousness, wickedness, greed, evil; full of envy, murder, strife, deceit, malice; they are gossips, slanderers, haters of God, insolent, arrogant, boastful, inventors of evil, disobedient to parents, without understanding, untrustworthy, unloving, unmerciful; and although they know the ordinance of God, that those who practice such things are worthy of death, they not only do the same, but also give hearty approval to those who practice them. (Romans 1:28-32)

Most of us would look at this scripture and say to ourselselves, "I would *never* hang around people who act like this!" But every day we can too easily be surrounded by negative influences. What kind of music do you listen to? Do you watch music TV channels? Of course it's by no means all bad. But a good portion of the secular media does promote the kinds of things mentioned in this scripture, either directly or indirectly. When we listen to secular music or watch movies, we should try to be selective. We should respect ourselves enough to stay clear of the bad influences. Often you don't even have to listen to music to know that it's bad news. You can tell just by looking at the album covers and titles!

Becoming a Christian doesn't mean that from now on you can listen only to Christian music, read only Christian books, and so on. But what you feed into your mind can make a big difference in how you live your life. If sinful thoughts or words go in, sinful actions come out. Think it over.

God of Steadfast Mercy,
Thank You for the forgiveness You have given us in the New Covenant in Jesus Christ. Teach me what sin is, so that I may avoid it and do Your good and gracious will. In Jesus' Name,
Amen.

April 5

For we must all appear before the judgment seat of Christ, so that each one may be recompensed for his deeds in the body, according to what he has done, whether good or bad. (2 Corinthians 5:10)

"I just can't help myself!"

Have you ever said that? Sometimes we use that as an excuse to keep on doing things that are wrong, but seem just too fun to give up. Well, according to the Bible, we'll have to think of a better excuse than that for our sins. This one just won't fly with God!

When you're making choices, keep in mind that you *will* have to answer for all that you do. No matter what we do,

God knows about it, and He will judge us all according to what we have done, or not done. Pretty scary, huh? But it's not a hopeless case. If you've asked for God's forgiveness, then He has indeed forgiven you, and removed your sins from you as far as the east is from the west. If you really want help in doing what is right, then ask God. He's always ready to help His children, if we are willing to be honest and go to Him.

Gracious God,
May I never boast about my good works, or be ashamed forever about my sins. Because of Jesus I will stand before You at the Judgment, forgiven and made righteous, and I will praise Your name for all ages. In Jesus' Name,
Amen.

April 6

I solemnly charge you in the presence of God and of Christ Jesus, who is to judge the living and the dead, and by His appearing and His kingdom: preach the word; be ready in season and out of season; reprove, rebuke, exhort, with great patience and instruction. (2 Timothy 4:1-2)

Have you ever been in this situation? You're with someone who asks a tough question about God, or says something critical about Christianity. You don't quite know how to answer, so you hem and haw, and beat around the bush, and finally give an answer that you're not totally sure is correct. Did you feel afterwards like you blew your opportunity? Didn't it make you almost want to memorize the entire Bible, so that you could be ready next time?

You never know if you might be the only Christian that person might see or talk to. You might be the person with the only chance to make a difference in their life. This is another reason that it's vital to know God's Word, and know it well. That way, we can be prepared "in season and out of season" (that is, both when we're ready for it and when we're not) to share our faith.

Heavenly Father,
Please give me the wisdom and knowledge that I need when I am asked challenging questions about hope and faith. In Jesus' Name,
Amen.

April 7

For our struggle is not against flesh and blood, but against the rulers, against the powers, against the world forces of this darkness, against the spiritual forces of wickedness in the heavenly places. (Ephesians 6:12)

It's so frustrating to try sharing your faith with someone whose mind is closed from the outset. Again and again they'll come back and challenge you, blasting you with their closed opinion on why Christianity is a waste of time, doesn't work, or whatever. I've had this experience with family members. It can drive you to distraction, make you want to argue, shake them up, *wake* them up!

The devil loves it when you end up getting exasperated and angry with such people, especially when you decide in frustration that they are not worth wasting your time on. When their minds are really closed to faith and reason, you should see them as blinded by the devil. Things may not be as simple as just trying to win them over with an argument. Don't try to do it yourself, because you can't. We need to pray for these people, asking God for the opportunity and the words to share His Good News. Keep in mind who the real enemy of our soul is, and pray for God's strength and guidance in being His witness.

God Most High,
There are spiritual battles around me that I often don't

know anything about. Thank You that Christ in me is more powerful than any evil force that I may encounter. In Jesus' Name, **Amen.**

April 8

The Spirit of the Lord God is upon me, because the Lord has anointed me to bring good news to the afflicted; He has sent me to bind up the brokenhearted, to proclaim liberty to captives and freedom to prisoners... (Isaiah 61:1)

Shame is a powerful force. Shame over something we are, something we did, or something done to us can make us captive to the embarrassment and guilt it causes. In this way, it can render us unable to experience the joy and freedom of life in Christ. Being a prisoner to our shame can make us desperate for approval, acceptance, and love from others. We become dependent on others for our own feelings of self-worth. Our shame can also cause us to doubt whether we are truly loved and accepted by Jesus.

Never doubt this.

After all, look what He endured for us: "*[Let us fix]* our eyes on Jesus, the author and perfecter of faith, who for the joy set before Him endured the cross, despising the shame, and has sat down at the right hand of the throne of God." (Hebrews 12:2). So that we could live a victorious life of joy and freedom, He took our shame upon Himself, proclaiming "liberty to captives and freedom to prisoners."

If you are living in guilt and shame, pray for deliverance. God will exchange that shame for the freedom and dignity purchased for us at the cross.

Sovereign Lord,

Inspire me with Your Holy Spirit to seek out and care for those lost and forgotten by the world, but for whom Christ gave his life. In Jesus' Name, **Amen.**

April 9

Bless the LORD, O my soul, and all that is within me, bless His holy name. Bless the LORD, O my soul, and forget none of His benefits... (Psalms 103:1-2)

Are there times when you just don't feel like praising God? Maybe things aren't going so well, and you can't think of any reason you *should* praise Him. If so, then look over Psalm 103. It reminds us that God is the One:

Who pardons all your iniquities, Who heals all your diseases; Who redeems your life from the pit,
Who crowns you with lovingkindness and compassion;
Who satisfies your years with good things, so that your youth is renewed like the eagle.
The LORD performs righteous deeds and judgments for all who are oppressed.
The LORD is compassionate and gracious, slow to anger and abounding in lovingkindness.
He will not always strive with us, nor will He keep His anger forever.
He has not dealt with us according to our sins, nor rewarded us according to our iniquities. **(Psalm 103:3-6, 8-10).**

All of this, and heaven too! *Now* can you think of a few reasons to give praise and honor to God?

Gracious Lord,
You have given me everything, and I owe You everything. With my heart, soul, mind, and strength I pledge myself to serve and obey You. In Jesus' Name,
Amen.

April 10

Therefore if anyone is in Christ, he is a new creature; the old things passed away; behold, new things have come. (2 Corinthians 5:17)

How many of us allow our past to dictate our present? I have a friend who, because of an unhappy childhood over 30 years ago, still lives his life very ineffectively. He never goes to church, even though he says he's a Christian. He doesn't have any friends because he has a hard time trusting people, and so he never socializes. He is very moody, has very little joy in his life, and he doesn't date. Never has. He can't let anyone get close to him. He's never allowed himself to move out of his old life; therefore, he's just as unhappy now as he was then.

Today's scripture says that anyone in Christ is a new creation. Do you realize what that means? Not that we put on a new cover to hide the old, but that the old doesn't exist anymore—it's completely gone! Don't allow your past to keep you in bondage; rejoice in your new life!

Almighty God,
I rejoice today that You have made me a new creation through the saving power of the Cross. Cleanse my heart of fear, suspicion, and guilt, and open me to the redemptive power of Your love. In Jesus' Name,
Amen.

April 11

"Truly I say to you, whoever does not receive the kingdom of God like a child will not enter it at all." (Luke 18:17)

Children are so trusting. They don't have to check out, prove, and verify every little thing; they just trust what they're told. If their parents tell them they'll get them ice cream, or a new toy, they don't question—they just get excited, and start looking forward to it! They *know* it will happen.

This is the way our faith should be. We should believe unreservedly in God's promises, because He is our heavenly Father and He keeps His Word. Part of having the faith of a child is believing that God knows what is best for us, and that our will is not always His. This is the difference between child-*like*—having a child's trust and confidence in our Heavenly Father—and child-*ish*—wanting everything our own way. If we would truly have the faith as a little child we would never be disappointed, "for he who promised is faithful" (Hebrews 10:23).

Heavenly Father,

I am a powerless child before Your divine majesty, power and love. You are my Creator, Redeemer and Sanctifier. In Jesus' Name,
Amen.

April 12

The Lord appeared to him from afar, saying, "I have loved you with an everlasting love; Therefore I have drawn you with lovingkindness..." (Jeremiah 31:3)

Have you ever seen Christians trying to "witness" to others? I mean the kind who get in other people's faces, telling them they're going to hell if they don't repent? They sometimes come across as angry or dictatorial. Do you think that kind of attitude will make unbelievers come to know the Lord? If I were them, I'd take one look at that nasty attitude and figure I had heard enough!

Christ never screamed condemnation at the prostitutes, adulterers, and other sinners He hung out with. Remember, "God is love, and the one who abides in love abides in God, and God abides in him" (1 John 4:16). People who don't yet know Christ are much more open to someone sharing God's love with them than being threatened with damnation.

Try sharing John 10:9: "I am the door; if anyone enters through me, he will be saved". Or tell them that God has a wonderful plan for their lives (Jeremiah 29:11), or how God gives us great joy (Luke 2:10), "peace...which surpasses all comprehension" (Philippians 4:7), and hope (Romans 15:4); strength (Isaiah 40:29), and wisdom, knowledge and happiness (Ecclesiastes 2:26). You can probably see what I'm getting at, and what a difference it would make to share God's love in a truly caring way.

Dear Lord God,
It's intimidating to be a witness sometimes. Please guide me and give me the words I need to express Your love and goodness. Help me see my witnessing as an opportunity to share with others the joy that I have found in You. In Jesus' Name,
Amen.

April 13

Do not be bound together with unbelievers...what has a believer in common with an unbeliever? (2 Corinthians 6:14-15)

This verse can save people from a lot of heartache in their dating relationships. Many people truly believe they can change the non-Christian they're dating, and somehow bring them to faith. However, this can end in disaster. For one thing, *you* can't bring someone to faith in Christ—it takes the Holy Spirit. Also, entering into a relationship with the expectation of forcing a major life-change upon the other person is almost always a bad idea...for both of you.

In the end, many get their hearts broken. You have to realize that a non-Christian might be a fun, caring, wonderful person—but if they're lacking a relationship with God, and as a result there's a void in their life, then you aren't going to be big enough to fill it.

A relationship with a Christian - with a strong foundation of Christian love - will bring you a lot of joy.

Heavenly Father,

Help me to be selective, without being judgmental, in choosing my friends and whom I date. Thank You for the cords of Your love that bind Christian relationships. In Jesus' Name,
Amen.

April 14

He who walks righteously and speaks with sincerity, he who rejects unjust gain and shakes his hands so that they hold no bribe; he who stops his ears from hearing about bloodshed and shuts his eyes from looking upon evil; he will dwell on the heights, his refuge will be the impregnable rock; his bread will be given him, his water will be sure. Your eyes will see the King in His beauty; they will behold a far-distant land. (Isaiah 33:15-17)

Most of us probably think (or hope) that we are fair and honest people. But it's pretty tempting when the check-out person at the store gives us too much change back, or doesn't charge us enough for something we bought. Maybe we just walk away and pocket the money, and justify it to ourselves: "Well, I'm sure they've overcharged me and others for something in the past." Or how many of us "borrow" something from school or work, thinking to ourselves, "They don't need this as much as I do," or, "It's just a pen (or candy bar, or T-shirt)—they'll never miss it." It's at times like this that our true colors come through, as this kind of action can be so easy and so tempting, especially if you know no one is watching at the time. But remember that God knows all and sees all; even if no one else knows, He does.

No matter how small the item or amount of money, the bottom line is, if it doesn't belong to us, then taking it is stealing. The Seventh Commandment is clear: "You shall not steal" (Exodus 20:15). Remember this scripture the next time you're tempted, and ask for God to help you avoid sin and "walk righteously."

Dear Lord God,

I ask that You strengthen me that I may resist the temptation to sin by taking what is not mine. Let me speak and do what is right. Thank You, my King, for the promise of seeing You face to face. In Jesus' Name,
Amen.

April 15

Only give heed to yourself and keep your soul diligently, so that you do not forget the things which your eyes have seen and they do not depart from your heart all the days of your life...(Deuteronomy 4:9)

When the Israelites experienced God's protection against the Egyptian plagues, and the shackles falling off of them to free them from slavery, and the miracle of the Red Sea parting, they were so excited about what God had done for them that they shouted hosannas to the Lord over and over again. But once they had been traveling in the desert for three days without water, they started complaining. It was as if they had totally forgotten all the miracles God had repeatedly performed for them!

Aren't we the same way? We see God do miraculous things in our lives, and then when one difficulty comes along, we act like we don't know how or if God will take care of it. We start doubting His protection and provision in our lives, and allow all of the wonderful things He has done to "slip from our hearts."

I encourage you to keep a journal, so that when a hardship comes along, you can refer back to it and see over and over again how God comes through. This is a real faith-builder. And don't forget to read the ready-made journal we already have of all the things God has done—the Bible.

Almighty and All-Powerful Father,
Thank You for Your miracles, especially the miracle of my salvation. Let me never forget what You have done for me and for all Your people, so that, with a thankful heart, I may sing Your praises. In Jesus' Name,
Amen.

April 16

When He arrived at the place, He said to them, "Pray that you may not enter into temptation." (Luke 22:40)

It's great to know that you're not the only one facing the kinds of difficulties and problems you have in your life. Others have experienced—and are currently experiencing—the exact same things, and God will give you the strength to say no to whatever is trying to bind you and hold you captive.

James 4:7 reminds us, "Submit therefore to God. Resist the devil and he will flee from you." Know this—as a child of God, you *do* have authority over Satan. This is His promise to you: "Behold, I have given you authority to tread on serpents and scorpions, and over all the power of the enemy, and nothing will injure you" (Luke 10:19). That authority is something you have according to God's Word, whether you feel like you have it or not. So whatever it is that's got you in its grip, remember that God is stronger. Use your God-given authority to overcome that sin.

Dear Heavenly Father,
Without You, I am powerless over sin. Let me submit myself to You and seek Your protection against the Evil One. Thank You for Your faithfulness. In Jesus' Name,
Amen.

April 17

Give thanks to the LORD, for He is good; for His lovingkindness is everlasting. (Psalm 118:29)

Lets face it, we all have bad days. And some of those bad days turn into hard weeks, even bad months. Isn't it wonderful to know that our God is good, and that His love endures forever? It doesn't stop when we hit our 100th sin, or when our grades are bad, or when we're not feeling very loveable. God's love will never run out!

We all need to be reminded from time to time that God loves us. Sometimes we're so hard on ourselves; we might actually get to thinking that there's no way God could keep on loving us after all the bad things we've done. *Not true*! God hates the sin, but loves the sinner.

Take a few minutes today in your prayer time and thank God for loving you.

Loving Father,
I cannot be good enough to deserve Your love, so I praise You all the more for Your goodness and Your wondrous love, which is beyond my comprehension. In Jesus' Name,
Amen.

April 18

Love the Lord your God with all your heart, and with all your soul, and with all your mind. This is the great and foremost commandment. The second is like it, 'you shall love your neighbor as yourself.' (Matthew 22:37-39)

Many pop-psychology books tell us we have to learn to love ourselves before we can love others. We're encouraged to take care of ourselves first, attend to our own needs and desires. Some people would go so far as to say that that it doesn't matter what we have to do to accomplish this. That's why the world can be a selfish place, with people often walking on others, using them to get ahead.

But God's view of success is very different. Jesus demonstrated God's love by serving others. That should be our attitude as well. If you're in a popular group at school or an important position at work, and you misuse that status by treating others like they're worthless, then all you're doing is loving yourself. You're certainly not loving your neighbor, and you're also failing to love God with all your heart.

Follow these two commandments of Jesus—if we love and serve God as we should, it's easy to reach out to others with His love. When we do this, we are fulfilling our true personhood in Christ.

O Lord,

I know what I must do to inherit eternal life: believe in You, and love You with all my heart and soul and mind; and through Your love, also love my neighbor. You have made the path to You so easy, Lord, but still I struggle against You through the desires of my own selfish will. Help me to love You and be obedient to You so that I may keep these two greatest commandments. In Jesus' Name,
Amen.

April 19

There is no fear in love; but perfect love casts out fear, because fear involves punishment, and the one who fears is not perfected in love. (1 John 4:18)

When we love God with our whole heart, soul, and mind, then fear has no place in our lives. We don't need to worry about self-image; we can just shrug off insults and rudeness. Because of God's perfect love, we know who we are in Christ. We don't need to worry about the future—we know that God will lead and direct us into whatever He has in store for us. In other words, we can trust God enough to believe that He always has our best interests in mind, and that whatever He calls us to do will be to our benefit.

There is no fear in God and there is no failure in God. Remember, fear has no authority over us—we have been set free from fear by God's perfect love for us.

God, My Strength,

Thank You for setting me free from fear. Grant that I may meet each new day in Your service boldly and joyfully. In Jesus' Name,

Amen.

April 20

See how great a love the Father has bestowed on us, that we would be called children of God... (1 John 3:1)

Most of us like to have the opportunity to share our interests with others. If we're in school, maybe we wear a letter jacket and love to talk about how our team is doing. If we're employed, some of us may wear buttons that say "Ask me about..." to have a chance to "talk shop."

But how many of us are that willing and eager to share our faith with others? Do you have any idea of the impact we as Christians could have on the world, if only we would be that pumped on Jesus? If we would use some of that excitement to tell people of what Jesus has done for us, we could really turn this world upside down!

When you share what's important in your life, don't forget the most important thing of all: the love the Father has lavished on us, making us children of God!

Father God,

You are the Source of all my abilities, gifts, and interests. Forgive me for sometimes putting those things above You in my heart. Help me to be willing and eager to share my faith,

so that others may know the joy I have found in You. In Jesus' Name,
Amen.

April 21

...the mind set on the flesh is hostile toward God; for it does not subject itself to the law of God, for it is not even able to do so, and those who are in the flesh cannot please God. (Romans 8:7-8)

It's easy to move too quickly, be rash. Maybe we buy something or do something that doesn't seem quite right, but we submit to our sinful nature anyway. When you settle for what the flesh wants now, instead of waiting for what truly satisfies your spirit, you end up missing God's best. Instead, you get a poor second-best.

We went car shopping one Friday night and found the car that we *knew* was a gift straight from God; it was perfect for us and the deal went totally smoothly. But then, rather than waiting to call the bank to find out what we still owed on our old vehicle, we took a stab at the figure ourselves. Well, on Monday after we had signed the papers, we found out that we were off $700, and we had to do some real scrambling to make it work. If we had just waited two days we would have known—but no, we just had to have that car that night! The car was the right one, but we jumped too fast.

This was just a car, but people rush into even more important things. Some get married because they feel they're getting older and won't have many more chances, so they go ahead and marry someone who isn't quite right, thinking, "Well, he/she could be worse...." In doing this, they settle for less, rather than wait for God's best.

God can do abundantly more than we can ask or think or imagine on our own. Don't listen to your sinful nature; submit to God's law. He will do what's best for you in His own time.

Gracious God,

My sinful nature can so easily lead me astray, leading me to follow my own will instead of Yours. Let me never be hostile toward Your law; instead, let me delight in submitting to You. In Jesus' Name,

Amen.

April 22

[The law] shall be with him and he shall read it all the days of his life, that he may learn to fear the Lord his God, by carefully observing all the words of this law and these statutes... (Deuteronomy 17:19)

It can be hard to have devotions on a daily basis; we have so many things going on in our lives that can keep us from it, if we allow them to. Here are several scriptures to show us why it is so important to read the Bible daily:

Psalm 119:105: Your word is a lamp to my feet and a light to my path.

Joshua 1:8: This book of the law shall not depart from your mouth, but you shall meditate on it day and night, so that you may be careful to do according to all that is written in it; for then you will make your way prosperous, and then you will have success.

Jeremiah 15:16: Your words were found and I ate them, and Your words became for me a joy and the delight of my heart; for I have been called by Your name, O Lord God of hosts.

John 8:32: And you will know the truth, and the truth will make you free.

John 12:50: I know that His commandment is eternal life.

Almighty God,

I thank You for the gift of the Bible. Open my mind and heart as I read it, that Your message may take root and grow in me. Let me always seek and find You in Your Word, which is my comfort and my guide. In Jesus' Name,

Amen.

April 23

[A]nd there must be no filthiness and silly talk, or coarse jesting, which are not fitting, but rather giving of thanks. (Ephesians 5:4)

Sometimes it happens. You get with some close friends, you let your guard down, and you get careless with your language, or maybe you start telling off-color jokes. Normally you wouldn't, but you think, "Hey, I'm with good friends—we're not hurting anybody."

But once we start, it's easy to let those inappropriate words and thoughts become habitual, part of our daily lives. We need to watch our tongues. Ask yourself, "Would I say this if Jesus were standing here?" If not, it probably shouldn't be said at all.

Almighty God,

Forgive me for the times I have dishonored You with the things I say. Grant me the self-control to think twice before I speak, so that my words will not lead anyone astray, but will instead be a reflection of Your love. In Jesus' Name,

Amen.

April 24

Be anxious for nothing, but in everything by prayer and supplication with thanksgiving let your requests be made known to God. (Philippians 4:6)

I've heard people say when they are going through a rough time, "All we can do is pray," as if it's a last resort that may or may not do any good.

Prayer is *powerful*. It does make a difference! Too often we give up and stop praying before the answer comes, because we think God isn't listening, or is saying no. Prayer is never in vain. If you start to feel during your prayer time like you're talking to yourself, remember—God is listening. He will answer in His own time, and according to His perfect will. "The effective prayer of a righteous man can accomplish much" (James 5:16).

Dear Heavenly Father,

You know all my needs before I do, and You meet them in Your own time. Strengthen my faith so that I am not anxious; help me to approach You with confidence and trust and a grateful heart. In Jesus' Name,

Amen.

April 25

For I am confident of this very thing, that He who began a good work in you will perfect it until the day of Christ Jesus. (Philippians 1:6)

Don't become discouraged because you're failing, in some areas in your life, to live according to God's Word. This isn't an excuse to say, "Hey, no one's perfect" and stop trying, but to let you know that God will give you the strength to work on these problem areas.

I certainly can't say that I have "arrived" in my Christian

walk—I know there are lots of ways that I fall short of what God wants from me. But I'm excited to know that He is going to continue the good work in me until it's complete on the "day of Christ Jesus." God is not going to leave me—or you—half-done!

We will not achieve perfection on this side of the grave, but we do need to try. God wants to continue His good work in you, if you will let Him. Confess your struggles to Jesus, ask Him to come in and do a good work in you, and then get ready, because He will! You can know, without a shadow of a doubt, that God is still working on you, and won't rest until you're completed.

God Most High,

I cannot help but fall short of perfection, but with You as my strength, I know that You will do good works in me and through me. Thank You for never giving up on me. In Jesus' Name,

Amen.

April 26

Now for this very reason also, applying all diligence, in your faith supply moral excellence, and in your moral excellence, knowledge, and in your knowledge, self-control, and in your self-control, perseverance, and in your perseverance, godliness, and in your godliness, brotherly kindness, and in your brotherly kindness, love. For if these qualities are yours and are increasing, they render you neither useless nor unfruitful in the true knowledge of our Lord Jesus Christ. (2 Peter 1:5-8)

All of us must be very careful not to judge others. I once went to a Christian concert, given by an artist who was fairly new to the faith. After the concert, I overheard some people ripping him to shreds for not singing all Christian songs; others were criticizing the way he was dressed. The poor guy never had a chance. Everyone assumed that because he had come to know Christ, he should have been Mr. Perfect.

And probably more to the point, they probably assumed that he should have been just like them.

There are as many ways to express our Christian faith as there are Christians. We all need room to grow spiritually and to strive toward that list of virtues given to us in 2 Peter. And we need to be able to do it without other Christians looking over our shoulder and being critical. Working on our own relationship with Christ, instead of worrying about that of others, is another way of showing brotherly kindness and Christian love.

Merciful Father,

Thank you for the grace You have shown me as I struggle with my own faith and Christian life. Let me show that grace to others who are similarly struggling, that we may support and encourage one another, and so be more productive and effective in Your service. In Jesus' Name,
Amen.

April 27

Do not love the world nor the things in the world. If anyone loves the world, the love of the Father is not in him. (1 John 2:15)

It's easy to let other things in our lives come before God. We get busy with school, work, our friends…and the next thing you know, we haven't prayed or read the Bible in days, or weeks.

We need to be vigilant about this. If anyone or anything in our lives becomes more important to us than God—and usually we don't even realize this has happened—then that person or thing is an idol, and we need to pray for the courage to part with it, and put our priorities in the proper order. We must remember the First Commandment, and always keep God first in our lives.

God of All,

You command us to have no other gods before You. Help me to remember that anything I place above You in my life is a false god, and so is causing me to be disobedient to You. Help me to keep everything in its proper perspective—with You above all things. In Jesus' Name,
Amen.

April 28

How blessed is he whose transgression is forgiven, whose sin is covered! How blessed is the man to whom the LORD does not impute iniquity, and in whose spirit there is no deceit! (Psalm 32:1-2)

God is always willing to forgive us our sins, but we must first admit to those sins and confess them. If you have problems admitting to sin and always have excuses for why you did what you did, be careful. God isn't fooled by our excuses. Instead, come clean with Him: "I acknowledged my sin to You, and my iniquity I did not hide; I said, "I will confess my transgressions to the LORD" and You forgave the guilt of my sin." (Psalm 32:5).

Don't allow sin to go on and on and build up; the longer it goes on unconfessed, the harder it is to admit to it.

Lord God,

If I think I am not sinful, I'm deceiving only myself. Let me not be so stubborn that I refuse the gift of Your forgiveness. Give me a contrite heart, willing to admit my faults and turn away from sin, toward You. In Jesus' Name,
Amen.

April 29

Do you not know that when you present yourselves to someone as slaves for obedience, you are slaves of the one whom you obey, either of sin resulting in death, or of obedience resulting in righteousness? But thanks be to God that though you were slaves of sin, you became obedient from the heart to that form of teaching to which you were committed, and having been freed from sin, you became slaves of righteousness. (Romans 6:16-18)

A lot of people get involved in things that end up controlling them. No one intentionally becomes a slave to something. People don't say, "Today I'm going to become an alcoholic," or "I want to have pornography control my life." Some believe that freedom is being able to do whatever you want, whenever you want. But the question is, can you *quit* whenever you want?

The only way to break slavery is to ask God for help and to submit yourself to His control; then you will be free. "For sin shall not be master over you, for you are not under law but under grace." (Romans 6:14).

Lord God, My Deliverer,

It's all too easy to become ensnared in sin. As You have already set me free from death, so free me from temptation to sinful acts and choices that would separate me from You. Thank You for the grace and mercy You show me every day. In Jesus' Name,

Amen.

April 30

Search me, O God, and know my heart; try me and know my anxious thoughts; and see if there be any hurtful way in me, and lead me in the everlasting way. (Psalm 139:23-24)

There are so many things that can keep God from being number one in our lives: boyfriend, girlfriend, sports, school, TV, friends, material things. It could be anything that you make time for even when you're too busy for prayer, devotions, or worship. Take a look into your own life to see what comes between you and God. None of those things, special as they may be, can lead you in "the way everlasting." Pray that God, who knows your heart, might help you put things right.

Lord,
Give me the courage to part with what I hold most dear, if it separates me from You. Please put into my heart the right desires and a thirst for You. In Jesus' Name,
Amen.

May 1

Jesus said to him, "I am the way, and the truth, and the life; no one comes to the Father but through me." (John 14:6)

People will try absolutely everything under the sun to look for peace and answers to their lives' questions. But real life comes only through Jesus. Even people who fill their lives with good works—feeding and clothing the poor and the hungry, crusading for human rights, and so on—can be left with a feeling of emptiness. That emptiness is the place where Christ belongs in all our lives.

Do you have that empty feeling? If so, then pray for God's forgiveness of your sins, and that He will fill you with His joy and peace. He can, and He will: "I came that they may have life, and have it abundantly." (John 10:10).

Lord God,
You alone can provide what's missing in my life. Let my good works come not from my own neediness, but from the

fullness of a heart overflowing with Your love. In Jesus'
Name,
Amen.

May 2

*I will give thanks to the LORD with all my heart; I will tell of all
Your wonders. I will be glad and exult in You; I will sing praise
to Your name, O Most High. (Psalms 9:1-2)*

Praise is supposed to be a regular part of our prayer life—
but it's hard sometimes, isn't it? Even when there's nothing
in particular that's bothering us and making praise difficult,
it just isn't an easy thing to do. We try—we tell God how
great He is, how amazing it is that He created us, and the
earth, and the heavens, etc…but then maybe we start to
feel a little silly, like we're gushing over Him. And anyway,
He already knows all the wonderful things He has done! So
before long, we're back to praying for what we want and
need from Him, instead of offering praise for what He has
already done.

God wants us to come to Him in prayer for *all* things:
confession, petition, thanksgiving…and praise. If you don't
know where to start, start right here in Psalms. Let those
beautiful words speak for you, until you find the words yourself to thank and praise God for all He is and does.

Almighty God
You know what is in my heart before I tell You. Accept
my praises, imperfect though they are, for my words can't
express Your wondrous love. In Jesus' Name,
Amen.

104

May 3

Blessed be the Lord, who daily bears our burden, the God who is our salvation. (Psalm 68:19)

For those of us who tend to have a hard time not worrying about things, no matter how big or small, this is something we need to be reminded of. God has no intention of letting us carry our burdens alone. No matter what it is, God cares, and will take from us our griefs, struggles, and problems, if we will just give up control of them. His invitation is always there: "Come to me, all you who are weary and burdened, and I will give you rest" (Matthew 11:28). This familiar hymn perhaps puts it best:

Have we trials and temptations? Is there trouble anywhere?
We should never be discouraged, take it to the Lord in prayer!
Can we find a friend so faithful who will all our sorrows share?
Jesus knows our every weakness, take it to the Lord in prayer.[1]

If you're carrying a heavy load, then it's time to turn it over to Him who knows our every weakness, who will carry for us our griefs and sorrows.

Loving Father,
I know You hear me when I cry. Teach me not to struggle alone with my sorrows, but to come to You for comfort and ease. Thank You for bearing my burdens. In Jesus' Name, **Amen.**

---

[1] Joseph Scriven, *What A Friend*, ed. Florence M. Martin. Miami, Florida: Paul A. Schmitt Music Company, 1940.

May 4

He who conceals a transgression seeks love, but he who repeats a matter separates intimate friends. (Proverbs 17:9)

Very clear message: *do not gossip!* We've all had someone do or say something to hurt our feelings or make us angry. And we don't always handle it well. Rather than going to that person and talking it out, we immediately storm off to someone else, and tell them what the person did to us. Usually we don't end it with the one incident; we go on to complain about other things too. The next you know, we've made the person out to be a complete monster.

"Concealing a transgression" doesn't mean letting others walk all over us, or pretending it didn't happen. And it doesn't mean we can't seek advice on the matter from a close friend or confidante. But it *does* mean resisting the temptation to broadcast to the world that you have been wronged, with the goal of making the other person look bad or getting people "on your side."

Take some time, cool off, and then go talk to the person directly. Usually that's enough to clear things up. If not, then at least you have done what is right. And don't forget, in this and all tough situations, to pray for strength and guidance. It helps.

Most Holy God,

Let me come to You when I am hurt and angry. Give me the strength to keep my own counsel, so that I may not injure my friends through my rash or careless words. In Jesus' Name,
Amen.

May 5

Lying lips are an abomination to the LORD, but those who deal faithfully are His delight. (Proverbs 12:22)

Have you ever promised someone you would do something, and then a "better" offer or opportunity came along? Did you keep your word, or did you make up an excuse? It can be so tempting to try to get out of that promise, but as Christians, it's especially important that we keep our word. If people can't trust us to keep our promises, then why should they trust us at all? They might think, "What else are they being untruthful to me about?" And don't resort to "little white lies" to make your life easier. It may seem that lying is the easiest way out of a situation, or the only way to avoid hurting someone's feelings. But usually, honesty early on will prevent you from getting into that kind of situation in the first place.

Remember the Eighth Commandment: "You shall not bear false witness against your neighbor." (Exodus 20:16). Be dependable and truthful.

Faithful God,
Help me resist the temptation to lie for the sake of my own convenience. Let me be kind in my truthfulness, honest whenever I can be honest, and silent if honesty seems too harsh. In Jesus' Name,
Amen.

May 6

Be hospitable to one another without complaint. (1 Peter 4:9)

I'm sure all of us have known the feeling of being "the new kid on the block," whether it was from starting at a new school, going to a new church, or moving to a new neighborhood. It's a pretty vulnerable and lonely feeling. Did you have someone reach out to you, introduce themselves, and show kindness to you? If so, then you know exactly how good it felt, what a relief it was to start feeling a sense of belonging.

That's the kind of hospitality we need to show others, even if it doesn't seem to be the "cool" thing to do, or if we fear we might look weird, or embarrass ourselves, or something. We are to love others as ourselves. A part of this is extending our hospitality and friendship to others, especially the new people who come our way. It's good for them, and it can be good for you, too: "Do not neglect to show hospitality to strangers, for by this some have entertained angels without knowing it." (Hebrews 13:2).

Dear Lord God,
I'm nervous sometimes of "hospitality," especially to strangers. Fear of being rejected or laughed at can hold me back. Strengthen me; let me reach out to others with Your love, so that no one in my life is made to feel a stranger. In Jesus' Name,
Amen.

May 7

My son, if sinners entice you, do not consent. (Proverbs 1:10)

If you're hanging out with some friends, and they all want to do something that you *know* is bad news, it can put you in a very difficult situation. You don't want to be the "different" one, or come across like a coward or "holier-than-thou." But usually, thinking through the consequences of the thing—whether it's stealing something just to see if you can get away with it, or watching an R- or X-rated movie, or going to a party your parents wouldn't want you to go to—you'll see, it just isn't worth it.

Keep your guard up. If you're in a questionable situation,

ask yourself, "What would my parents want me to do? What would Jesus want me to do?" What can at first seem like no big deal can turn into a *very* big deal, and end up getting you into trouble. Resist the pressure; do not give in.

Saving Lord,

I cannot resist temptation without Your strength. Help me to avoid situations that tempt me to sin, and give me the courage to be "different" for Your sake. In Jesus' Name, **Amen.**

May 8

Know therefore that the LORD your God, He is God, the faithful God, who keeps His covenant and His lovingkindness to a thousandth generation with those who love Him and keep His commandments... (Deuteronomy 7:9)

Isn't this wonderful to know? No matter what happens, God is faithful; He will never forsake those who love him and keep his commands. I've been told by friends who are suffering that they felt God had abandoned them, but that's impossible. Though we may feel alone, we are not. Remember, we don't depend on our feelings, but on what the Word of God says, and we don't judge the Word of God by our lives, we judge our lives by the Word of God. So be encouraged, and know that whatever you are facing, our faithful God is right by your side, and that nothing can ever separate us from the love of Christ.

Gracious, Electing God,

Out of Your pure divine mercy and goodness You have chosen me and all other Christians to be righteous and holy in Your sight. In Your love grant me faithfulness, even as You are faithful toward Your children. In Jesus' Name, **Amen.**

May 9

In this case, moreover, it is required of stewards that one be found trustworthy. (1 Corinthians 4:2)

Have you ever felt that you deserved *more*? More freedom at home from your parents, or maybe more promotions at work? We all have. But if you've ever abused your parents' trust, or abused your position at work, maybe this is the reason you haven't received anything more. How would you feel if you loaned someone your car to run an errand, and later you found out they had picked up a bunch of friends and gone joyriding all around town? You'd probably feel like they had taken advantage of your kindness, abused your faith—and you would be wary of loaning your car, or anything else, to them again.

This parallels our relationship with God. As we are faithful with a few things, He puts us in charge of more and more. Along with that comes more responsibility, more trust, and more respect. So next time you start wondering why you haven't received *more*, stop and examine how you have handled things in the past, and start being a better steward of the trust people place in you.

God my Father,

You have given me so much in my life. Teach me to be a faithful steward of Your trust, that I may acknowledge You as the ultimate Provider for everyone. In Jesus' Name,
Amen.

May 10

[Cast] all your anxiety on Him, because He cares for you. (1 Peter 5:7)

How can it be possible for us *not* to be anxious when things are turning upside-down in our lives? Our grades go down, we get laid off from work, our boyfriend or girlfriend breaks up with us, or there's trouble at home. There's probably always something going on that could keep us off balance.

God knew that along with this life comes trouble, and that His children need to have something they can count on in the midst of their problems. He tells us that if we turn everything over to Him by praying and giving Him thanks, then His peace will keep our hearts and minds steady.

So give to God your prayers and petitions with thanksgiving. Not only will you be a happier, more relaxed person, but what an example to others you will be when, in the midst of your troubles, you still have God's joy and peace!

Lord,
I had looked for Your peace for a very long time, and now I have found it in Your Son Jesus Christ and the Way of His Cross. Prepare my heart and mind and soul as I walk His Way, and give me His peace. In Jesus' Name,
Amen.

May 11

you have left your first love. (Revelation 2:4)

You know how it is when you get something new. At first, you spend all your time with it. If it's a new car, you wash it and wax it when it's not even dirty. If it's a new outfit, you get it home and immediately try it on to see what shoes go with it. If it's a CD, you listen to it over and over and over.... Do you remember as a kid getting new toys for Christmas that you'd play with every waking moment...until suddenly, they weren't new anymore? From then on, you didn't pay as much attention to them, only getting them out once in a great while.

We tend to do the same in our relationship with God. When we first come to faith, it can be so exciting—you're pumped up and ready to save the world! Then, after a while, we start taking God for granted, especially if things are going well. Our attitude becomes, "I'm busy right now—I'll pray and read my Bible later."

Don't forsake God like He's a worn-out Christmas toy. He is our Creator, our Heavenly Father, our first love. Make Him first in your life, and everything else will fall into place.

Almighty God,

I want to love others, but I know that You have commanded us to love You first and above all else. It is hard enough to do this, but easier when I think of Your great love toward us: You even gave Your one and only Son, so that we may find our way back to You. Kindle in us, Your children, the fire of Your eternal, divine love! In Jesus' Name,
Amen.

May 12

They profess to know God, but by their deeds they deny Him... (Titus 1:16)

Being an example is important. People who profess to be Christians and attend worship regularly, but live a distinctly un-Christian lifestyle the rest of the week, are examples of the worst sort. One of the biggest criticisms of Christianity by non-Christians is that kind of "hypocrisy." It makes it easy for those who see it not to become Christians themselves.

How about you? Are you one of those people who claim to know God, but say something very different through your actions? If so, it's never too late to start afresh. "'Come now, and let us reason together,' Says the LORD, 'though your sins are as scarlet, they will be as white as snow; though they are red like crimson, they will be like wool.'" (Isaiah 1:18).

We all know that Christians aren't perfect—we never will be, because we're human. But even so, we need to set as good an example as possible, trying to make our actions reflect Christ's love, rather than denying Him.

Living Lord,
Make me conscious of my actions, so that whatever I do will be to Your glory and honor. In Jesus' Name,
Amen.

May 13

For I am not ashamed of the gospel, for it is the power of God for salvation to everyone who believes... (Romans 1:16)

How do you react when you're with non-Christian friends or family members and the conversation turns to "religion?" Do you shrink back and keep quiet, or do you feel free to share God's Word? It can be very intimidating to be the only Christian in the group, especially when you're put on the spot about your faith.

I used to feel that intimidation deeply, but I came to realize that I have something those people needed and wanted—they just didn't know it. That made it easier for me to stand out in the crowd, to not be intimidated, and to actually use my "differentness" as an example of what Christ can give us all—"salvation of everyone who believes."

Loving Father,
You weren't ashamed to claim me as Your child, even sending Your own Son to die so that I might live. Give me the courage proudly to share with everyone I know Your Good News and the salvation You bring. In Jesus' Name,
Amen.

May 14

Therefore leaving the elementary teaching about the Christ, let us press on to maturity... (Hebrews 6:1)

The message here is certainly not that we should *abandon*

the elementary teachings about Christ, but that we should learn them and move forward.

When we learn math in school, we start with the basics (addition, subtraction), then move onto more challenging work (multiplication, division), and with that foundation, into even more complicated areas (algebra, trigonometry, calculus). We build on the "elementary" teachings, and go forward from there.

Likewise with our faith. We learn the "basics" (that God gave His Son to die for our sins, and that we who believe in Him may have eternal life), then we move on into a more mature faith. "As a result, we are no longer to be children, tossed here and there by waves and carried about by every wind of doctrine, by the trickery of men, by craftiness in deceitful scheming; but speaking the truth in love, we are to grow up in all aspects into Him who is the head, even Christ" (Ephesians 4:14-15).

Dear Lord God,
Life in You is always new and exciting. Grant that I may never stop learning, adding joy upon joy as I continue to grow in Your Word and live out Your will. In Jesus' Name, **Amen.**

May 15

Be angry, and yet do not sin; do not let the sun go down on your anger, and do not give the devil an opportunity. (Ephesians 4:26-27)

Anger is a problem for a lot of people. Or rather, *handling* anger is a problem for a lot of people. When we become angry, we aren't able to handle the situation properly; we end up saying or doing something that is inappropriate and un-Christian.

I have a neighbor, a married man with children, who dislikes like my cats. We've even caught him throwing rocks at them. When I first found out he was doing this, I was furious. I wanted to knock his block off! However, after prayer and consideration, I realized my attitude was as inappropriate as his actions. I had to come up with a different way to handle the problem. Can you imagine what kind of witness I would have been if had acted out in my anger? That would truly have been sinning in my anger, which we are warned against in Ephesians. As Christians we need to think—and pray—before we act or speak. If we do this, we will save ourselves a lot of trouble, and avoid giving the devil a foothold.

Loving Father,

Help me to control my anger so that I don't sin against You or others through thoughtless words or actions. Thank You for being slow to anger and abounding in steadfast love. In Jesus' Name,
Amen.

May 16

And we know that God causes all things to work together for good to those who love God, to those who are called according to His purpose. (Romans 8:28)

Have you ever heard one Christian say to another who is facing some difficulty, "God is trying to teach you a lesson"? This kind of response shows an amazing lack of compassion, love, and good sense. If your family is falling apart, or you were robbed, or your house burned down, that is *not* God's will, nor is He trying to teach you a lesson through those events. God is our loving Heavenly Father, and no parents intentionally cause those things to happen to their children and say, "Well, I hope that will teach you a lesson."

Bad things do happen to us, but they're not God's way of punishing us. We live in a fallen creation where sin and evil are a part of life. But God can take those things and redeem them, drawing good from the bad.

When you're hurting, never believe you are being punished. Instead, remember that in *all things*—even bad things—God will work for our good.

Merciful God,

I know the problems I face are the result of our fallen world or my own mistakes. Strengthen my faith during times of difficulty, so that I never doubt that You are in perfect control over the situation and will redeem it according to Your will. In Jesus' Name,
Amen.

May 17

...because by the works of the Law no flesh will be justified in His sight; for through the Law comes the knowledge of sin. (Romans 3:20)

Sometimes when we've been tempted to do wrong, we beat ourselves up with what could have been, even when we didn't give in to the temptation. Stricken by fear and shame, we think, "*What if...*" We are all sinners, and knowledge of God's Word can be knowledge of how close we sometimes come to disobeying it.

Instead of feeling guilty about how close we came, we should rejoice when we stand the test of temptation. And remember, avoiding sin isn't the only important thing. Repenting of sins actually committed, and turning away from them, are other ways of doing God's will.

For this, God will reward us with "the crown of life"— eternal life with Him.

My Heavenly Father,

As I struggle with my problems, keep me mindful that You are my loving Father, and that You will, at the appointed

time, gather me and all the faithful to live with you eternally. In Jesus' Name,
Amen.

May 18

Whenever you stand praying, forgive, if you have anything against anyone, so that your Father who is in heaven will also forgive you your transgressions. (Mark 11:25)

This is not a request. This is a commandment, and not an easy one. But keep in mind that forgiveness is not something we always *feel*; it's an action we must take.

If you're having a hard time, ask God to help you—He will. He's in the heart-changing business. Admit to Him that you don't feel forgiving (He already knows this), but that out of obedience to His Word, and with His help, you are making the choice to do it.

After all, Jesus died on the cross for each of us while we were yet sinners, and we are forgiven daily for our own sins. It's our duty to show that same forgiveness toward others.

Gracious Lord,
I must come to You for help in forgiving others; I can't do it on my own. Enable me sincerely to forgive those who have sinned against me, as I have been forgiven and redeemed by the blood of Your Son Jesus. In Jesus' Name,
Amen.

May 19

I will sing of the lovingkindness of the Lord forever; to all generations I will make known Your faithfulness with my mouth. For I have said, "Lovingkindness will be built up forever; in the heavens You will establish Your faithfulness." (Psalm 89:1-2)

These beautiful words remind us that the Lord is faithful.

The Psalmist is so full of joy at the Lord's love and faithfulness that he can't keep it to himself; he's going to sing it, declare it, and make it known through all generations. All this joy in only two verses!

We should show the same joy, that we—unfaithful, undeserving—daily receive this love and faithfulness established for us in heaven.

Rejoice!

Almighty God,
I give You thanks for Your love and faithfulness. Let me never forget that everything good in my life is a gift from You. Praise be to You forever! In Jesus' Name,
Amen.

May 20

Now the word of the LORD came to me saying, "Before I formed you in the womb I knew you, and before you were born I consecrated you; I have appointed you a prophet to the nations." (Jeremiah 1:4-5)

The first time I read this verse, I was blown away. It was hard for me to imagine that before I was born, before I was even in my mother's womb, God already knew me, and had a plan for my life! Just think about that for a moment. Before God created the world, He already knew you—what you were like, the needs you would have—and He set you apart to be His own.

If you ever feel like you're nothing special, this should encourage you. God hasn't forgotten about you! As a matter of fact, He has great plans for you, and He's not making it up as He goes, but has had it all laid out since the beginning of time.

You are a special person, with a special purpose. Spend time in prayer, and ask God what He has planned for your life.

Dear Lord God,
When I feel lost, help me to remember that You have a perfect plan for my life. Let Your will be done through me; make me willing to follow Your path instead of my own. Thank You for setting me apart as Your own. In Jesus' Name, *Amen.*

May 21

Let your gentle spirit be known to all men. (Philippians 4:5)

People almost always respond better to gentleness than force. If you're trying to get someone to see your point of view by insisting that they're wrong and you're right, that you know better because you're older, smarter, more experienced...you probably won't get very far. That kind of attitude is not only a sure way to alienate and annoy the person you're trying to help; it's also an indication that you have an attitude problem. Remember the words of St. Paul, and make every effort to "walk in a manner worthy of the calling with which you have been called, with all humility and gentleness, with patience, showing tolerance for one another in love" (Ephesians 4:1-2). So leave the rough and tough attitude at home, and let God's light shine through you.

Loving Father,
Help me to see gentleness not as a weakness, but as a strength born of Your love. Let me humble myself before You so that I don't feel I have to prove myself, but instead demonstrate to others the care and compassion You have shown me. In Jesus' Name,
Amen.

May 22

do not grow weary of doing good. (2 Thessalonians 3:13)

This can be tough sometimes, especially when we see others who are definitely *not* doing what is right, but seem to be doing just fine anyway. Sometimes it's almost like they're being rewarded for behaving badly. We look at the effort it takes sometimes to do the right thing instead of the easy thing, and maybe we just want to give up—after all, what's the use?

Our reward is the joy that is to be found in obedience to God, the satisfaction of knowing we have done the right thing, the pleasure of having a reputation as a good, honest person—and, ultimately, eternal life.

It *is* worth it. Never tire of doing what is right.

Holy God,
The temptation to do the easy thing instead of the right thing is very strong sometimes. Keep me on the right path of obedience to You, always endeavoring to follow the example of Your Son, who always did right. In Jesus' Name,
Amen.

May 23

See to it that no one comes short of the grace of God; that no root of bitterness springing up causes trouble, and by it many be defiled... (Hebrews 12:15)

We must never allow bitterness to take root in our hearts. Bitterness not only separates us from God, it doesn't do us any good. It never proves anything to the person we're holding the grudge against, and it just makes us more unhappy. When anger is in our hearts, our hearts become hardened, and bitterness settles in. Bitterness robs us of our joy, and as

Christians, the joy of the Lord is our strength.

Ask God to remove the bitterness from your heart so that you'll be free to experience His grace.

Dear Lord God,

Holding a grudge is just a sign of my insecurity. Help me to remember that human relationships are imperfect; make me willing to overlook slights and offenses; and free me from the bitterness that would diminish my joy in You. In Jesus' Name,
Amen.

May 24

The foolishness of man ruins his way, and his heart rages against the Lord. (Proverbs 19:3)

It can be easy to blame others when things go wrong in our lives. It can also be easy to blame others when we've made a mistake; we try to talk our way out of it by blaming someone else.

It started with Adam and Eve. They both had sinned, but when caught, they both tried shifting the blame. Adam blamed Eve, saying she had given him some fruit, and he ate it. Eve blamed the serpent, saying it had deceived her. There they were, talking to God, the One who knows and sees all, and they were still trying to cast blame for their disobedience!

Even worse, sometimes we blame God for troubles caused by our own disobedience—how dishonest is that? When it comes right down to it, we need to be mature enough to stop placing blame, and to admit that we made a mistake. Then we can ask for forgiveness and go on with our lives.

Almighty God,

Thank You for forgiving my foolish mistakes. Help me to avoid them through obedience to You, but when I fail, help me to hurry to repent and turn away from my sin. In Jesus' Name,

Amen.

May 25

For the mouth speaks out of that which fills the heart. (Matthew 12:34)

Do you want to know the areas of your life that need work? Try this. When you're frustrated with your parents, do you remind yourself of the Fourth Commandment—"Honor your father and your mother" (Exodus 20:12)—or do you ridicule them and complain about them to your friends? When you're angry, do you try using the "gentle answer" that turns away anger (see Proverbs 15:1), or do you let it all out with foul language and cruel words? When someone wrongs you, do you curse them and swear revenge, or do you say to yourself, "I can do all things through Christ" and begin to forgive?

Listen to yourself. If you don't like the idea of those words reflecting what's in your heart, work on it.

Lord,

Too often I don't pay attention to what I say, and what comes out is unkind words and complaints. How can this be the reflection of my heart, which You have made clean through the blood of Christ? Help me to guard against speaking thoughtlessly; let my words build up others and glorify You. In Jesus' Name,

Amen.

May 26

In Him we have redemption through His blood, the forgiveness of our trespasses, according to the riches of His grace...
(Ephesians 1:7)

What a wonderful verse! Many of us still struggle with things we did in the past. Even after we've asked for and received forgiveness, still we carry the burden. No one can make us let go of these things. If we want to continue allowing our past sins to make us feel like failures and weigh us down, then we can, but there's no need to. As a matter of fact, in doing this, we're actually saying that Jesus' death on the cross wasn't enough.

It *was* enough. As Galatians 5:1 says, "It was for freedom that Christ set us free; therefore keep standing firm and do not be subject again to a yoke of slavery." One of the greatest sins is believing that our sin is unforgivable, that somehow it's too big for God.

Receive the forgiveness that is ours when we repent. It is for this that Jesus gave us His all...His life.

Redeeming Lord,
I know that the sacrifice of Your Son has saved me. Let me never sin against You by refusing to accept Your gracious forgiveness. Through You I am forgiven of all my wrongdoing; through You I am truly free. In Jesus' Name,
Amen.

May 27

Answer me, O LORD, for Your lovingkindness is good; according to the greatness of Your compassion, turn to me... (Psalms 69:16)

Do you ever feel like your prayers are bouncing off the ceiling? Like you're praying and praying, but getting nowhere?

Maybe you need to do an examination of your life. Do you have some built-up anger or bitterness toward someone? Are you harboring some resentment over a situation, and won't let it go?

We can cut off our own blessings by not having a right heart, yet we blame God, even become angry with Him, as if *He's* the problem.

Ask God for the strength to let go of the thoughts and feelings that are getting in the way, and He will—once again—bestow upon you his love and mercy.

Dear Lord God,
Create in me a clean heart, O God,
And renew a steadfast spirit within me.
Do not cast me away from Your presence
And do not take Your Holy Spirit from me.
Restore to me the joy of Your salvation
And sustain me with a willing spirit. *(Psalm 51:10-12)*
In Jesus' Name,
Amen.

May 28

Do not be deceived, God is not mocked; for whatever a man sows, this he will also reap. (Galatians 6:7)

I've heard Christians blame God for things they got themselves into, things that didn't go as they had expected. *We* are the ones who make the decisions concerning our lives. We can choose to take or not take a job, to attend or not attend college; we can choose to hold on to or let go of anger or unforgiveness. These are choices that we make with our lives.

We must remember that every choice we make has consequences. We will reap what we sow, good or bad. To help us make the right decisions, we have God's Word and His Holy Spirit for guidance.

Heavenly Father,

Thank You for the guidance of the Holy Spirit which You give me through Your Word the Bible and the guidance of fellow Christians. Please help me to sow only what is good and honorable, for Your glory. In Jesus' Name,
Amen.

May 29

...be like-minded, live in peace; and the God of love and peace will be with you. (2 Corinthians 13:11)

We need to respect others, even when we don't totally agree with the way they believe. Christians often argue with each other over petty little differences. Some even refuse to socialize with Christians of other denominations, which must look pretty silly to the rest of the world.

How sad this is, and how dangerous. If the devil can keep us fighting with each other, we will forget who the real enemy is. We need to focus on our mission in life—that is, to preach the gospel to the world—and stop arguing with our brothers and sisters in Christ over unimportant matters. If we can join together in this way and do what God has called us to do, just think how much we can accomplish.

So even if we can't "be of one mind" with everyone, over everything, all of the time, at least let's behave toward others with the love of God, and so live in peace.

God of Peace,

When we take our eyes off of You, we focus too much on ourselves and the differences between us. Let all Your children be of one mind, and together offer You praise. In Jesus' Name,
Amen.

May 30

We have come to know and have believed the love which God has for us. God is love, and the one who abides in love abides in God, and God abides in him. (1 John 4:16)

Did you know that there is nothing at all that you can do to make God love you more? He already loves us with pure, perfect, unconditional love.

Everybody is searching for love. People do all sorts of things trying to get others to love them. This is sad, because no matter how good the relationship, human love always involves some measure of hurt and disappointment. Only God's true love will never fail us.

We all want to be loved; we all want that inner peace and feeling of belonging. Isn't it wonderful to know that God loves us just the way we are? And that while we were yet sinners, God sent His son Jesus to die on the cross for each of us? Now *that* is unconditional love. Share that with someone who needs to hear it today.

Dear God,
You love me so much that You sent Your only begotten Son to die, that I might live. That perfect, unconditional love far surpasses my human understanding of love. With all that is in me, I give You thanks for that precious gift of salvation. In Jesus' Name,
Amen.

May 31

I have wiped out your transgressions like a thick cloud and your sins like a heavy mist. Return to me, for I have redeemed you." (Isaiah 44:22)

Have you slid back to your sinful ways after knowing the love and forgiveness of God? Maybe you slipped away from

Him gradually, inch by inch, or maybe you decided to turn your back on Him. Either way, you end up feeling the same: guilty, alone, so far away from God.

I want you to know that no matter what, He still loves you with the same love as always, and is waiting for you. There is nothing so terrible that puts you beyond the power of God's forgiveness...except refusing to be forgiven.

Return to God; allow Him to sweep away your sins. Remember, true freedom is found only in Him.

Compassionate God,

You always offer pardon and relief to a repentant sinner. When I stray, let me always return to You. Thank You for the tender mercy You show me. In Jesus' Name,
Amen.

June 1

The Spirit of the Lord GoD is upon me...He has sent me to bind up the brokenhearted...to comfort all who mourn... (Isaiah 61:1-2)

Grief touches us all sooner or later, whether it's the grief of a broken relationship, or a death in the family, or some other ending or parting that causes us pain. At these times, the Holy Spirit is sent to comfort us in our time of need. Those times are still painful; we still mourn what is lost—but the Spirit of God binds up our broken hearts, gives us hope, and makes it bearable.

If you're in need of that comfort right now, remember, "The LORD is near to the brokenhearted and saves those who are crushed in spirit." (Psalm 34:18). Know that the Spirit of the Lord is with you.

God of Comfort,

I know that You are with me in good times and in bad. When I am overcome by sorrow, help me to turn to You for

comfort and peace. In Jesus' Name,
Amen.

June 2

Therefore you are to be perfect, as your heavenly Father is perfect. (Matthew 5:48)

"That's just the way I am." Have you heard that excuse? People who are negative, embittered, angry, reckless, and hurtful with their words use that as a justification for not bothering to change.

Do you think that works with God? That He looks at us and says, "It's all right that you never bothered to love your neighbor…that's just the way you are." No—because it's *not* "just the way we are." God didn't create us to be angry, hurtful, or uncaring; He created us in His own image.

No, He doesn't expect us to be perfect in this life. After all, we are human, and so by our very nature are imperfect. But through His grace and love, we do need to strive to emulate that perfection which He alone has.

Father in Heaven,
I am not perfect, nor can I be, but You did create me in Your own image. Help me to be aware of my behavior so that my words and actions support and encourage those around me, and serve as a witness to Your love. In Jesus' Name,
Amen.

June 3

In the same way the Spirit also helps our weakness; for we do not know how to pray as we should, but the Spirit Himself intercedes for us with groanings too deep for words… (Romans 8:26)

Sometimes we *want* to pray, but don't have a clue how or

where to begin. Isn't it comforting to know that the Holy Spirit will lead us? Entering prayer time in stillness can allow the Spirit to speak for us far more eloquently than we could do ourselves. He voices our fears and hurts with "groanings too deep for words."

If you don't know what to say or how to say it, don't try—let the Spirit speak for you and through you, and help you in your weakness.

Lord God,
There are times that I want to talk to You, but I just don't know what to say; times that I want to praise You, but I don't have the words. When my feelings are beyond my power to express, let Your Holy Spirit speak for me. In Jesus' Name, **Amen.**

June 4

Be strong and courageous, do not be afraid or tremble at them, for the LORD your God is the one who goes with you. He will not fail you or forsake you. (Deuteronomy 31:6)

We all go through times where we are uncertain, afraid, worried, even terrified. Our Lord knew from the beginning that this is something we would face. Being a loving God, He doesn't want us to live with that kind of anxiety, which is why He gave us this verse. It reminds us that we don't have to be afraid, that He will go with us, and will not leave us.

When I was fifteen, I got my first job working at a grocery store. I was thrilled...*a real job!* After working for some time, I got up the nerve to ask for one Saturday off; and my boss fired me on the spot. Crushed, I went home and described what had happened to my father. He immediately offered to go back down to the store with me to talk to my boss about what had happened. I cannot tell you what peace I felt. Knowing my dad was going to go with me, I knew it would be all right; I knew that no matter how unpleasant or scary the situation, my dad would never leave me, but would fight on my behalf.

You can count on God in the same way. Perhaps you are facing things in your life right now that have you worried or afraid. Give it to God, and receive the peace He wants you to have. He loves you and cares for you...lean on him!

(By the way, I got my job back.)

God Omnipotent,

I am humbled before Your power and might. Help me to run to You when I need help, drawing my strength and courage from You, instead of trying to rely only on myself. Thank You for Your faithfulness. In Jesus' Name,

Amen.

June 5

It will also come to pass that before they call, I will answer; and while they are still speaking, I will hear. (Isaiah 65:24)

There are times when we have a need that we feel isn't worth praying about. Maybe we feel it's too insignificant to bother God with; on the other hand, maybe it's so great that we feel there's no way it would ever get answered, so we don't even take it before God.

This attitude is actually a lack of faith. God is bigger than our biggest needs and problems, but He cares about even the "trivial" issues in our lives. He wants us to come to Him with *everything*.

Psalm 102:17 says, "He has regarded the prayer of the destitute and has not despised their prayer." Don't ever think your prayers don't make a difference. God hears us even while we are still speaking to Him, and will answer our prayers according to His good and gracious will.

All-Knowing Father,

You hear my prayers before I even utter them, and You know my every need. Thank You for caring about even the smallest details of my life. Let me always approach You with confidence, offering my prayers and thanksgiving. In Jesus' Name,

Amen.

June 6

What do you desire? Shall I come to you with a rod, or with love and a spirit of gentleness? (1 Corinthians 4:21)

Have you ever had someone try to show you how to do something? Someone with very little patience, who when you didn't catch on right away became irritated with you and made you feel foolish, like you didn't have a brain?

Fortunately for us, God is kind, gentle and infinitely patient. When we make mistakes—and we always do—He never demeans us or punishes us, as long as we repent and try again.

Remember, people respond much better to loving persuasion than to impatient pushing. Treat others the way you would like to be treated; the way God treats us.

Dear Lord,

Grant me the grace to face my everyday problems and irritations with patience, and learn from Your example to be thoughtful and considerate of others, even when I am provoked. Thank You for Your gentleness and compassion toward me and all Your children. In Jesus' Name,

Amen.

June 7

[I pray] that the God of our Lord Jesus Christ, the Father of glory, may give to you a spirit of wisdom and of revelation in the knowledge of Him. I pray that the eyes of your heart may be enlightened, so that you will know what is the hope of His calling, what are the riches of the glory of His inheritance in the saints, and what is the surpassing greatness of His power toward us who believe. (Ephesians 1:17-19)

How much time do you spend with the Lord each day? Three minutes? Ten minutes? An hour? Do you spend time with Him every day, or just once in a while, when it's convenient or when problems come up?

An acquaintance of mine often talks about wanting to do some kind of ministerial work. The odd thing is, he doesn't have a home church and he hardly ever attends worship. He very rarely reads the Bible, and doesn't seem to spend too much time in prayer; yet he wants to preach God's Word. How can he, when he doesn't even know the Word himself?

We must spend time with God, and get to know Him and His voice. Life has many challenges and difficulties, and there are important decisions we face every day. How can we know we are doing the right thing when we aren't familiar with God or His Word? How can we know where he's leading us?

Get to know God better, that you may know the hope to which he has called us.

God of my Hope,
Grant that I may, through prayer, worship, and the study of Your Word, know You better and come to a clearer understanding of Your will for me. In Jesus' Name,
Amen.

June 8

Therefore, take up the full armor of God, so that you will be able to resist in the evil day, and having done everything, to stand firm. Stand firm therefore, having girded your loins with truth, and having put on the breastplate of righteousness, and having shod your feet with the preparation of the gospel of peace; in addition to all, taking up the shield of faith with which you will be able to extinguish all the flaming arrows of the evil one. And take the helmet of salvation, and the sword of the Spirit, which is the word of God. (Ephesians 6:13-17)

The "armor of God" is something you may have heard or read about but don't totally understand. Here is some help:

· The *belt of truth* is God's Word. If we know the truth, then we cannot be deceived.

· The *breastplate of righteousness* is God's righteousness. Our self-worth is under constant attack, but if we know that we have been made righteous through the blood of Jesus, we cannot be made to feel worthless.

· The *gospel of peace* is the Good News of Jesus Christ that we are to spread wherever we go—the news that everyone needs to hear.

· The *shield of faith* is seeing beyond our circumstances and knowing what God's Word has to say about our situation and the victory that is ours through faith.

· The *helmet of salvation* is our protection against doubt and fear for the future; it keeps us sure of God's saving love.

· The *sword of the Spirit* is also God's Word. Jesus used it to do battle against Satan (Luke 4:1-13), and we need to do the same.

Knowing the Bible can help us to stand strong against whatever comes our way.

Dear Lord,
I give You thanks for the many tools with which I can fight temptation and live a fuller life in You. Let me depend on Your armor to carry me safely through the dangers of this life. In Jesus' Name,
Amen.

June 9

"For my thoughts are not your thoughts, nor are your ways my ways," declares the LORD. "For as the heavens are higher than the earth, so are my ways higher than your ways and my thoughts than your thoughts." (Isaiah 55:8-9)

Ever had something go differently than you had planned? I know I have, and it's not easy. But we have to believe by faith that God knows more than we do and that He has our best interests at heart.

I applied for a job once that had much better pay and benefits than what I had at the time. I had hoped it would work out, and was disappointed when I didn't get the job. Later on, I discovered that the man who told me about the job had lied; it wouldn't have been what I thought it was. If I had taken that job, I would have moved halfway across the country for it and then been terribly disappointed.

"My thoughts are not your thoughts, nor are your ways my ways"…humbling, but true. Sometimes it's easy to see why God did things a certain way; sometimes we will never understand. But remember that His ways are higher than our own, and that everything He does, He does for a reason.

Extra time in the Word: **Isaiah 55**

Most High God,

It's not always easy to depend on You, especially when things are going well; I sometimes get over-confident and think I can do it all on my own. I ask that You guard me against that arrogance and keep me close to You, for You know and see far beyond what I know and see. Let Your will be done in me. In Jesus' Name,

Amen.

June 10

always [be] ready to make a defense to everyone who asks you to give an account for the hope that is in you, yet with gentleness and reverence; and keep a good conscience so that in the thing in which you are slandered, those who revile your good behavior in Christ will be put to shame. (1 Peter 3:15-16)

This verse instructs us always to be ready to share Christ, the reason for our hope, and to do it with gentleness and respect. You don't have to be pushy, or impatient, or condescending. Just give credit where credit is due, that Christ in your life has given you peace and hope.

If you proclaim this Good News with gentleness and respect, you are truly a good witness for Him.

Dear Lord God,

Help me not to push people away with a rude or condescending attitude, but instead share Your Good News, demonstrating the same patience and kindness You have shown me. Let Your gentleness and light shine through me, drawing others to You. In Jesus' Name,

Amen.

June 11

Since we have gifts that differ according to the grace given to us, each of us is to exercise them accordingly...he who leads, with diligence... (Romans 12:6, 8)

Do you believe you have the qualities of a good leader? Here is a list of those qualities according to the Bible. See if you have these:

Diligence (Proverbs 12:24): The hand of the diligent will rule, but the slack hand will be put to forced labor.

A trustworthy messenger (Proverbs 13:17): A wicked messenger falls into adversity, but a faithful envoy brings healing.

Just, fair (Proverbs 17:26): It is also not good to fine the righteous, nor to strike the noble for their uprightness.

Thoughtful (Proverbs 18:13): He who gives an answer before he hears, it is folly and shame to him.

Able to discern (Proverbs 18:15): The mind of the prudent acquires knowledge, and the ear of the wise seeks knowledge.

Listens to both sides of the story (Proverbs 18:17): The first to plead his case seems right, until another comes and examines him.

Able to stand up under adversity (Proverbs 24:10): If you are slack in the day of distress, your strength is limited.

Able to stand up under praise (Proverbs 27:21): The crucible is for silver and the furnace for gold, and each is tested by the praise accorded him.

Dear Heavenly Father,
Thank You for the gifts and abilities You have given me. Help me to recognize them, and cheerfully use them in Your service and to Your glory. In Jesus' Name,
Amen.

June 12

Therefore be on the alert, for you do not know which day your Lord is coming. (Matthew 24:42)

Most of us wonder from time to time when Jesus will return. We've all heard different people and groups say that *they* know the day…and this is nothing new, it's been happening since the time of the earliest Christians.

But according to the Bible, no one *really* knows when He will come again—that's why those people and groups are always wrong! The Bible does say that His return will be unexpected, "like a thief in the night" (1 Thessalonians 5:2), and that there are different signs to look out for: famine, increase of crime, increase of knowledge as the world has never seen before, wars and rumors of wars, people who are lovers of themselves. But those things too have happened for hundreds, thousands, of years.

So how can we know? *We can't.* All we can do is be faithful to him now, and prepare ourselves for His glorious return.

Mighty God,
It's a little scary to think of Christ's return. Will it happen in my lifetime? Will I be prepared? What will happen? I know I believe in You, but is that enough? Strengthen my faith; give me a contrite heart and replace my anxieties with a spirit of joyful anticipation as I look forward to seeing You face to face. In Jesus' Name,
Amen.

June 13

Beloved, do not believe every spirit, but test the spirits to see whether they are from God, because many false prophets have gone out into the world. (1 John 4:1)

It is important to make sure that what we are being taught is from God. There are many people out there with messages contrary to God's Word, teaching half-truths or falsehoods. This is why this scripture tells us to "test the spirits to see whether they are from God."

There are several ways to determine this. The first is by what they say about Christ: "Every spirit that confesses that Jesus Christ has come in the flesh is from God; and every spirit that does not confess Jesus is not from God" (1 John 4:2-3). The second is whether what they are telling you agrees with God's Word. Finally, check out their lifestyle and the fruits of their ministry. If their messages are truly from God, they will be consistent with Jesus' teachings.

God of Wisdom,
Thank You for giving us Your Word through the Bible. I ask that You give me the gift of discernment, so that I can determine what is from You and what is a false teaching, and not be led astray. In Jesus' Name,
Amen.

June 14

Be strong and let your heart take courage, all you who hope in the LORD. (Psalm 31:24)

Are you going through something right now that seems hopeless, like there's no way out? One person who had a "hopeless" situation was Jonah, someone who ran from God because God had a task for him that he didn't want to do.

He ended up in the middle of a whale's stomach—I can't imagine a more hopeless looking situation than that!

But keep in mind that we don't look to our circumstances when things seem to be disastrous; we depend on God's promises. Our God is the God of the "how much more"; "If you then, being evil, know how to give good gifts to your children, how much more will your Father who is in heaven give what is good to those who ask Him!" (Matthew 7:11).

Remember that your Heavenly Father has not forgotten about you and what you're going through, and put your hope in Him.

Dear Lord,
Help me to keep my trust in You, even when things seem hopeless. Let me take heart in the "how much more" that You can do for me. In Jesus' Name,
Amen.

June 15

The angel of the LORD encamps around those who fear Him, and rescues them. (Psalms 34:7)

Angels are created by God, and act to communicate and carry out God's will, whether to protect or advise the righteous, or to destroy evil. Not all angels appear in flowing robes and wings; while Balaam was busy beating his donkey (see Numbers 22), he was unaware of the presence of an angel, who at the time was invisible to him. Or an angel may appear to be a regular person, just like you or me.

You may have experienced a time when you were somehow helped in some way, and you wonder if it might just be luck or coincidence, but something tells you it was more. It may have been an accident that you narrowly avoided, or a feeling that you should do something right there and then that turned out to be of great help to others. Whatever the experience, an angel may well have been looking after you.

God in Heaven,
Thank You for sending Your holy angels to earth to do Your will and come to the aid of Your children. Let them guard and keep me safe from all harm. In Jesus' Name, **Amen.**

June 16

As obedient children, do not be conformed to the former lusts which were yours in your ignorance, but like the Holy One who called you, be holy yourselves also in all your behavior; because it is written, "You shall be holy, for I am holy." (1 Peter 1:14-16)

Many of us began the new year with a renewed commitment to God. Part of this can be striving to be holy in all that we do.

Unfortunately, many of us hang on to the old sin we embraced before we were Christians. According to this scripture, we are not to continue to sin like we did when we lived in ignorance, before we knew better. God is commanding us to be holy, and we cannot do that while we still practice old sins. God's grace doesn't give us the right to sin, but the grace to resist sin.

Turn away from your sins, keep your body and mind pure, and love the Lord your God with all your heart, mind, and strength. Only God is truly and perfectly holy, but we, as His obedient children, must resist evil desires and heed the Lord's call to holiness.

O Lord God,
I am a sinner, undeserving of Your mercy. For the sake of Your Son, cleanse me of my sins; cast out of my heart all selfishness, anger, and greed, and replace it with love for

You and a spirit of service toward all people. In Jesus' Name,
Amen.

June 17

*but you will receive power when the Holy Spirit has come upon
you; and you shall be My witnesses both in Jerusalem, and in
all Judea and Samaria, and even to the remotest part of the earth.
(Acts 1:8)*

Do you know that being a witness is not optional for Christians? We have been *commanded* to witness to others; as a matter of fact, we have been called to take God's Good News to the ends of the earth.

Many Christians feel shy, or don't want to "offend" others by sharing their faith, but God isn't offering us a choice. Don't allow fear to keep you from talking with others. Remember: "For God has not given us a spirit of timidity, but of power and love and discipline." (2 Timothy 1:7). Pray and ask the Holy Spirit to use you, to give you the words and boldness. Now, "boldness" doesn't mean getting in people's faces and yelling at them that they are going to hell; the Holy Spirit doesn't work through condemnation and making people feel like losers. Tell of the joy, peace, and hope that is yours—and can be theirs—in Christ. So be obedient to God's will, and no matter where you are, ask God to help you share your faith.

Good Shepherd,
You do not desire any to be lost. I ask that You use me as Your witness; let my conduct reveal Your presence in my life and every word bear witness to You and Your love. Open the eyes of those around me to see the joy, satisfaction, and blessed peace of life in You. In Jesus' Name,
Amen.

June 18

How precious also are Your thoughts to me, O God! How vast is the sum of them! (Psalm 139:17)

The Lord is thinking about you constantly. Sometimes destructive thoughts can enter our heads, making us believe we are just a bunch of nothings; that God has so many other, more important things to contend with; that we are only wasting our time, because He couldn't possibly have the time to listen to our prayers, much less answer them. As if when we went to Him in prayer, He would say, "Now, what is your name again?"

Isn't it wonderful to know that we are His precious children, and that He knows us inside and out? Often when we see a crowd of people, all we see is a crowd...but Jesus sees each of us as individuals; He knows each of us by name.

"O Lord, You have searched me and known me. You know when I sit down and when I rise up; You understand my thought from afar. You scrutinize my path and my lying down, and are intimately acquainted with all my ways." (Psalm 139:1-3). Don't ever think for one second that you aren't important, but rest in the precious knowledge that God's thoughts are always with us.

Precious Lord,

I offer You thanks and praise for all Your blessings, especially the gift of salvation, which You have given me through the precious blood of Your Son. Teach me to remember daily the blessings You have given me, and, out of gratitude and joy, to rededicate myself to Your service. In Jesus' Name,
Amen.

June 19

...for the accuser of our brethren has been thrown down, he who accuses them before our God day and night. And they overcame him because of the blood of the Lamb and because of the word of their testimony, and they did not love their life even when faced with death. (Revelation 12:10,11)

Have you ever heard or sung "There is Power in the Blood" at church? *"There is power, power, wonder-working power, in the precious Blood of the Lamb."*

Think about those words. Do you know that the blood of Jesus has not lost its power, even today? I'm speaking not only of salvation, but also about ways to defeat the devil in your life and start living a victorious life for Christ. A life full of abundance, as the Word talks about. This scripture clearly tells us how the Enemy is defeated. First, by telling Satan that he has already been defeated through the Blood of Jesus. Second, by using the Word of God, as Jesus did when He was dealing with Satan (see Matthew 4). Third, by making sure our commitment to God is without compromise (not allowing God to come in second place in our lives).

You are free through the precious Blood of the Lamb...rejoice!

O God,

I thank You for the freedom and saving faith in Jesus Christ and for the privilege of being a Christian. Give me a deep and abiding faith, and let my actions show to others that You are the Ruler of my heart and mind and soul. In Jesus' Name,

Amen.

June 20

Therefore let us draw near with confidence to the throne of grace, so that we may receive mercy and find grace to help in time of need. (Hebrews 4:16)

I used to be absolutely *terrified* to pray out loud in front of people—I could barely even pray by myself in my own room! I was so fearful of saying the wrong thing, or sounding silly in front of others. Then one Sunday at church I heard my pastor describe praying as sharing your heart with God, just telling Him your needs and what's on your mind, and then thanking Him for the answers.

It was like a light came on. I realized then that I didn't have to "thee and "thou" God, or try to sound "holy" or "spiritual." After all, we don't talk to our parents like that, so why should we think our Heavenly Father requires fancy language from us?

Talk to him in plain words, fancy words, song, whatever...*just talk to Him*. Don't allow fear to keep you from approaching the throne of grace with confidence, where you can pray, share your heart with God, and receive His blessing.

My Lord and King,
Please give me the confidence and courage to approach You wherever and whenever I need to. Thank You for allowing me to share my heart with You, for always hearing me when I pray. In Jesus' Name,
Amen.

June 21

Do you not know that you are a temple of God and that the Spirit of God dwells in you? (1 Corinthians 3:16)

It's hard to imagine our bodies as God's temple, that the Holy Spirit dwells within each of us. That's a wondrous thought...but also a little intimidating. After all, it's quite a bit of pressure. How can we be good enough to be God's temple? Well, we can't—but we can try.

Start with knowing the fruits of the Spirit—"love, joy, peace, patience, kindness, goodness, faithfulness, gentleness, self-control" (Galatians 5:22-23)—and strive for those. Also, take care to keep your bodies free of alcohol, drugs, sexual immorality, and other impurities, so you don't defile the dwelling-place of the Spirit.

What greater honor could there be than to be God's temple? Do your best to provide for Him a worthy home.

Dear God,
Thank You for making my body Your dwelling-place. Please help me to resist temptations that will be harmful to it, and keep myself pure for Your service. In Jesus' Name, **Amen.**

June 22

Children, obey your parents in the Lord, for this is right. Honor your father and mother (which is the first commandment with a promise), so that it may be well with you, and that you may live long on the earth. (Ephesians 6:1-3)

It's hard sometimes to understand our parents' reasoning. Believe it or not, your parents were teenagers once, and probably faced a lot of the same situations that you are facing now. They know what peer pressure is all about—pressure to have sex before marriage, pressure to drink alcohol or use drugs, pressure to engage in other risky or inappropriate behavior. "Been there, done that"—they've seen all that before. Therefore, they have insights that can be valuable, if you will take the time to listen.

Listen to your parents. Yes, they're human; yes, they'll make mistakes—but they love you and have your best interests at heart…and they may be wiser than you think!

Dear Heavenly Father,

Help me to honor my parents, even when I don't agree with them. Please help us to love and respect one another and serve You together as a family. Thank You for being our Heavenly Father. In Jesus' Name,
Amen.

June 23

Therefore let him who thinks he stands take heed that he does not fall. (1 Corinthians 10:12)

Have you ever had someone tell you about a temptation they were really struggling with? And maybe you thought, "What's the big deal?" because their temptation wasn't tempting to you. If so, be careful. When we start feeling overconfident, we let our guard down and can easily be overcome.

Look at Peter—he was adamant that he would never deny Jesus: "Even if I have to die with You, I will not deny You." (Matthew 26:35). But that very night he not only denied Him, but denied knowing Him three times! Even with Jesus' warning, Peter never saw that coming until it was too late.

Stay on your toes constantly, and never think that you are above temptation.

Almighty God,

Please help me to recognize temptation and avoid it, and protect me from the temptations I don't even see. And when I do make mistakes, please give me the strength to admit it, and bring me back to You. Thank you for Your protection and Your forgiveness. In Jesus' Name,

Amen.

June 24

Truly, truly, I say to you, he who believes in me, the works that I do, he will do also; and greater works than these he will do; because I go to the Father. (John 14:12)

Have you ever heard someone say "I don't want to be a Christian—it's so *boring*"?

Anyone who finds his or her faith boring isn't doing it right. According to this scripture, Jesus enables His followers to do even greater things than He did, in order to bring glory to the Father. Is seeing someone come to faith and the resulting change in their life boring? What about seeing someone healed from sickness? Seeing families restored? Or seeing someone set free from addiction? This is true excitement!

Dear Lord God,

Thank You for Your miracles, especially the "everyday" miracle of faith in You. Help me to recognize those everyday miracles, and never lose the joy and excitement of life in Your service. In Jesus' Name,

Amen.

June 25

"I am the good shepherd, and I know my own and my own know me, even as the Father knows me and I know the Father; and I lay down my life for the sheep." (John 10:14-15)

The Good Shepherd is just one name used to describe Jesus. Here are some others from which we can further understand Him:

Name	Meaning	Scripture Background
Son of Man	divine	*As they were coming down from the mountain, Jesus commanded them, saying, "Tell the vision to no one until the Son of Man has risen from the dead."* (Matthew 17:9).
Bread of Life	The life-giver	*Jesus said to them, "I am the bread of life; he who comes to me will not hunger, and he who believes in me will never thirst...." (John 6:35).*
Light of the World	The answer to our need for spiritual truth	*Then Jesus again spoke to them, saying, "I am the Light of the world; he who follows Me will not walk in the darkness, but will have the Light of life." (John 8:12).*
Door of the Sheep	The only way into the Kingdom of God	*So Jesus said to them again, "Truly, truly, I say to you, I am the door of the sheep. All who came before Me are thieves and robbers, but the sheep did not hear them. I am the door; if any one enters through Me, he will be saved, and will go in and out and find pasture. (John 10:7-9)*

148

The Good Shepherd	*the source of love and guidance*	*I am the good shepherd, and I know my own and my own know me, even as the Father knows me and I know the Father; and I lay down my life for the sheep. (John 10:14-15).*
Resurrection	*the source of life*	*Jesus said to her, "I am the resurrection and the life; he who believes in me will live even if he dies, and everyone who lives and believes in me will never die..." (John 11:25-26).*
The Way and the Truth and the Life	*the method, message, and meaning for all people*	*Jesus said to him, "I am the way, and the truth, and the life; no one comes to the Father but through me. "If you had known me, you would have known my Father also; from now on you know Him, and have seen Him." (John 14:6-7).*
The Vine	*Our life-force-- we (the branches) are completely dependent on Him*	*"Abide in Me, and I in you. As the branch cannot bear fruit of itself unless it abides in the vine, so neither can you unless you abide in Me. (John 15:4).*

Eternal God,

You are my Shepherd, my Light, and my one way to eternal life. Thank You for all the ways You give us to understand You and what You have done for us. In Jesus' Name,
Amen.

149

June 26

Do not let your heart be troubled; believe in God, believe also in me. "In my Father's house are many dwelling places; if it were not so, I would have told you; for I go to prepare a place for you. If I go and prepare a place for you, I will come again and receive you to myself, that where I am, there you may be also. (John 14:1-3)

We have been promised a place in heaven that Jesus has prepared for us, where we will live eternally; and that He will come back to take us there. We are also told not to allow our hearts to be troubled, but to trust in God and in His Son. With all of the troubling things that go on in this world, that seems hard to avoid.

This is why we need to keep trusting and placing our hope in God. The knowledge that there is prepared for us a room in the house of God is comforting indeed. Hold that hope in front of you, and don't let your heart be troubled.

Eternal Father,

Sometimes I am troubled, and my sorrow and fear makes me forget Your presence. Help me always to remember that You are my God and I am Your beloved Child. You have graciously given me all that I have and daily defend me from all evil. In that knowledge, let me live confidently and joyfully. In Jesus' Name,
Amen.

June 27

Therefore, putting aside all filthiness and all that remains of wickedness, in humility receive the word implanted, which is able to save your souls. (James 1:21)

If you have ever been frustrated at not being able to

understand the Bible (and *all* of us have at one time or another), there are a few things that you should look at.

If you want to be able to understand God's Word better, you need to prepare yourself and come into it with the right attitude. You must truly want to understand God and His principles, not just be someone who comes to Him occasionally when things become difficult. You must also have a sincere desire to learn, a "teachable attitude," and a sense of reverence as you approach God through His Word. The only way all these things will happen is if you put God first in your life, spending "quality time" with Him on a daily basis.

Just as with any relationship, if you really want to get to know the other person, you must spend time with them. Spend time with God today.

Holy Father,
Instill in me the desire to learn Your Word and Your will. Cleanse my heart of impurity; let me come before You with reverence and humility, so that I may have a more right relationship with You. In Jesus' Name,
Amen.

June 28

Marriage is to be held in honor among all, and the marriage bed is to be undefiled; for fornicators and adulterers God will judge. (Hebrews 13:4)

This scripture is very clear about staying pure sexually. Don't be fooled into thinking, "It's OK if we love each other," or "What's the harm in just trying it once?" Or, most dangerous of all, "The Bible is outdated—that may have been wrong then, but not now." If you're not married, you need to keep yourself pure—period. You may get lots of messages about sex being a healthy, natural part of a "committed relationship." Well, it is...*within marriage.*

Don't give in to peer pressure. If someone is pressuring

you to have sex, either by trying to persuade you that it's right, or by threatening to leave you if you don't, then that person is not for you—he or she doesn't have your best interest at heart. If someone tells you that they love you so much that they can't wait, know that they are giving you the world's biggest line. True love is not that selfish. A person who really loves you will help keep you from sin.

Righteous God,

Help me to control my body and resist the temptation to sin by having sexual relationships before I am married. Let me find other ways, productive and pleasing to You, to show my love for my boyfriend or girlfriend. Let us support and encourage each other, keeping each other from sin, and have a stronger relationship based on shared love in Christ. In Jesus' Name,
Amen.

June 29

Let no one say when he is tempted, "I am being tempted by God"; for God cannot be tempted by evil, and He Himself does not tempt anyone. But each one is tempted when he is carried away and enticed by his own lust. (James 1:13-14)

Let's face it, temptation is hard to overcome. And sometimes we don't even want to overcome, because whatever is tempting us is something we really want, something we really *need* (or so we tell ourselves).

God has given all of us the power to resist temptation. When we give in, it is our choice; it is *not* God's fault. Yes, He is all-powerful and all-knowing, but He isn't the one who tempts us—it's our own sinful nature. The Bible tells us that God doesn't do wrong, and He wouldn't try to make us fall.

God will give you the power to resist whatever temptations come your way. If we can just stand strong and not give in, we will be rewarded. Hang in there!

Lord,

Sometimes temptation is hard to recognize; it's often very hard to resist. I ask that you give me the strength to avoid temptation whenever possible, and to withstand it when it presents itself to me. In Jesus' Name,

Amen.

June 30

I will instruct you and teach you in the way which you should go; I will counsel you with my eye upon you. (Psalm 32:8)

So many people want to know what God has planned for their lives. They're trying to figure out things such as what school to go to; what to do when they get out of school; whom to hang around with and whom to date; what church to attend…the list goes on.

Isn't it a relief to know that God is willing to instruct and guide us along the way? And the best thing is that He doesn't only instruct us; He also looks out for us, carefully and lovingly watching our progress.

God will give you the wisdom you need in whatever you're trying to figure out. Ask Him to instruct you on whatever it is you have to decide, and then get ready for His answer.

Wonderful Counselor,

Sometimes it's hard to know what to do. Help me to hear Your counsel through prayer, devotion, and the advice of Christian friends. Thank You for Your loving guidance. In Jesus' Name,

Amen.

July 1

O fear the LORD, you His saints; for to those who fear Him there is no want. (Psalm 34:9)

How many times have we Christians gone to the world looking for answers to our problems? When we have fears or phobias, we go to doctors to get prescription drugs or therapy, spending thousands of dollars to figure out why we are the way we are. When we have a financial need, we go to the bank for a loan, or use credit cards to get one instantly. We live in a world of instant gratification. What if instead we took our problems to the Lord and kept seeking Him, waiting patiently until the answer came?

How different our lives would be if we went to God for our answers! According to this scripture, whatever may be troubling us, he will take care of those who "fear" (love and obey) Him.

There's nothing wrong with a Christian using doctors and banks, but we should take everything to God as well, and *first,* and see if He would like to do something supernatural in our life. You just might be surprised!

God, My Provider,
You know my every need, and meet each one according to Your will. Let me always come first to You. In Jesus' Name, **Amen.**

July 2

The effective prayer of a righteous man can accomplish much. (James 5:16)

Do you ever feel that your prayers aren't being answered, like you're just talking to yourself? This scripture reminds us that we need to keep at it and not give up.

In the book of Daniel, after Daniel had fasted and prayed for three weeks, he received a visit from a man whose "body also was like beryl, his face had the appearance of lightning, his eyes were like flaming torches, his arms and feet like the gleam of polished bronze, and the sound of his words like the sound of a tumult." (Daniel 10:6). From this amazing being, Daniel learned that because he had humbled himself before God and set his mind to gain understanding, his prayers had been heard. Despite all opposition, God's messenger eventually arrived.

The answers to our prayers may be slow in coming, but follow Daniel's example, and don't give up.

Everliving God,
I am not a righteous person, but for the sake of Your Son, Whose sacrifice has made me righteous in Your sight, hear my prayers. In Jesus' Name,
Amen.

July 3

Blessed is a man who perseveres under trial; for once he has been approved, he will receive the crown of life which the Lord has promised to those who love Him. (James 1:12)

Do you find it more difficult to keep your faith when hard times come? I've heard people say, when facing hard times, thinks like: "What's the use? God must not be all that great if He's allowing me to deal with this stuff on my own."

Well, God never told us that becoming a Christian would end all trouble in our lives. In fact, He tells us in James that we should consider it pure joy when tests and challenges come at us from all sides (see James 2:4). I know it seems pretty strange to take joy in our problems. But just try a joyful attitude, and see what happens.

Too many folks give up just before the miracle arrives. If you feel like giving up today, I encourage you to hang in there, just one more day. You can make it!

Faithful Lord,
I don't want to be a "fair-weather" Christian. Increase my faith so that it does not falter when I'm going through times of trial; instead of sinking into doubt and despair, let me find contentment and peace, safe in the knowledge that You are taking care of me. In Jesus' Name,
Amen.

July 4

[If] my people who are called by my name humble themselves and pray and seek my face and turn from their wicked ways, then I will hear from heaven, will forgive their sin and will heal their land. (2 Chronicles 7:14)

Happy 4th of July !!
It may be easy to remember to pray for our elected leaders during election time, but we should pray for those in authority in government around the world all the time. We need to pray for wisdom for them, and that they will know Christ, and through Him be wiser, kinder, and more just leaders.

1 Timothy 2:1-2 says, "First of all, then, I urge that entreaties and prayers, petitions and thanksgivings, be made on behalf of all men, for kings and all who are in authority, so that we may lead a tranquil and quiet life in all godliness and dignity." On this celebration of our country's birthday, remember to pray for our country and our leaders.

Ruler of the Nations,
Thank You for the blessing of liberty. Let me use the freedoms I am given as a citizen of this country to serve You, my neighbor, and my nation. Grant wisdom and faithfulness to our leaders, and peace to our country. In Jesus' Name,
Amen.

July 5

For God has not given us a spirit of timidity, but of power and love and discipline. Therefore do not be ashamed of the testimony of our Lord... (2 Timothy 1:7-8)

God gives every Christian the necessary tools to use for the Christian life. One of these is the gift of prayer.

Can you imagine if we used that particular gift all the time? I don't know how many times I've told someone I would keep him or her in my prayers. Well, that's great, but why not pray right then and there? I am a rather shy person, so praying for someone in public or even on the phone wasn't easy at first. I was more comfortable doing it in private. But this scripture tells us not to be timid, and to testify about our Lord without shame. What better way to testify than through open prayer? Now instead of saying, "I'll pray for you," I just do it!

I encourage you to try praying for your friends when they need it. It doesn't have to embarrass them or you. Just quietly, in a loving and caring manner, pray for and with them. Can you image how it would make someone feel to know you care enough to pray for him or her on the spot?

Give it a try. There's no time like the present, especially for prayer!

God Almighty,
What a blessing it is to know that I can come to You in prayer any time, for any reason. Fill me with Your power, so that I am never too shy to share Your Good News with others. In Jesus' Name,
Amen.

July 6

Now flee from youthful lusts and pursue righteousness, faith, love and peace, with those who call on the Lord from a pure heart. (2 Timothy 2:22)

Temptation isn't something that happens only to "bad" people, and it's certainly not only a problem for young people. But youth, especially adolescence, can be a particularly difficult time in terms of the choices, problems, and decisions we face daily.

Temptation gets us all, at one time or another, but there are some tactics to make things a little easier for yourself: 1) Avoid awkward situations where it would be easy to sin. 2) Have Christian friends, because they will be less likely to put you in situations at odds with Christian teaching. 3) Be familiar and comfortable with the Word of God; knowing it will help you to keep it.

Finally, whenever you face temptation, get out of there—fast! Don't choose that time to pray and ask God to remove the person or situation that is tempting you. Save that for later. The Bible tells us to flee, and the sooner the better! Remember, it's much easier to get out of trouble in the early stages than later on. There is always a way to escape temptation.

Merciful Father,

Thank You for always providing a means to avoid and escape temptation. Let me call on You for help, and, strengthened by Your love, pursue the path of righteousness. In Jesus' Name,
Amen.

July 7

I know your deeds, that you are neither cold nor hot; I wish that you were cold or hot. So because you are lukewarm, and neither hot nor cold, I will spit you out of my mouth. (Revelation 3:15-16)

Too many youth groups today are full of Christian teenagers who are lukewarm. They certainly don't want to reject God, but they're not too keen on following Him and His commandments, either. Well, those who are lukewarm about following God just may find God, on the last day, lukewarm about their eternal life! Don't risk that.

God expects no more and no less from teenagers than from any other Christian. Turn your life completely over to Him! Stop playing the game of coming to church and acting like Perfect Young Christian, and then going to school the next morning and living a totally different life. If this is your life, you know it's empty.

Renew your commitment to God—tell Him you want Him as Lord of your life. Jesus wants to use you in a big way. Are you ready?

Dear Lord God,

I am sometimes afraid of alienating my friends by being "too Christian." I ask that You replace my fearfulness with confidence; my selfishness with compassion; and my timidity with boldness, so that I may not be "lukewarm," but instead serve You with enthusiasm. In Jesus' Name,
Amen.

July 8

For if a man comes into your assembly with a gold ring and dressed in fine clothes, and there also comes in a poor man in dirty clothes, and you pay special attention to the one who is wearing the fine clothes, and say, "You sit here in a good place," and you say to the poor man, "You stand over there, or sit down by my footstool," have you not made distinctions among yourselves, and become judges with evil motives? (James 2:2-4)

Have you ever been to a rock concert? When that artist comes to town, people rally around, getting them whatever they need, wanting to be as close to them as possible. But what about the people who come in beforehand to set up for the concert? Or the people who clean up after everyone, especially those with the non-glamorous jobs like cleaning the restrooms or emptying the trash? They don't get the special treatment, even though they play a big part in making things go well.

How about at church? Our pastors do so much for the congregation, and they get some recognition because they're in the "spotlight," but what about the nursery workers, janitor, church secretary…are they shown much appreciation? We need to keep in mind that no matter what our calling in life, we are *all* equal in the body of Christ. No one is better than the other, and we should not show favoritism. Showing favoritism, choosing who is and is not important, insults people made in God's image. Make a special effort today to appreciate those "behind the scenes" people in your life.

Mighty Lord,

I know that I have judged people by their appearance. Help me to show love and acceptance to people regardless of their appearance, just as You love me no matter what I look like. In Jesus' Name,
Amen.

July 9

Blessed are you when people insult you and persecute you, and falsely say all kinds of evil against you because of me. Rejoice and be glad, for your reward in heaven is great; for in the same way they persecuted the prophets who were before you. (Matthew 5:11,12)

Sometimes all this "be happy when bad things happen" stuff may seem hard to take. But the key words here are "because of me."

Most of us who have really tried to live a Christian life and be a good witness have, at one time or another, been "persecuted" for our efforts (taunted, excluded from certain groups, etc.). No doubt it's embarrassing, painful, and upsetting. But from now on, just don't allow it to hurt you! It's all about attitude. Being looked down on for your Christian faith is nothing new. Christians have always experienced this kind of trouble. The reward in heaven is great for those who have had to take a lot of abuse for their faith.

Make the decision that it's not going to get to you, and keep in mind that people ridicule what they fear and envy. Stand tall, and be proud of your faith!

Heavenly Father,

I have a hard time being glad when people insult and hurt me. Help me to see these painful times as learning opportunities, making me more careful not to hurt others. Comfort and strengthen me, that I may handle these situations gracefully. In Jesus' Name,

Amen.

July 10

For we do not have a high priest who cannot sympathize with our weaknesses, but one who has been tempted in all things as we are, yet without sin. Therefore let us draw near with confidence to the throne of grace, so that we may receive mercy and find grace to help in time of need. (Hebrews 4:14-16)

We have all been tempted to sin. Sometimes, we fall. And sometimes, when we fall, we just can't seem to get over it.

Satan, whom the Bible calls "the accuser of our brethren" (Revelation 12:10), always brings up our sins to us in order to make us feel guilty and ashamed, as if our sin is too great ever to ask God for forgiveness.

This is a lie. As this scripture tells us, Jesus understands our weaknesses. We need to go *with confidence* to the throne of God to find grace and mercy to help us when we need it. *Never, ever* feel that you cannot receive forgiveness of any sin, or that it's ever too late to ask.

Lord God,

You know the struggles I face every day, and I know that You care. Keep me ever mindful that You understand, and that You are with me every step of the way, offering forgiveness and redemption. In Jesus' Name,

Amen.

July 11

If we live by the Spirit, let us also walk by the Spirit. (Galatians 5:25)

Once we become Christians, we need to turn our backs on sin. This, of course, doesn't mean evil desire will never rear its ugly head again, or that we will never sin. But we need to renounce sin and our old selves and start anew. The Holy Spirit is in constant opposition to our sinful desires. If we rely on our own wisdom we will make wrong choices, but if we live a life guided by the Holy Spirit, the power of Jesus will help us control selfish desires. It will help us to control such impulses and feelings as fits of rage, jealousy, impurity, hatred, selfish ambition, and envy. Conversely, "the fruit of the Spirit is love, joy, peace, patience, kindness, goodness, faithfulness, gentleness, [and] self-control..." (Galatians 5:22-23).

Which list best describes your life?

Most Holy God,
Let Your Holy Spirit dwell in me, empowering me with Your love and replacing my selfishness, jealousy, and anger with kindness, patience, and peace. In Jesus' Name,
Amen.

July 12

For our heart rejoices in Him, because we trust in His holy name. Let Your lovingkindness, O LORD, be upon us, according as we have hoped in You. (Psalm 33:21,22)

A lot of people try to get their fulfillment and satisfaction from the world. Some pour their energy into their work in order to be prosperous materially, because that's how the world measures success. Others focus only on relationships—boyfriend, girlfriend, wife, husband—thinking another person can meet all their needs. People work hard on these earthly things, hoping they will bring happiness.

God alone is the foundation of all joy and success. The only way to be totally happy is to have a continued relationship with God. The greatest joy we as Christians can have is when we abide in Christ, allowing His love to flow through us, enabling us to reach out to a hopeless world to show all in it that there is hope and purpose in life.

Put your hope in the Lord, trust Him, and rejoice.

Father God,

Thank You for Your unfailing love. Let me rededicate myself daily to Your service, loving and serving others because You first loved me. In Jesus' Name,

Amen.

July 13

"As for the person who turns to mediums and to spiritists, to play the harlot after them, I will also set my face against that person and will cut him off from among his people." (Leviticus 20:6)

Isn't it amazing where we try looking for answers to life? Psychics on television encourage people to call them for encouragement and comfort; in the newspaper, horoscopes offer vague warnings and promises.

This shows that people are seeking help. They feel hopeless or frightened, and want answers. The above are the sorts of places they might look if they don't know God. This is an easy way for Satan to deceive people and get them hooked into the occult without their even realizing it. Satan is always offering people a quick fix, a dark alternative to what God has for them.

We don't need to look to the occult for information. We don't need to look to psychics and astrologers for guidance. God has given us the Bible for all the answers and information we will ever need, and the Bible is totally trustworthy.

Lord God Almighty,

Protect me against the darkness of this world and the power of the Evil One. Let me look to You for the answers, for only in You will I find wholeness and protection from all harm. In Jesus' Name,

Amen.

July 14

The LORD is good to those who wait for Him, to the person who seeks Him. It is good that he waits silently for the salvation of the LORD. (Lamentations 3:25,26)

Have you ever had a situation that almost seemed impossible? That seemed it would take a miracle to resolve it?

Miracles do happen. There's a story in the book of Mark in which Jesus raised up a little girl from the dead. Even though it seemed impossible, the dying girl's desperate father went to Jesus and told him his little daughter was dying, and asked him to put his hands on her so that she would be healed and live (see Mark 5:23). And indeed, though the little girl had died by the time Jesus arrived, he took her by the hand and told her to rise, and she lived again, to the amazement of all.

Can you see this father's faith? Even after other people told him his daughter was dead, he didn't give up. He didn't let his situation dictate his faith; rather, his faith secured the outcome of the situation.

And miracles still happen, even today. What situation are you going through that seems beyond hope? Place your hope in God and wait quietly for salvation. You may just be surprised with a miracle.

Saving Lord,

I believe that You still perform miracles every day. Grant that my faith may be stronger than the difficulties I face; let me put my hope in You, my salvation. In Jesus' Name,
Amen.

July 15

You have taken account of my wanderings; put my tears in Your bottle. Are they not in Your book? (Psalm 56:8,10)

God cares. He cares about you and about your problems, whether big or small, so much that He sees and keeps track of every tear that falls. Don't ever think that we have an impersonal God, one who either doesn't notice or doesn't care when we're hurting. Our God loves us. Go to Him with your sorrows, and He will comfort you.

God, My Comforter,

There are times when my grief and fear overwhelm me; I feel beyond the reach of all help. Help me to remember that You see every tear I cry; You hear my every groan of anguish. Draw me close to You at those times, and send Your Holy Spirit to ease my suffering and quieten my soul. In Jesus' Name,

Amen.

July 16

For as the rain and the snow come down from heaven, and do not return there without watering the earth and making it bear and sprout, and furnishing seed to the sower and bread to the eater; so will my word be which goes forth from my mouth; it will not return to me empty, without accomplishing what I desire, and without succeeding in the matter for which I sent it. (Isaiah 55:10-11)

When you have the opportunity to share your faith, make sure you take that opportunity. Don't feel that what you say is insignificant, or that it won't make a difference, because you never know how God will use you in any given situation.

Before I became a Christian, I went to a movie with a Christian friend. The movie we were seeing was about the end times, and while we were waiting for the movie to begin, my friend made a comment about how it was really going to happen one day. Though we never discussed it any further, her words stayed with me, and it was a short time later that I became a Christian. God used my friend and her words to help bring me to faith.

Remember, His Word will accomplish what He wants it to accomplish, but we need to be obedient and keep sharing it with others.

O God,
I give You thanks for another day of life in You. Strengthen me in Your service; let Your will be done in me, that I may be a bold and faithful witness for Christ. In Jesus' Name, **Amen.**

July 17

Humble yourselves in the presence of the Lord, and He will exalt you. (James 4:10)

Pride, in the worst sense, is a common problem in the world, including, unfortunately, among Christians. Pride tells us that we need more because we deserve it. It can make us self-centered, making us place ourselves above other people in our minds. Then our own selves and needs become more important to us than anyone or anything else.

God calls us to be His servants, and He chooses us not because He's impressed by our accomplishments, but because we're sinners in need of His love and mercy.

If you find yourself being prideful, ask God to forgive you and humble yourself before Him. Only then will you be lifted up to true happiness.

God of Power and Might,
Your son died for a lost and sinful world, a gift we do not deserve. Thank You for my deliverance. In Jesus' Name, **Amen.**

July 18

Therefore whoever resists authority has opposed the ordinance of God; and they who have opposed will receive condemnation upon themselves. (Romans 13:2)

God put authority figures here on earth for our own good. As long as we are not asked to do something that is contrary to God's Word, we need to be obedient to that authority. Teachers, parents, law enforcement, pastors, and others are there for our guidance, protection, and instruction. Can you imagine what it would be like on earth if there was no one in charge, and people could do whatever they wanted? What a mess!

God tells us that people who rebel against authority will bring judgment upon themselves. Earthly authority figures are human, so no one is saying they're perfect, or even always right. But in general, they're older, more experienced people who know what they're talking about. Don't rebel just for the fun of being rebellious. Try listening to the people God has put as authority figures in your life, and you will benefit from it.

Supreme Lord,

I am grateful for the good government with which you have blessed our land. Help me to be a good citizen and respect the authority figures in my life, never forgetting that You are the Ruler of us all. In Jesus' Name,
Amen.

July 19

How lovely on the mountains are the feet of him who brings good news, who announces peace and brings good news of happiness, who announces salvation, and says to Zion, "Your God reigns!" (Isaiah 52:7)

How does it look to the rest of the world when Christians walk around complaining, acting like the world is a terrible, hopeless place? It certainly wouldn't inspire hope in anyone else. After all, if we, who have the hope of eternal life, don't have any good news to share, why should anyone else?

We need to bring happy news to people, and tell them that God reigns and that He has the answers. He's not in heaven pacing back and forth in fear, wondering what to do. We have been redeemed, and we need to start declaring the good tidings and salvation of God.

Gracious Father,

Keep me from becoming negative or discouraged by my problems. Help me to be cheerful, trusting, and confident. In gratitude for the salvation You have given me, let me take delight in sharing Your Good News with everyone around me. In Jesus' Name,
Amen.

July 20

He gives strength to the weary, and to him who lacks might He increases power. Though youths grow weary and tired, and vigorous young men stumble badly, yet those who wait for the LORD will gain new strength; they will mount up with wings like eagles, they will run and not get tired, they will walk and not become weary. (Isaiah 40:29-31)

I really love this chapter of the Bible for so many reasons, partly because it talks about how awesome God really is and what He can do for us. He gives strength to the "weary," which can mean physical, mental, or emotional weariness, any of which can afflict people of any age.

If we put our hope and trust in God, He will help us back on our feet and give us the strength to keep going. If we rely on the Lord for our strength, we will do incredible things. God never asked us to stand with our own strength alone. He wants to give us His strength and power to be a good witness for Him. If you are weary in body or spirit, ask God to renew your strength.

Sustaining Lord,
I am tired, worried, dissatisfied. I come before You seeking consolation and encouragement. Go with me through my days; ease my mind and fill my soul with Your peace. In Jesus' Name,
Amen.

July 21

I will give you a new heart and put a new spirit within you; and I will remove the heart of stone from your flesh and give you a heart of flesh. (Ezekiel 36:26)

This is what God says He will do for His children, not for our sake but for the sake of His holy Name. When we follow Him, He washes away our old selves and old sins, and gives us clean hearts and new spirits.

Rejoice in God's power to make you a new creation!

Righteous God,
Through the sacrifice of Your Son, I have a new and purified heart. Make me a living branch on the Vine which is Christ the Lord; help me to bear fruit for Your glory and for the benefit of all, living in Your favor until the day of Jesus Christ. In Jesus' Name,
Amen.

July 22

He Himself has said, "I will never desert you, nor will I ever forsake you"... (Hebrews 13:5)

The verse is short, but to the point. So often we get in the middle of a hard time and wonder, is God really here with me? The answer to that question is YES! The Bible doesn't say God will never leave you unless you do something really stupid, or that He will be with you as long you remain an "A" student in school and never miss church. Rather, we are told He will *never* leave us.

Maybe you're wondering right now if God is really with you. Again, the answer is yes. He will never leave you.

Faithful God,

Sometimes I am filled with fear, and I start to doubt Your presence. Forgive my lack of faith. Help me to meet each challenge with confidence born of the knowledge that You are with me always, and nothing can separate me from Your love. In Jesus' Name,
Amen.

July 23

With Him are wisdom and might; to Him belong counsel and understanding. (Job 12:13)

Sometimes we have to admit that we lack wisdom. True wisdom, in the sense of God's Word, is God's; earthly "wisdom," which unfortunately we more often attain, can do no better than lead us astray. But asking for God's wisdom can seem scary; what if He tells us something we don't want to hear, something that might interfere with our agenda, something that might not be convenient?

It's hard sometimes to remember and really comprehend that God is all-knowing. He knows what is best for us even when we can't see it. So be brave and wise enough to know when you need God's wisdom and guidance, and ask Him. He gives generously.

God of Wisdom,

I confess that I often am confused and uncertain. You know all and see all, and never have to wonder what to do next. I ask that You enlighten me and help me to recognize

Your will. Give me the courage to do Your will to the best of my ability and leave the outcome in Your hands. In Jesus' Name,
Amen.

July 24

Now He was telling them a parable to show that at all times they ought to pray and not to lose heart... (Luke 18:1)

The parable Jesus tells is about a judge being pestered by a widow who kept coming to him with a complaint against her neighbor. This judge put her off and put her off, but she was so persistent that finally he said to himself, "Even though I do not fear God nor respect man, yet because this widow bothers me, I will give her legal protection, otherwise by continually coming she will wear me out." (Luke 18:4-5).

The point of this story is not that if we pester God enough, He will give in to our demands. After all, God is not a customer service representative, there for our satisfaction. Rather, the point is that the judge, who neither feared God nor respected other people, did the right thing simply because of the widow's faith in his ability to help her. So how much more will God, who loves and cares for us, do for us when we put our faith in Him?

Always pray; never give up. God is listening.

Father in Heaven,
Help me to remain faithful even when the answers to my prayers seem long in coming, never losing my confidence that You are my God and I am Your child. Let me diligently seek You and not give up, knowing always that You hear my every prayer. In Jesus' Name,
Amen.

July 25

Then Asa called to the LORD his God and said, "LORD, there is no one besides You to help in the battle between the powerful and those who have no strength; so help us, O LORD our God, for we trust in You, and in Your name have come against this multitude. O LORD, You are our God; let not man prevail against You."
(2 Chronicles 14:11)

In this chapter of 2 Chronicles, King Asa had only a small army of men against Zerah the Cushite with his "vast army." But because King Asa relied on the Lord, he won the battle. In order for this to happen, he "did good and right in the sight of the LORD his God," (2 Chronicles 14:2), removing from his kingdom anything that was offensive to God.

We need to do the same. Like King Asa, we need to rely totally on God, and remove from our lives anything offensive to Him. Do that, and no matter what the "battle" you are facing, you can depend on God to help you.

O Lord my God,

I know that You have redeemed me from sin and death, and that this is reason enough to trust in You. When I am facing difficulties, show me the best course of action, and help me to await with confidence Your help, guidance, and comfort. In Jesus' Name,
Amen.

July 26

...we also exult in our tribulations, knowing that tribulation brings about perseverance; and perseverance, proven character; and proven character, hope... (Romans 5:3-4)

When problems develop, we want God to take them away immediately and make everything all right. But think about this. If parents always rushed to get their children out of

173

jams, even those of their own making, what would the children learn? That no matter what they do, Mommy and Daddy will fix everything and make things right?

Likewise, if God always rushed to get us out of trouble, what would we learn? Nothing. Our patience would not develop, nor would our faith. It's not that God wants us to suffer—it hurts a parent to see his child in pain. Nor does he make bad things happen to us just to "teach us a lesson." But sometimes we can grow and learn through tough situations, partially redeeming the suffering.

So when you don't understand what is going on, do understand that God will walk with you through it.

Loving Father,

I am sometimes upset by the problems I face, and I find it difficult to rejoice because of them. I don't ask to understand why these things happen to me, for I know Your ways are beyond my understanding. Let my faith be strong enough to know that You love me and will redeem every situation according to Your will. Help me to follow the example of Your Son. In Jesus' Name,
Amen.

July 27

When Gideon saw that he was the angel of the Lord, he said, "Alas, O Lord God! For now I have seen the angel of the Lord face to face." (Judges 6:22)

It's wonderful to know that God has sent His angels to watch over us. Some of the ways angels serve God are by protecting us, proclaiming God's message, and executing God's judgment.

So what are angels? It's important to realize that angels are from God and of God. They are not merely friendly spirits who exist only to do our bidding. Angels are God's messengers, created by God and under His authority. And the great thing is that they are supernatural, not bound by human limitations. Just another way God takes care of us.

Almighty God,
I am grateful for the many ways You care for me and all Your children, including through the protection of Your holy angels. Let me approach each new day with the assurance that You are watching out for me and will defend and guide me. In Jesus' Name,
Amen.

July 28

"Is not my word like fire?" declares the LORD, "and like a hammer which shatters a rock? (Jeremiah 23:29)

The Bible is not just a bunch of words; it is powerful and life-changing. God's Word reveals who and what we are, and who and what we are not. It is something against which we can judge the thoughts and attitudes of our hearts.

There are three uses of scripture for us as Christians, known as the three uses of the law:

1.   To maintain civil order in the world.

2.   To make us aware of our sins and drive us to the mercy of Christ.

3.   To provide rules by which Christians should live.

The Bible is more than a historical document or a collection of pretty words; it is God's message to us. Listen to it, and live by it.

Heavenly Father,
Let the Bible be my comfort and guide; grant that I may love it, believe it, and live according to it. Through study of Your Word, allow me better to worship and glorify You. In Jesus' Name,
Amen.

July 29

And there is no creature hidden from His sight, but all things are open and laid bare to the eyes of Him with whom we have to do. (Hebrews 4:13)

If we kept this scripture in front of us at all times as a reminder, we probably would not do some of the things we do, knowing we will someday have to give an account for it. We can have no secrets from God. Even when we are not aware of His presence, He is still there. We can take comfort in knowing that God sees when we are hurt or wronged, even if no one else is aware of it. But He also sees us at all times. His love for us is unfailing, but we must be responsible for our thoughts and actions, so that we can face God with no shame.

The true joy is in the knowledge that He knows all about us and He still loves us. "I am with you always, even to the end of the age." (Matthew 28:20).

All-Knowing God,

You know all that I do: what is worthy of praise, and what is clearly not. Remove from me the desire to sin. When I do sin, create in me a repentant spirit that I may receive Your forgiveness. In Jesus' Name,

Amen.

July 30

...you laid aside the old self with its evil practices, and have put on the new self who is being renewed to a true knowledge according to the image of the One who created him—a renewal in which there is no distinction between Greek and Jew, circumcised and uncircumcised, barbarian, Scythian, slave and freeman, but Christ is all, and in all. (Colossians 3:9-11)

When God looks at us, He sees His children, made in His

image and made perfect through the One who is perfect—Jesus. Never let anyone tell you you're not smart enough, good-looking enough, thin enough, Godly enough, rich enough, or anything else. The new covenant of Christ's love is for all who believe, regardless of age, gender, or any other classifications we use to separate ourselves from others.

We are all equal in Christ. Know who you are in Him—nothing else matters.

Lord,
You have re-created me; I am no longer what I was. Let me rejoice in my new self. Grant me the self-confidence and patience to recognize others as Your creation as well. Let me be a blessing to others at all times, treating them with respect and compassion, letting Your love shine through me. In Jesus' Name,
Amen.

July 31

and let us consider how to stimulate one another to love and good deeds... (Hebrews 10:24)

It can be easy to take our family for granted. After a bad day, it's too easy to come home and take it out on those closest to us.

We need to start taking the time to show our families that we love them. We need to be forgiving, and not allow the little things to mount up and cause anger or resentment. Instead of focusing on the trivial annoyances and conflicts present in every family, we should think of ways to provide loving support to our family members. Supporting and encouraging your mom, dad, brother, sister, grandma, or grandpa in his or her Christian walk is a wonderful way to show your love.

God of All Goodness,

Help me not to take my family for granted. Let me love and cherish each family member, that we may encourage each other in Your saving faith. Let Your Holy Spirit keep us strong in You, that we may be together in Your kingdom. In Jesus' Name,

Amen.

August 1

For you have not received a spirit of slavery leading to fear again, but you have received a spirit of adoption as sons by which we cry out, "Abba! Father!" The Spirit Himself testifies with our spirit that we are children of God... (Romans 8:15-16)

This should give you a great indication of how much God loves and cares for us. The word Abba means "Daddy." God wants us to trust Him and know that we can come to Him with everything, no matter how big or small, and He wants to be not only our God, but also our Daddy—a word that implies an intimate, loving relationship.

With so many families being torn apart through divorce, God wants you to know that in Him you have a Daddy, and that He will always be there for you. No matter what disappointments or hurts may be present in our personal relationships, God is always faithful—"For my father and my mother have forsaken me, But the LORD will take me up." (Psalm 27:10). Our God, our Abba, will never leave us.

Father God,

Through the sacrifice of Your Son Jesus, You have drawn me, a sinner, to You, not as a slave but as Your own dear Child. Thank You for being there for me at all times; thank You for my hope of eternal life; thank You for being my loving Father. In Jesus' Name,

Amen.

August 2

Jesus Christ is the same yesterday and today and forever.
(Hebrews 13:8)

A lot of people put God in a box. They believe that what He did for people in the Bible, He did only for those people. They believe Him to be bound by time, trapped back in "those days," when He still performed miracles and spoke to His people. But God, the Author of time, cannot be bound by His own creation.

This scripture tells us that God hasn't changed. He still performs miracles and speaks to His children. Take joy in the knowledge that God is still the God who spoke to Moses from the burning bush, parted the Red Sea, and raised Jesus Christ from the dead. He is our all-powerful God, the same yesterday and today and forever.

Eternal Father,
You are the same yesterday, today, and forever. In this world, where there is so much doubt and cynicism, help me to remain confident in Your power and authority; let me recognize and rejoice in the miracles You perform every day. In Jesus' Name,
Amen.

August 3

No temptation has overtaken you but such as is common to man; and God is faithful, who will not allow you to be tempted beyond what you are able, but with the temptation will provide the way of escape also, so that you will be able to endure it. (1 Corinthians 10:13)

It can be a real comfort to know that whatever temptation we face is nothing new. We are not the first to struggle with it. The part of this verse that really stands out is that we can

179

trust God to show us a way of escape when temptation comes along.

When you think about it, it almost seems there is no reason to sin. God tells us that no temptation will come our way that we can't beat with His strength. No temptation is as strong as God, and He will show us how to escape. This is good news!

The next time you are struggling with temptation, immediately stop and pray for God's escape plan...He will help you out.

Saving Lord,
Strengthen me, that I may resist temptation in whatever form it appears; please hear me when I call upon You for help, and come swiftly to my aid. When temptation is strong, let me remember that You are stronger. In Jesus' Name, **Amen.**

August 4

Before I formed you in the womb I knew you, And before you were born I consecrated you; I have appointed you a prophet to the nations. (Jeremiah 1:5)

This verse is worth a second glance. In the past, while going through tough times, I have asked myself, *"Does God really have a plan for me? Can He really use me?"* That's when I go to this scripture. It reminds me that I am not going it alone, nor is God "winging it." He has had a plan for my life, and yours, since the beginning of time.

Read this verse, and then sit and think about it for a while. Before you were born, before you were even in your mother's womb, God knew you. You were not a surprise to Him. He knew you since the beginning of time, and has set you apart and chosen you for His own. That is great news!

O God,
What a joy and comfort it is to be Your child. Sustain me

with the knowledge that you have a perfect plan for my life, which You will bring about in Your own time. Grant me the faith and patience to wait for Your will to be done in me. In Jesus' Name,
 Amen.

August 5

But godliness actually is a means of great gain when accompanied by contentment. For we have brought nothing into the world, so we cannot take anything out of it either. (1 Timothy 6:6-7)

I'm sure you've heard the expression "the grass always looks greener on the other side." Well, it's true. So many of us look to other people or things to satisfy us—our jobs, boyfriend or girlfriend, sports, or money.

But real satisfaction is knowing who you are in Christ. If you have that, you don't need anyone or anything else in life to try to fill you up. No person or possession can make you truly complete, nor can they help you after you have left this world. If you find yourself constantly trying to find fulfillment in other things, then pray and ask for God's peace and contentment to fill your life.

God, My Wholeness,
I confess that, because of self-absorption and lack of faith, I am sometimes too focused on "me"—my wants, my desires, how I appear to others. I pray that You take from me these selfish concerns and replace them with a desire only for You. I give You thanks for completing me through the death and resurrection of Your Son, Jesus. In Jesus' Name,
 Amen.

August 6

My son, observe the commandment of your father and do not forsake the teaching of your mother; bind them continually on your heart; tie them around your neck. When you walk about, they will guide you; when you sleep, they will watch over you; and when you awake, they will talk to you. For the commandment is a lamp and the teaching is light; and reproofs for discipline are the way of life (Proverbs 6:20-23)

As I get older, I find myself more and more saying things that my parents used to say to me (something I never thought would happen!) This scripture tells us that we need to follow our parents' advice and listen to what they tell us. We need to be willing to receive counsel from others who are older and wiser in the Lord than we are.

We all tend to think, "This is my life—I know what's best for me." But don't make the mistake of thinking that others don't know what they're talking about. The chances are, they've been in your shoes. Be wise enough to learn from the wisdom of others.

God of Wisdom,

It's hard for me to take advice, when I feel I already have the answers. It's even harder to accept criticism, which so often can feel like a personal attack. Help me to remember that people who take the time to offer me advice are doing so out of concern. Guard me against the arrogance that can make me feel that I always know better. Thank You for putting those caring and knowledgeable people in my life. In Jesus' Name,
Amen.

August 7

Do not be afraid, little flock, for your Father has chosen gladly to give you the kingdom. Sell your possessions and give to charity; make yourselves money belts which do not wear out, an unfailing treasure in heaven, where no thief comes near nor moth destroys. (Luke 12:32-33)

So many people fear that serving God means they will have to give up many of the things they hold dear. This scripture simply tells us we are not to be afraid of missing out. God wants us to have the very kingdom itself.

Worldly possessions are so insignificant compared to the Kingdom of God that Jesus even tells His disciples, "Sell your possessions and give to the poor." Though most of us don't go that far, we are to concentrate on the "money belts which do not wear out," and the indestructible "treasure in heaven"—eternal life.

This is the kingdom our Father wants to give us. What earthly possession could possibly compare?

Heavenly King,

Even if I am never required to give away all that I own, grant me the willingness to do so. Let me never put material possessions above other people; let me be generous in sharing what I have with those less fortunate; and create in me a heart that holds You most dear of all. In Jesus' Name, **Amen.**

August 8

How can a young man keep his way pure? By keeping it according to Your word. With all my heart I have sought You; do not let me wander from Your commandments. (Psalm 119:9-10)

This scripture tells us very simply how to stay pure. If we pray, read, study God's Word, and seek only Him and His will, then it is possible to live a godly life.

This sounds more difficult than it is. It doesn't mean we will never stumble, or that we ourselves will be pure, but it gives us a "road map." Stay on the path set out for us in God's Word, and don't forget to ask for directions in prayer.

My Comfort and my Guide,
No one can be truly godly but You, but create in me the desire to live according to Your Word. In Jesus' Name,
Amen.

August 9

Why do you look at the speck that is in your brother's eye, but do not notice the log that is in your own eye? Or how can you say to your brother, 'Let me take the speck out of your eye,' and behold, the log is in your own eye? You hypocrite, first take the log out of your own eye, and then you will see clearly to take the speck out of your brother's eye. (Matthew 7:3-5)

It can be very easy to judge others—after all, their faults are so obvious, aren't they?

But what about our own faults? We all have our weaknesses, after all, so before we worry about other people's problems and shortcomings, we need first to make sure our own lives are in order.

None of us is perfect. We are all sinners in need of Christ. Instead of being harsh and critical, try looking at your brothers and sisters through the eyes of mercy and love, and hope that they will do the same for you.

Holy God,
Though my own faults are many, I'm far too quick to notice other people's shortcomings. Because You graciously forgive me whenever I ask, please help me to be more understanding of others. Instead of being judgmental or

harshly critical, let me offer them the support and encouragement they deserve as my brother or sister in Christ. In Jesus' Name,
Amen.

August 10

from the same mouth come both blessing and cursing. My brethren, these things ought not to be this way. (James 3:10)

You can tell a lot about someone by listening to what comes out of his or her mouth. Our words are a reflection of what is in our hearts and minds. This means there's no such thing as "just words." What we say can be as important as what we do.

One thing we all need to practice is self-control, a gift of the Holy Spirit which can help us control our tongues and actions. Poorly chosen words have the power to divide people and keep them at odds with one other. A few words spoken in anger can destroy a relationship.

Keep in mind that loving words will help keep peace, and God loves the peacemakers: "Blessed are the peacemakers, for they shall be called sons of God." (Matthew 5:9).

God of Peace,
Grant me the self-control to consider carefully the words I say and what effect they will have on others. Let everything I say and do be pleasing to You, a reflection of Your love and goodness, and a witness to others. In Jesus' Name,
Amen.

August 11

Then you will call, and the LORD will answer; you will cry, and He will say, 'Here I am.' (Isaiah 58:9)

Isn't it great to know that God is always available to us?

He never goes on break. You never get a busy signal. You don't have to pay $4.99 a minute to talk with Him. Even if we abandon him, He waits patiently for us to come back. He is faithful. Don't ever fall into the trap of thinking it's too late for you to go back to God, or that you have sinned too much. It is never too late, and no sin is too great for God to forgive a repentant sinner.

Faithful God,

I know You are always with me. Break through my stubborn will that makes me want to pull away from You; ease my fears that make me doubt Your love. Draw me ever closer to You and give me peace. In Jesus' Name,
Amen.

August 12

If anyone thinks himself to be religious, and yet does not bridle his tongue but deceives his own heart, this man's religion is worthless. (James 1:26)

We've talked about our words and the damage we can do when we don't watch what we say to others. We need to try to keep our speech pure at all times.

This is true even when we're only joking around. Sometimes when we're with close friends, it may seem OK to say something a little "dirty." But before you speak, be aware that all our words have consequences: "But I tell you that every careless word that people speak, they shall give an accounting for it in the day of judgment. For by your words you will be justified, and by your words you will be condemned." (Matthew 12:36-37). Remember to make every effort that what comes out of your mouth be to the benefit of those who listen.

Dear Lord,

I confess that I am affected by what I hear around me— what I hear on TV and the movies, and by the way some

people talk at school. Sometimes I slip. Guard me against the temptation to sound "like everyone else." Let my words never injure or offend or lead anyone astray. Instead, let them be a benefit and a blessing to others and bring glory to You. In Jesus' Name,
Amen.

August 13

What shall we say then? Are we to continue in sin so that grace may increase? May it never be! How shall we who died to sin still live in it? (Romans 6:1-2)

Unfortunately, there are a lot of people out there who live like the devil and still call themselves Christians, living by the credo "it's easier to ask for forgiveness than permission."

God did not give us *suggestions* to live by. He gave us *commandments.* Yes, we can take comfort in the knowledge that because of the cross, we can seek and receive forgiveness when we sin. But not even to bother trying to live by God's commandments is lazy. It's also a horrible abuse of God's grace and the sacrifice Christ made for us. Not only that, but what kind of witnessing is it for someone to see you living a careless lifestyle?

Don't contribute to someone else's stumbling by being a poor example to them. And never take God's grace for granted.

Dear Heavenly Father,
Let me obey Your commandments even when they're not comfortable or "convenient." I give You thanks for Your saving grace, which strengthens and sustains me. In Jesus' Name,
Amen.

August 14

Anxiety in a man's heart weighs it down, but a good word makes it glad. (Proverbs 12:25)

Once again, we're talking about our words—this time words of encouragement. Think about how genuine words of encouragement from someone you care about can turn your day around. You can do the same for others, too.

We need to lift each other up and not be negative. When we need answers, we go to God's Word, because there is life in His Word. Since we are His children and represent Him, we also need to speak life into others through kind and sincere words of encouragement.

Use the power of your words to support and cheer someone struggling under the burden of an anxious heart.

Sustaining Lord,
When I see people struggling, let me have the compassion to ease their burden. Help me to know whether to keep silent and listen, to speak words of encouragement, or to pray with them. Through every word and action, let me offer them Your mercy and kindness. In Jesus' Name,
Amen.

August 15

Beloved, let us love one another, for love is from God; and everyone who loves is born of God and knows God. The one who does not love does not know God, for God is love. (1 John 4:7-8)

When we become Christians, we receive the Holy Spirit, which gives us the power to love others; even people who aren't very loveable. We need to be reminded that love is not a feeling. It is an action and a choice. The world has a warped view of love, viewing it as just an emotion, something that happens to us. The pursuit of this kind of love can be very selfish.

Our love needs to be like the love of Christ. He is the perfect example of unselfish love, as He gave up His life for each one of us. In loving others as Christ loved us, we touch others with His love.

Loving Father,

I don't always feel very loving, especially when it comes to people who aren't very loveable. Because I am imperfect, please take possession of my heart. Cast out all bitterness, resentment, and selfishness, and fill it with Your perfect love, that I may love others and so know You better. In Jesus' Name,
Amen.

August 16

And lovingkindness is Yours, O Lord, for You recompense a man according to his work. (Psalm 62:12)

When you read this, what do you think? Does it make you think "I had better get my act together!" Or do you think, "Keep up the good work"—that you are already doing what God wants you to do, by being obedient to His Word? Which describes you?

The Bible says that God rewards those who earnestly seek him. It tells us that whatever we do, we should work at it with all our hearts, because we work for the Lord, not for men.

O God,

Let me delight in performing acts of charity and kindness for those around me, spreading Your love and serving You. In Jesus' Name,
Amen.

August 17

But whatever things were gain to me, those things I have counted as loss for the sake of Christ. More than that, I count all things to be loss in view of the surpassing value of knowing Christ Jesus my Lord, for whom I have suffered the loss of all things, and count them but rubbish so that I may gain Christ, and may be found in Him, not having a righteousness of my own derived from the Law, but that which is through faith in Christ, the righteousness which comes from God on the basis of faith...
(Philippians 3:7-9)

When you first became a Christian, it seemed like other things didn't matter nearly as much as they used to; your priorities changed. Maybe you felt "on fire" and wanted to tell others about the change in you, and what Jesus had done in your life.

Do you still have that "first love" that you had when you first became a Christian? If you don't, maybe its time to take spiritual inventory and find out why not. Our goals should always be to strive to become more like Jesus, to keep spreading His Good News. That way, we may help others to gain Christ and the righteousness that comes only through Him. Keep that fire burning.

Righteous Lord,
Nothing compares to You; Your power, wisdom, and lovingkindness are beyond measure. Let my light shine brightly for You, now and forever. In Jesus' Name,
Amen.

August 18

And He looked up and saw the rich putting their gifts into the treasury. And He saw a poor widow putting in two small copper coins. And He said, "Truly I say to you, this poor widow put in more than all of them; for they all out of their surplus put into the offering; but she out of her poverty put in all that she had to live on." (Luke 21:1-4)

Many times, we feel that if we can't give a large sum of money or do some huge, impressive task as a volunteer, then it's not worth giving or doing. We think, "How can $2, or half an hour out of my day, make a difference?"

But it can! If you've ever thought you'd like to help out in some way, ask around. Maybe your church could use someone to help with grounds upkeep, or nursery care, or folding monthly newsletters. Maybe your community is holding a canned food or clothing drive. They would certainly welcome your contribution, no matter how small. All of these things help, so don't be fooled into thinking that your contribution won't make a difference. After all, look how Jesus rejoiced in the widow's small gift in Luke 21:4.

The next time you want to help out in some way, don't hold back: go ahead, take that step of faith, and contribute your gift of time or money.

God of All,

I confess that I am not always generous with the gifts You have given me: I tend to want my time and money all for myself. Help me to conquer this selfishness; let me seek and find opportunities to serve You through service to others. In Jesus' Name,

Amen.

August 19

When Jesus heard this, He said to him, "One thing you still lack; sell all that you possess and distribute it to the poor, and you shall have treasure in heaven; and come, follow me."
But when he had heard these things, he became very sad, for he was extremely rich. (Luke 18:22,23)

What would you do if, like the rich young man in this story, Jesus asked you to sell everything you have, give the money to the poor, and follow Him? You might say, "I can't—I have to go to school," or "I can't leave my family and friends."

Well, there are sacrifices that come with service to Christ. You probably won't be required to empty out your room, sell all your stuff, and abandon your family. But the point is, you must love God so much, and be so obedient to Him, that you would be willing to do all this if He asked You. There must be nothing more important to us than God.

He held back nothing from us, even sacrificing His only begotten Son for our sake—don't hold back from Him.

Almighty God,
Your Son came down from heaven and gave His life for our sinful world. Make me willing to be obedient to You, whatever You require of me. In Jesus' Name,
Amen.

August 20

...for the gifts and the calling of God are irrevocable. (Romans 11:29)

This is so true! If God has truly called you, that call will always be there. You can try to ignore it, or you can try to run from it, as some people called by God have done (just read the book of Jonah!)—but it never goes away. If you do manage to ignore it and go down a path God has not called you to, you may find you're not totally fulfilled, that there's always an empty spot inside that needs to be filled.

It may not always be a simple thing to know God's plan for us, but at some point in our lives, through prayer, devotions, and the advice of fellow Christians, His calling will be made known. Whether that call be to business, the ministry, marriage, or parenthood, follow it and glorify God through that calling.

Blessed Lord God,

I rejoice in the knowledge that You have a plan just for me. Let me be open to hearing You through prayer, study of Your Word, and the counsel of fellow Christians. Give me the patience to wait for Your will instead of pursuing my own, and when I do hear Your call, let me be obedient to it. In Jesus' Name,
Amen.

August 21

A new commandment I give to you, that you love one another, even as I have loved you, that you also love one another. (John 13:34)

A lot of us struggle with love, not sure if anyone truly loves us. Whenever you wonder if you are loved, read these verses. They are reminders of God's perfect and unfailing love for us.

"*He*...was delivered over because of our transgressions, and was raised because of our justification." (Romans 4:25).

"For the mountains may be removed and the hills may shake, but my lovingkindness will not be removed from you, and my covenant of peace will not be shaken" (Isaiah 54:10).

"By this the love of God was manifested in us, that God has sent His only begotten Son into the world so that we might live through Him. In this is love, not that we loved God, but that He loved us and sent His Son to be the propitiation for our sins." (1 John 4:9-10).

God, My Redeemer,

I sometimes take it for granted that Christ died for me, a sinner. Maybe it's because the full magnitude of that sacrifice is beyond my comprehension. Father, let me never forget that Your Son died an agonizing death and descended into hell for my sake, that I would be free from sin and death, and then rose from the dead and ascended into

heaven, that I may live eternally. Thank You for this wondrous love. In Jesus' Name,
Amen.

August 22

The LORD is for me; I will not fear; what can man do to me? (Psalm 118:6)

There are people who say that some fear is healthy. That's not quite true. Caution is healthy; for example, we are cautious of touching a hot stove, talking to strangers, and other things we know can be harmful to our well-being. But being afraid is never a good thing.

Fear is the opposite of faith. If we are afraid, it's because we aren't putting all our faith in God. Reading God's Word increases our capacity for faith and squeezes out fear as your faith and trust in God grows.

Remember, fear has no authority over you unless you allow it to! God is with us; we don't have to be afraid.

Lord God of Hosts,
When You are with me, I have nothing to fear, for nothing is stronger than You. Help me to strengthen my faith in You through faithful study of Your Word, and I pray that You watch over me and protect me from all harm. In Jesus' Name,
Amen.

August 23

But each one must examine his own work, and then he will have reason for boasting in regard to himself alone, and not in regard to another. (Galatians 6:4)

With school starting soon, you may soon feel great pressure to try to fit in with whatever everyone else is doing—good or bad. This pressure may make it easy to cave in, to say or do things that you wouldn't ordinarily say or do, just so you won't be "different."

I encourage you to stay strong in your morals and beliefs. Doing so may not always make you more "popular" at the time, but I promise you, you won't regret it in the long run. And doing the right thing may bring surprising results. There are always one or two people who may ridicule you because they feel threatened, but most people respect someone willing to think on his or her own, to do their own thing. You may even find that you become a leader—all just for doing what's right.

Almighty God,
Sometimes I just want to be like everyone else, but help me not to be afraid to be "different" for Your sake. Let me take joy in obedience to Your good and gracious will, and never fail to do what is right. In Jesus' Name,
Amen.

August 24

If I take the wings of the dawn, If I dwell in the remotest part of the sea, even there Your hand will lead me, and Your right hand will lay hold of me. (Psalm 139:9-10)

These are wonderful verses of hope and encouragement. God has promised us that He will guide us and show us which way to go. The best thing about these verses to me is the promise that God will be with us everywhere we go: no matter when, no matter where, God will be there to guide us and to hold on to us.

Maybe you find yourself in a new place this fall—a new school, a new town, even a new state—and you're really having a tough time with it. Well, good news! God has traveled with you; He hasn't forgotten you, and He will guide you through this tough time in your life.

Be encouraged. God is with you always, wherever you go.

Gracious Lord God,

I know You are with me everywhere and always. Hold me fast and guide me through the new situations I face in life. Thank You for the comfort of Your presence. In Jesus' Name,
Amen.

August 25

We know love by this, that He laid down His life for us; and we ought to lay down our lives for the brethren. But whoever has the world's goods, and sees his brother in need and closes his heart against him, how does the love of God abide in him? (1 John 3:16-17)

We need to be sensitive about the last part of these verses. Often, while sitting in worship, I've heard about a need and thought, "I'll help out with that." But by the end of the service, I've totally forgotten about it.

We tend to take for granted how we have been blessed. This makes it easy to overlook others who are struggling, while at the same time we assume that someone will help us in our own time of need.

What would happen if everyone had such an attitude? The Bible makes it very clear that we are to do good deeds, not for our salvation but for the glory of Christ. So help your brothers and sisters, for the sake of Jesus Christ, who laid down His life for you.

Eternal Father,

I give You thanks for the true, perfect love I have found in You and for the blessings and material goods You have bestowed upon me. I pray that You guard me against indifference to the suffering of those less fortunate around me. Stir in me a compassion for other people and an eagerness

to serve You and them. In Jesus' Name,
Amen.

August 26

Therefore everyone who confesses Me before men, I will also confess him before My Father who is in heaven. But whoever denies Me before men, I will also deny him before My Father who is in heaven. (Matthew 10:32-33)

What if you had been dating someone for six months or so, and one day you found out they had never told any of their friends or family that the two of you were dating? How would you feel if the two of you were with a group of his or her friends and he or she didn't introduce you to any of them? Your feelings would probably be hurt; you might even wonder how important this relationship was to the person if he or she didn't even tell any of his or her friends about you.

Do you ever wonder how God feels when we do that to Him? I want to challenge you this upcoming school year not to be hesitant in telling others of your faith in God. The Bible doesn't say, "If you know me or hint of knowing me on earth, I will hint of knowing you to my Father in heaven"—it says you must acknowledge Him before others.

Acknowledge Christ boldly through your words and actions, and He will do the same for you on the last day.

Merciful Father,

Forgive me for the many times I have failed to acknowledge You through shame, weakness, or indifference. Let me make You known through my words and actions, that others may know the joy and hope of life in You. In Jesus' Name,
Amen.

August 27

Brethren, even if anyone is caught in any trespass, you who are spiritual, restore such a one in a spirit of gentleness; each one looking to yourself, so that you too will not be tempted. (Galatians 6:1)

Wouldn't it be wonderful if we really lived this way? If we would stretch out our hand to other sinners in love instead of criticizing or condemning them?

This doesn't mean you condone their sin. If someone is not living as God wants, you can be assured that the Holy Spirit is dealing with them. God, our Creator, says He has seen our ways but will heal us. If that is the case, then who are we to sit in judgement on another person? We need to restore that person gently, as this scripture says, and hope our brothers and sisters will do the same for us when we fall.

Lord God,
When I see someone caught up in sin, help me to be concerned instead of smug. Let me offer help instead of judgement. And when I am the one sinning, I pray that You send a brother or sister in Christ to offer the same loving guidance to me. In Jesus' Name,
Amen.

August 28

Do you not know that those who run in a race all run, but only one receives the prize? Run in such a way that you may win. (1 Corinthians 9:24)

When things get tough, it's tempting to get going—away from our problems. We're tempted to give up rather than persevere.

We must not give up if we are going to get that prize God has promised us. We must keep our eyes on Jesus Christ and

His Word, so we don't get sidetracked. When we do, we start looking at our circumstances, focusing on ourselves rather than on Him. If God has called you to a task, then set your heart and mind on finishing it, and don't lose faith or give up...He won't give up on you.

So don't allow discouragement to set in. Keep pressing on.

Holy God,

I'm not always strong enough to stand up against the day-to-day challenges life presents to my faith: disappointment when it seems my prayers aren't being answered; the feeling sometimes that You are very far away. When I am disheartened, send Your Holy Spirit to me. Encourage and comfort me, that my faith will be strong enough to stay in the race. In Jesus' Name,

Amen.

August 29

I can do nothing on my own initiative. As I hear, I judge; and my judgment is just, because I do not seek my own will, but the will of Him who sent me. (John 5:30)

These are the words of Jesus—even He was totally dependent on God. Can you imagine the great things that would happen if we were to seek God out for answers to every situation, realizing that He knows far more than we do, no matter what? You see, we are not wise enough to do things on our own. The Lord is all-knowing; He knows the answers to all the situations you and I face every day. He can save us from spinning our wheels and wasting time, if we seek Him first.

In order to do this, we need to have the discipline to spend quality time with Him every day. We need to know that by ourselves we can do nothing.

God, My Strength,

My judgement is subject to my human shortcomings; Yours is limitless. Grant me the wisdom to know my limitations, and come to You with all my needs. In Jesus' Name, **Amen.**

August 30

because you are not of the world, but I chose you out of the world, because of this the world hates you. (John 15:19)

Sometimes, when we see the inexplicable or tragic things that happen in the world, our only comfort is our hope in God. It can be easy to feel despair when watching the news or reading the paper. This is one reason that it's so very important to stay connected with God through prayer and devotion, so that we don't lose the joy and peace that is ours through Him.

When things look down, don't focus on what you see going on around you; stay focused on God.

Lord God Almighty,

Heaven and earth rejoice in You. Let me not be frightened by the violence and uncertainty of this world, but put my hope and trust in You, that You will redeem all things according to Your will. Thank You for Your watchful and loving care, and the precious hope of eternal life. In Jesus' Name, **Amen.**

August 31

For we do not have a high priest who cannot sympathize with our weaknesses, but one who has been tempted in all things as we are, yet without sin. (Hebrews 4:15)

Temptation often doesn't appear boldly showing itself for what it is. It shows up looking very attractive, reasonable, and convincing. It can even appear to be the right thing to do.

No matter how it shows up, recognize it for what it is, and remember that there is a way of escape if we look for it. Whatever temptations you are facing, realize that Jesus—fully God and fully man—was tempted in every way, just as we are. Being perfect, He did not give into that temptation, and will always help us out of our own difficulties if we ask.

Merciful Lord,
I give You thanks for the victory over sin that is mine through the death and glorious resurrection of Your Son, Jesus Christ. To You be all glory and honor, now and forever! In Jesus' Name,
Amen.

September 1

For this is the love of God, that we keep His commandments; and His commandments are not burdensome. (1 John 5:3)

The sooner we learn this, the better off we are. We need to remember who's really in charge. Have you ever seen the bumper sticker that says "God is my co-pilot?" Wrong! He's the pilot!

We are told in Proverbs 3:6, "In all your ways acknowledge Him, and He will make your paths straight." Likewise, Proverbs 16:3 says, "Commit your works to the LORD and your plans will be established." These scriptures don't mean that you should do whatever you want and then expect God to give you His blessing; rather, that we must take our orders from God. If we do, our plans will succeed, because they are ultimately His plans.

So in everything, through prayer, devotion, and the counsel of Christian friends, seek God's will. He has a plan for us and knows what is best.

Lord God, Captain of My Soul,

You are in charge of my life and my destiny—and what a relief that is! I pray that you guard me from the overconfidence that sometimes leads me to think I can do it all on my own. Give me a humble heart, grateful for your guidance and wisdom. In Jesus' Name,

Amen.

September 2

I am the true vine, and my Father is the vinedresser. Every branch in me that does not bear fruit, He takes away; and every branch that bears fruit, He prunes it so that it may bear more fruit. You are already clean because of the word which I have spoken to you. Abide in me, and I in you. As the branch cannot bear fruit of itself unless it abides in the vine, so neither can you unless you abide in me. (John 15:1-4)

Have you known someone who became a Christian but then was unwilling to change his or her life? Or have you yourself struggled with giving up your old ways? This scripture lays down the law: the Father cuts off every branch that bears no fruit.

God "prunes" us so that we will be more fruitful. Sometimes this is no fun, but it makes us stronger and more mature.

If you know someone whose life doesn't appear to be bearing fruit, try talking to that person, and share this scripture with them gently but firmly. Perfection isn't expected of Christians, but there should be a change of the heart. Work at making and maintaining that change of heart yourself, so that you won't become a branch that is pruned and discarded. Instead, "remain in the vine" and bear the fruit of a joyous life in Christ.

God of Mercy,

You have cleansed, pardoned, and renewed me. Let my life reflect the newness of life I have in You; cut out from my heart all that is dishonorable and impure. Shine the light of

Your love through me, that others may be drawn to You. In Jesus' Name,
Amen.

September 3

His master said to him, "Well done, good and faithful slave. You were faithful with a few things, I will put you in charge of many things; enter into the joy of your master." (Matthew 25:21)

We all have a tendency to want to start at the top. When we start a new job, we immediately want the best hours or the highest pay. In a new relationship, we want all the other person's faith and trust from the beginning. But it doesn't usually work that way, does it? We have first to show ourselves to be responsible and trustworthy, and then we are rewarded.

It's the same with God. If you are faithful with a few things, then He will put you in charge of many. God wants His people to be faithful and trustworthy in all things, no matter how insignificant they seem to us. Through this, we will be rewarded and allowed to share in His happiness.

Heavenly Father,
You are always faithful to Your children. Help me, too, to be faithful with all my responsibilities, going about my work diligently and with a good attitude, sharing in Your happiness. In Jesus' Name,
Amen.

September 4

everyone who acts unjustly is an abomination to the LORD your God. (Deuteronomy 25:16)

Have you ever been told or promised something that you counted on, and then been disappointed? Undoubtedly it has happened to you; it happens to all of us. It's a shame, especially when it happens among Christians. I recently had a friend tell me that the Christians she had dealt with professionally were more difficult to do business with than the non-Christians. In her experience, Christians were the ones who complained about the bill, or even tried to get out of it, even though they had signed a contract.

Though my friend's experience certainly isn't true across the board, I found this embarrassing, sad, and a very bad witness. We should be especially careful of what we say and do in order to set a good example of what Christians are about.

God of Truth,
Make me desire to uphold truth and righteousness at all times, especially for the sake of being a good witness. Let me be honest and trustworthy, my conduct always reflecting Your glory, that people may experience Your love and truth through me. In Jesus' Name,
Amen.

September 5

And the Lord opened the mouth of the donkey, and she said to Balaam, "What have I done to you, that you have struck me these three times?" (Numbers 22:28)

Can you imagine having a donkey speak to you? I should think Balaam was rather surprised. The animal actually saved Balaam's life, but made him look foolish in the process, so Balaam lashed out angrily at the donkey. An angel of the Lord stood in the way to oppose Balaam, who was disobeying God and pursuing a reckless path. But Balaam didn't get it, so God had to open the donkey's mouth to get Balaam's attention.

We should hope we don't have to go through something like that for God to get our attention, but that we will be listening carefully for God's direction. "I will instruct you and teach you in the way which you should go; I will counsel you with my eye upon you. Do not be as the horse or as the mule which have no understanding, whose trappings include bit and bridle to hold them in check, otherwise they will not come near to you." (Psalm 32:8-9). (In this case, we should be like Balaam's donkey, who obeyed the angel of God more than her master!)

Heavenly Father,
Obedience to Your will isn't easy sometimes, especially when I'm not always sure what Your will is. I pray that You do whatever it takes to get my attention—even a talking donkey!—and give me a humble, obedient heart so that I will obey Your wise and loving commands. In Jesus' Name,
Amen.

September 6

For whoever is ashamed of me and my words in this adulterous and sinful generation, the Son of Man will also be ashamed of him when He comes in the glory of His Father with the holy angels. (Mark 8:38)

This is a pretty strong verse that we often don't want to think about. I know that when I get to Heaven, I don't want Jesus to be ashamed of me. That's why it's so important to stand tall for Jesus Christ while on earth.

Many of you have just started the school year. Maybe last year you weren't as strong in your faith as you'd have liked to be. This year, however, you really have a desire to witness for Jesus on campus and make a difference in your school. Here are five things that will help make you a better witness for Christ:

1. Read the Bible daily. I encourage you to read one chapter of the Bible each day. That may sound tough, but it doesn't take that long, and it's well worth the effort. We will never really know how to witness for Christ if we don't read

His Word and spend time in devotion.

2. Have a daily prayer life. Each day, spend some time in prayer. Prayer can move mountains in our life, so let's get busy moving them! I'm convinced that the reason people don't have a regular prayer time in their life is because they don't understand how powerful prayer is. Share with God your hurts and disappointments; he can handle it!

3. Have Christian friends. Make sure that your inner circle of friends are Christians who will help you in your Christian walk. I suggest forming an "accountability group," friends who help you walk the walk.

4. Get rid of the "nasty stuff" in your life. Ask God to let you know what He doesn't want in your life...but beware, He will show you things that you need to deal with, and it may not be easy! Remember, whatever God shows you to throw out, it's for your own good.

5. Get involved in church. You can't be fully effective for the Kingdom if you're not active in church. And don't just "go to church." Get involved, in youth group, Bible study, service groups, and family activities. You can learn so much from being in church, and grow spiritually in leaps and bounds.

Stand strong for Jesus this school year, and really make a difference!

O Lord,

Forgive me for the times that I'm not bold enough in my faith. Strengthen me and help me be an effective witness, so that my friends may see Your love through me, and that I may cause You no shame. In Jesus' Name,
Amen.

September 7

Do not fear what you are about to suffer. Behold, the devil is about to cast some of you into prison, so that you will be tested, and you will have tribulation for ten days. Be faithful until death, and I will give you the crown of life. (Revelation 2:10)

At the time this was written, being a Christian was a dangerous thing. The Church was facing severe persecution, and a lot of Christians were being killed for their faith.

How strong is your faith? Most of us will never be called upon to be faithful to the point of death, as were many early Christians (and Christians in some parts of the world still are today). But persecution happens on a smaller scale, too. If people make fun of you for your faith, how do you handle it? Do you back down and try to act like everyone else? Or do you stay strong and risk the teasing?

Remember that insults and ridicule, though hurtful, are insignificant compared to the rewards of being a Christian; so don't back down. "Blessed are you when people insult you and persecute you, and falsely say all kinds of evil against you because of me. Rejoice and be glad, for your reward in heaven is great; for in the same way they persecuted the prophets who were before you." (Matthew 5:11-12).

Lord God, Strength of the Weary,

I confess that I am afraid of suffering—it's difficult to handle people talking about me or making fun of me. For the sake of Your Son, Who suffered so much for me, strengthen my faith, so that I don't allow my daily challenges to separate me from You. In Jesus' Name,
Amen.

September 8

Woe to those who call evil good, and good evil; who substitute darkness for light and light for darkness; who substitute bitter for sweet and sweet for bitter! (Isaiah 5:20)

A lot of people, even Christians, say that they can't judge what is right for someone else: "That's right for you and this is right for me—you have your 'value system' and I have mine." But when we make these kinds of excuses for ourselves or someone else, we blur the line between right and wrong.

The Bible has no such blurring. It's very clear on a lot of issues, and when we don't use it as our guide, we get a warped view of what is morally right. In today's society, there's no such thing as sin. This is called moral relativism—there is no absolute right or wrong, only what's right or wrong for me!

Don't fall into this way of thinking. Look to the Bible to know what is right.

God of All Goodness,

You have given Your children many ways to discern what is right, including the Bible. I give You thanks for all the forms in which You give us Your wisdom. Sometimes, though, it's not so easy to know; sometimes, the wrong thing feels right. For those times, I pray that You take away my confusion and give me a clear sense of right and wrong, and let Your Holy Spirit guide me in the right path, the path to eternal life. In Jesus' Name,
Amen.

September 9

preach the word; be ready in season and out of season... (2 Timothy 4:2)

Have you heard people say they are going through a "dry season" in their walk with God, or that they feel "distant" from Him? Can you imagine going to church one Sunday and your pastor telling the congregation that there was no sermon that day, because he or she was going through a dry season? What if you went in for counseling and your pastor told you he couldn't counsel you because he felt distant from God?

There is no dry season with God, and it isn't His will for anyone to feel distant from Him. God never distances Himself from us. If we feel distant from Him, we should look in to our own lives to see what we've put between ourselves and Him. Stay close to Him through His Word and prayer, and it will be impossible to have a dry season.

God, Author of Life,

Give me the strength to search my soul for the cause of my feelings of distance from You. Am I resisting Your will? Coming to You only when I am in trouble? Neglecting my prayer or worship life? I ask that when I feel alone, You draw me even closer to You, and lead me into the fellowship of other Christians. Restore my heart and soul to You, and help me to be a blessing to others. In Jesus' Name,
Amen.

September 10

The Spirit Himself testifies with our spirit that we are children of God, and if children, heirs also, heirs of God and fellow heirs with Christ, if indeed we suffer with Him so that we may also be glorified with Him. (Romans 8:16-17)

This is great news! When we're going through rough times,

sometimes all we can see are the bad things that are happening. But look at the wonderful things we're going to receive! As children of God, we are heirs to eternal life with Him; a reward greater than any earthly treasure.

Saving Lord,

When the requirements of discipleship seem too much, let me remember what Jesus Christ suffered to bring me into Your kingdom, into everlasting glory and life eternal. Thank You for making me Your child. In Jesus' Name,
Amen.

September 11

Shout joyfully to the LORD, all the earth. Serve the LORD with gladness; come before Him with joyful singing. (Psalm 100:1-2)

Here's an obvious statement: God is worthy of our praise and worship. If you are finding it difficult to praise and worship Him, then stop and think—do you have any unconfessed sins, or is your relationship with Him not what it once was?

Worshiping God is our duty, our way of showing gratitude and remembering all His goodness. But it's also our delight. A heart that is full of the love of Christ cannot help but praise Him! If you're having trouble, look into your heart, find the problem, and pray for help. And then praise Him! "Say to God, 'How awesome are Your works! Because of the greatness of Your power Your enemies will give feigned obedience to You. All the earth will worship You, and will sing praises to You; they will sing praises to Your name.'" (Psalm 66:3-4).

Almighty God,

You are indeed worthy of praise! Give me a heart overflowing with gratitude; let me ever sing of the wonders You

have done in my life and in the world, that all may know of Your majesty and love. In Jesus' Name,
Amen.

September 12

For the one who sows to his own flesh will from the flesh reap corruption, but the one who sows to the Spirit will from the Spirit reap eternal life. (Galatians 6:8)

The more we give in to bad habits, the more we become enslaved to them. Satan wants us to keep giving in to these habits to defeat us and keep us in bondage, away from the love of Christ. Don't do it! Don't let yourself be enslaved to sin, which, as we are warned in the verse above, leads to destruction. Stay close to God through prayer, devotion, and Christian fellowship. Whatever you're tempted with—smoking, drugs, drinking, overeating, bulimia, promiscuity, pornography, bad temper, rebellion, worrying, fear, pride, gossiping, swearing—there is a way out. "God...will not allow you to be tempted beyond what you are able, but with the temptation will provide the way of escape also..." (1 Corinthians 10:13).

If you seek it, God will show you the escape from temptation's power, so that you can bear up patiently against it. Remember, your freedom was provided at the cross—you need to keep what God has already provided for you.

Lord God,
Without You I can do nothing, but through You, all things are possible. For the sake of Your Son, free me from the bondage of my sin. Cut away from me my rebelliousness and defensiveness; guard me against temptation, and give me the faith to lean on You. In Jesus' Name,
Amen.

211

September 13

Do not be wise in your own eyes; fear the LORD and turn away from evil. It will be healing to your body and refreshment to your bones. (Proverbs 3:7-8)

This is so true! We need to avoid thinking we're so wise, strong, and self-sufficient that we can play around with temptation and handle it alone.

No matter how smoothly things may be going, never think you're above temptation and that you can't fall. All of us will fail if we try to do it alone, without God. Shun evil and run to God!

Gracious Lord God,
You have given me a lot, and I still need You, and if I forget that, I'm in trouble. Keep me mindful that You are the source of all my strength and wisdom; let me always seek Your will in all things. In Jesus' Name,
Amen.

September 14

Truly I say to you, all sins shall be forgiven the sons of men, and whatever blasphemies they utter; but whoever blasphemes against the Holy Spirit never has forgiveness, but is guilty of an eternal sin... (Mark 3:28-29)

Some people wonder whether they may have committed this eternal sin: the sin of rejecting God himself.

If you are a Christian, then you are not guilty of this, because you are saved through Christ's sacrifice. If you're not sure whether you are a Christian, you don't have to wonder any longer—take a few minutes right where you are and pray this:

Lord Jesus,

I believe that You died on the cross for me and I ask that You forgive my sins. Come into my life and cleanse me. Acts 2:21 says "And it shall be that everyone who calls on the name of the LORD will be saved." I believe that I am saved and a new creation in Christ. Thank You for loving me and thank You for forgiving me. In Jesus' Name,

Amen.

September 15

You are the light of the world. A city set on a hill cannot be hidden; nor does anyone light a lamp and put it under a basket, but on the lampstand, and it gives light to all who are in the house. Let your light shine before men in such a way that they may see your good works, and glorify your Father who is in heaven. (Matthew 5:14-16)

People are hungry for God, whether they realize it or not. They're looking for something that is real and solid, something they can count on and really believe in. They're tired of seeing people who call themselves Christians, but who are no different from anyone else.

How bright is your light? When people get to know you, do they know you are a Christian? When you hear an off-color joke, do you join in on it, or do you walk away and let people know you're not interested in hearing that kind of stuff? How is your language? Do you swear when you talk, or do you take the Lord's name in vain? Are you a good representation of Christ? Or are there too many areas in your life in which you compromise?

These are hard questions. None of us is perfect; we all make these or other mistakes. Fortunately, we don't have to try to deserve our salvation, since "all have sinned and fall short of the glory of God, being justified as a gift by His grace through the redemption which is in Christ Jesus" (Romans 3:23-24).

If your light could be brighter, ask God to forgive you and

help you be a stronger Christian. That way, others "may see your good works, and glorify your Father who is in heaven."

Heavenly Father,

Support me with Your power as I witness to others. Give me a loving heart, sincere speech, and a godly life, so that my light will shine brightly, and through me, Your kingdom will increase. In Jesus' Name,
Amen.

September 16

I will heal their apostasy, I will love them freely, for my anger has turned away from them. (Hosea 14:4)

Do you know that no matter what you do, God still loves you? Sometimes it may seem that we've messed up so badly that God couldn't possibly love us. When we do something bad, we may "feel" that God doesn't love us; we may "feel" unworthy, like a failure.

The key word here is "feel," because we don't depend on our feelings, we depend on what God's Word says. "'For the mountains may be removed and the hills may shake, but my lovingkindness will not be removed from you, and my covenant of peace will not be shaken,' Says the LORD who has compassion on you." (Isaiah 54:10).

God always forgives a repentant sinner—ask, and you will see that His love for us is unfailing.

Merciful Father,

I pray that You forgive me of all my sins and fill my soul with peace. Go with me through all my days; let Your loving presence ease my mind and speak peace to my soul. Thank You for Your gracious forgiveness. In Jesus' Name,
Amen.

September 17

*But they, in their own kingdom, with Your great goodness which
You gave them, with the broad and rich land which You set
before them, did not serve You or turn from their evil deeds.
(Nehemiah 9:35)*

It's easy sometimes to fix our eyes on what we don't have,
rather than keep in mind all that God has done for us and
given to us.

When I became a prayer partner at church, people would
call in for prayers and encouragement. I had thought I had
troubles—until spending a few days answering the phones
and talking with others about their needs. Then I realized
how blessed I was. It made me thankful to God, rather than
dissatisfied or resentful about what I thought was so terribly
wrong in my life.

Always be aware of God's great goodness, and take joy
in loving and serving Him all the more because of it, and
because of His love for us.

Heavenly King,
It's so easy to take my blessings for granted. Please take
ungratefulness and self-centeredness from me. You have
given me so much; let me be grateful, and want to share my
joy and good fortune with those who are in need. In Jesus'
Name,
Amen.

September 18

*The LORD is my rock and my fortress and my deliverer, my God,
my rock, in whom I take refuge; my shield and the horn of my
salvation, my stronghold. (Psalm 18:2)*

The world believes that people need to be strong, self-
reliant; but the Bible tells us that God is our strength. Even

Christians have bought the lie that we are to be the strong ones. The problem is, the more we feel that we have to carry things on our own and rely on our own abilities, the more difficult it is to trust God.

When we try to do things on our own, we can make a real mess of it. Then, after we have messed things up, we go to God, so He can take over and get us out of it. He can get us out of it, of course; but why not save yourself a step, and go to Him in the first place?

God works things out when we trust in Him as our rock; it is only through Him that we are strong.

O Lord, My Strength,
Give me the faith to depend only on You, and strengthen me when my power fails. In Jesus' Name,
Amen.

September 19

So Peter was kept in the prison, but prayer for him was being made fervently by the church to God. (Acts 12:5)

Do you sometimes feel that your prayers aren't doing any good? Well, you're not the only one. Even the first Christians had such doubts.

In Acts 12, the church was praying hard for Peter while he was in prison. But when he got out of prison and went and knocked on their door, nobody believed he had been released! As a matter of fact, the servant girl who opened the door to Peter and ran to tell those praying inside was told she must be out of her mind (see Acts 12:15). When she kept insisting that it was so, they said it must be his angel. This doesn't say much about their faith that God was going to answer their prayer!

Believe that God hears our prayers, and be ready for miracles.

Almighty and Everliving God,

I believe You hear and answer my prayers—but not always when and how I want You to. Help me to be patient enough to wait for You with a calm and trusting heart. I know You will do what is best for me in Your own time. In Jesus' Name, **Amen.**

September 20

You shall therefore impress these words of mine on your heart and on your soul; and you shall bind them as a sign on your hand, and they shall be as frontals on your forehead. (Deuteronomy 11:18)

Everyone wants other people to recognize their rights. People march, picket, and protest, going to the newspapers and government offices if they have to, until they are recognized.

As a child of the living God, do you know what your rights are? If you fix God's Word in your hearts and minds as this scripture tells us to, then you will know:

Forgiveness (1 John 2:12): " …your sins have been forgiven you for His name's sake."

Salvation (Romans 10:13): "Whoever will call on the name of the LORD will be saved."

New Life (2 Corinthians 5:17): "Therefore if anyone is in Christ, he is a new creature; the old things passed away; behold, new things have come."

Joy (Psalm 16:11): "…In Your presence is fullness of joy; in Your right hand there are pleasures forever."

Hope (Colossians 1:27): "[To the saints] God willed to make known what is the riches of the glory of this mystery..., which is Christ in you, the hope of glory."

Life Eternal (1 John 2:25): "This is the promise which

He Himself made to us: eternal life."

O God,

These words remind me of all You have given me, which is far beyond what the world can give. I give You thanks for the benefits of being Your child. Let me share Your glory with all the world, that all may know the joy and hope of life in You. In Jesus' Name,

Amen.

September 21

It is good not to eat meat or to drink wine, or to do anything by which your brother stumbles. (Romans 14:21)

This is another reminder that we must be very careful in all that we do. It's easy to let our guard down, especially if we are away from home and are not around people we know. We might think, "Who will ever know?" But we never really know who is watching.

I have a pastor friend who, while at an airport changing planes, saw an article on a magazine cover that caught his eye. There was nothing wrong with the article itself, but there was something wrong with the kind of magazine it was in. He really would have liked to have seen what this article had to say, but just didn't feel right about buying and reading that type of magazine, for any reason. He left the magazine on the shelf. He was glad he had done so when, just a moment later, someone recognized him, came up to him, and told my friend that he had come to know Christ through his ministry.

Can you imagine what that person might have thought, what it may have done to his newly-found faith, if he had seen my friend with this magazine in his hand? What kind of witness would that have been? Even innocent mistakes and misunderstandings can cause a brother or sister to fall. Be careful.

Dear Lord,
New-found faith can be so fragile. Please guard me against saying or doing anything, even in jest, that would destroy the faith of a brother or sister in Christ. Let my life be an example to others, and help me support and encourage others in any way I can. In Jesus' Name,
Amen.

September 22

Put away from you a deceitful mouth and put devious speech far from you. (Proverbs 4:24)

Some Christians use bad language, with the excuse that it's not really bad language unless they take God's name in vain. It certainly is true that blaspheming is expressly forbidden in the commandments, but it says right here in Proverbs that "corrupt talk" is not OK either.

I wonder what non-Christians think when they hear a Christian use that kind of language? A lot of people say they just can't help it, but the Bible says otherwise.

Swearing and cursing, like any bad habit, can be hard to stop, but it's worth working at. Don't just say, "I can't help it"—do it, with the help of God.

Most Holy God,
You have called me out of darkness to live in Your light, and I want my words and conduct to reflect that light. Remove from me the desire to impress other people with shocking language, and if it has become my habit, make me aware of each offense. In Jesus' Name,
Amen.

September 23

...it is appointed for men to die once and after this comes judgment... (Hebrews 9:27)

Who comes to mind when you think about someone you need to share Jesus with? Your parents, cousin, aunt, uncle, friend, or neighbor? Sometimes we get so "busy" that we forget our commission in life: to preach the gospel. Fear is another reason we put off sharing the Good News with others, fear that you won't say the right thing, or that they might reject your message—or you.

It's not your fault if people reject your message, but it is your fault if you never share your faith with them, never even give them the chance. Don't allow fear to hold you back. After all, it is wonderful news we have to share with others! They can be set free from guilt, fear, worry, anger, and discouragement, and receive the blessings of peace, contentment, hope, strength, love, forgiveness, and mercy...just to name a few.

If someone knew that you were in debt, and they had won a billion dollars but never shared with you, wouldn't you wish they had? Well, you have something even better than that to share, and it's free—eternal life!

Righteous Father,

I pray that You give me the desire to witness. Let my strength be Your strength, and my words, Your words. Fill my heart with the joy of Your presence, and let it overflow to everyone around me. In Jesus' Name,
Amen.

September 24

For You formed my inward parts; You wove me in my mother's womb. I will give thanks to You, for I am fearfully and wonderfully made; wonderful are Your works, and my soul knows it very well. My frame was not hidden from You, when I was made in secret, and skillfully wrought in the depths of the earth; Your eyes have seen my unformed substance; and in Your book were all written the days that were ordained for me, when as yet there was not one of them. (Psalm 139:13-16)

God knows everything we say, do, and think. Nothing is hidden from Him—and He loves us anyway. He values us more than we can imagine, and far more than we deserve.

Never doubt that God watches over us at all times. "Are not two sparrows sold for a cent? And yet not one of them will fall to the ground apart from your Father. But the very hairs of your head are all numbered. So do not fear; you are more valuable than many sparrows." (Matthew 10:29-31).

My Lord,
You see me wherever I go and whatever I'm doing, but sometimes I still feel alone. I come to You with my fears and insecurities; let me find reassurance in You. In Your precious hands I put my well-being. In Jesus' Name,
Amen.

September 25

Little children, let us not love with word or with tongue, but in deed and truth. (1 John 3:18)

Has someone ever shared a problem with you, and you told them you would pray for them, but then you forgot? Or have you known of a need that you could have helped with, but you didn't make time for it, and the opportunity passed? We mean well; we're filled with good intentions, but we let ourselves and others down all the same.

Next time, take the opportunity to show your love through your actions. If someone comes to you with a prayer request, pray with them, right then and there. If you see someone with a need—an elderly neighbor who needs her walk shoveled, a friend who could use help studying for a test— jump in and help. "Carry each other's burdens, and in this way you will fulfill the law of Christ" (Galatians 6:2).

Loving God,

I want to do my part in Your service. I pray that You show me opportunities to proclaim Your glorious name and Your wonderful works, and grant me the courage to witness for You at home, at school, and wherever I may be. In Jesus' Name,
Amen.

September 26

But they lie in wait for their own blood; they ambush their own lives. (Proverbs 1:18)

It's easy to blame others for our own evil or foolish actions. We may even try blaming God: "If He hadn't wanted me to do it, He wouldn't have allowed me to be in this situation." In reality, we need to take responsibility for our own actions.

In 2 Samuel, we read of how David allowed himself to fall deeper into sin. Instead of fleeing when he saw Bathsheba, he entertained and acted on thoughts of lust. I'm sure he had no idea he would end up murdering someone to cover up his wrongdoing, but that's how sin works. Once it gets started, it gets harder and harder to stop. And it always takes you farther than you had planned on going.

In the moment of temptation, we overlook the inevitable consequences. In David's case, though he asked for and received God's forgiveness, he still had to suffer the consequences of his actions. Do you think if David had known all that was going to happen beforehand, he still would have pursued the pleasures of the moment? Don't allow sin to get started.

Dear Lord God,

You know that I have sinned, and that no matter how hard I try to do right, I will sin again. Please help me to resist the temptation to blame my own sinful actions on other people or on You. Let me instead take responsibility for my actions and come to You with a humble and contrite heart, seeking Your gracious forgiveness. In Jesus' Name,
Amen.

September 27

Now the word of the LORD came to me saying, "Before I formed you in the womb I knew you, and before you were born I consecrated you; I have appointed you a prophet to the nations." Then I said, "Alas, Lord GOD! Behold, I do not know how to speak, because I am a youth." (Jeremiah 1:4-6)

Can you imagine how Jeremiah felt when he found out what God had planned for him? I think the sentences above pretty much sum it up. It's probably the way most of us feel when God tells us what He has planned for us. We probably feel inferior—"Who am I?" But whenever God has a job for us, he also equips us to do it, and He promises to be with us and to watch over us at all times. God is looking for people who are willing to be obedient and be used by Him. Remember that whatever God has planned for you, He will see you through it. "For we are His workmanship, created in Christ Jesus for good works, which God prepared beforehand so that we would walk in them." (Ephesians 2:10).

Father in Heaven,

It's hard to think of myself as Your workmanship. But I am; You created me in Your own image. Remove my insecurities,

and let me not offend You by disrespecting Your creation. In Jesus' Name,
Amen.

September 28

For rebellion is as the sin of divination, and insubordination is as iniquity and idolatry. Because you have rejected the word of the LORD, He has also rejected you from being king." (Samuel 15:23)

From this scripture you can tell what God thinks of rebellion and arrogance, serious sins that go far beyond just being independent and strong-willed. We are to submit to God's authority and also to pray for those in authority over us on earth.

The following are Biblical examples of rebellion and its consequences:

Genesis 3: Adam and Eve rebelled against God and were expelled from Eden.

Numbers 14: Israelites rebelled against God and Moses; they had to wander in the desert for 40 years.

Judges 2: The Israelites rebelled against God; God removed His protection from them.

2 Samuel 15-18: Absalom rebelled against his father, King David, and was killed in battle.

Almighty God,
The consequences of rebellion against You are serious indeed. I am grateful for the spirit and intellect You gave me, but let me not become arrogant. Humble me, I pray, and let me joyfully submit to Your authority, for my own sake and for the sake of Your Kingdom. In Jesus' Name,
Amen.

September 29

What the wicked fears will come upon him, but the desire of the righteous will be granted. (Proverbs 10:24)

With the school year underway, a lot of you will be wanting to date someone. That's a natural desire. We all want someone to care for and who will care for us.

But choose carefully. I encourage you not to settle for second best. I know it's hard to sit at home on the weekends while your friends are going out on dates and to dances, but stay strong. Don't go out with someone just for the sake of going out; just so you won't be lonely. And remember the special value that a truly Christian relationship can bring. God wants to meet your every need, but you must keep Him first in your life. Wait for the right person. God will send him or her your way sooner or later, and you'll find a Christian relationship that is well worth waiting for.

Dear Lord God,
Thank You for the joy of Christian relationships. Please keep me from making bad choices, and help me to wait for the right person, so that we can have a stronger relationship through shared faith in You. In Jesus' Name,
Amen.

September 30

You shall love the LORD your God with all your heart and with all your soul and with all your might. (Deuteronomy 6:5)

It's all too easy to put God on the back burner when our lives are going smoothly. When we're prospering financially, getting good grades, getting along with our parents and peers, we tend to feel self-sufficient.

It can be too easy to forget that we need to keep God first at all times. We have the mentality that we'll let God know if we need Him—sort of "don't call us, we'll call you" on a grand scale. But once a crisis hits us, we're on our knees immediately, crying out to God for help. It is important to remember that we need God in bad times and good.

Merciful Father,
You are my God, in good times and in bad; and at all times I am a sinner in desperate need of Your mercy. Preserve me from the pride that struggles against Your will, and draw me close to You. In Jesus' Name,
Amen.

October 1

For I am the LORD your God, who upholds your right hand, who says to you, "Do not fear, I will help you." (Isaiah 41:13)

Most of you are back in school by now, or will be going back soon—maybe even today. Sometimes fear begins to creep in when we go back to school in the fall; fear of our new classes, the challenges that come with a higher grade or college, new people we don't know.

I would encourage you to claim this verse for the school year. God has promised you that He will help you and that you don't need to fear. He will help you get through whatever you are facing this year in school. Take it one day at a time, have your daily devotions, and make sure you have a daily prayer time. And do not fear.

Dear Lord God,
Daily pressures and challenges sometimes make me focus too much on myself, turning me away from You. Take hold of me; guide and comfort me through this school year. Thank You for the freedom from fear that You have given me, and help me to meet each challenge with the confidence that comes only through You. In Jesus' Name,
Amen.

October 2

Therefore I am well content with weaknesses, with insults, with distresses, with persecutions, with difficulties, for Christ's sake; for when I am weak, then I am strong. (2 Corinthians 12:10)

It can be tough when you are surrounded by people who do not understand your faith. For example, you may be the only Christian in a family who may not understand your faith, or the only minority in a group. When you're insulted or ridiculed, it probably makes you angry. You might even start thinking about ways to get even.

But even in those difficult situations, we have to remember that we are the light of the world. How you react under pressure may well make a difference in someone else's life. And remember, God sees everything: He knows when You suffer, and if you suffer for the sake of Your faith, you will be rewarded in full in His Kingom.

My God and King,

I'm not able to rejoice at being hurt, but with Your strength, I can get through it. Strengthened by Your love, grant me the courage to handle these situations gracefully. In Jesus' Name,
Amen.

October 3

the one who says he abides in Him ought himself to walk in the same manner as He walked. (1 John 2:6)

Have you ever met someone who you thought was a great person, until you saw them with their family? A person's real character usually comes through when they are around their family. Are they short-tempered, impatient, and rude, or are they loving, respectful, and kind?

I've heard it said that no amount of success or talent

matters as much as how a person treats his or her spouse and children behind closed doors. What does your character say about you?

God in Heaven,

I give You thanks for every blessing You have given me and my family. Teach me to love and honor each member of my family, and let me find it easy to forgive when I am hurt by them. Keep me from hurting them, too; help me to recognize that everyone in my family has his or her own rights and privileges that deserve my respect. Unite us in Your love, I pray. In Jesus' Name,

Amen.

October 4

The steadfast of mind You will keep in perfect peace, because he trusts in You. Trust in the LORD forever, for in GOD the LORD, we have an everlasting Rock. (Isaiah 26:3-4)

In this world of turmoil, isn't it wonderful to know that we can be kept in perfect peace? No matter what it is you're going through, if your trust is in the Lord, you can know that you will have His peace. If you're feeling anxious about something, here are some great scriptures on God's peace for His children:

Psalm 4:8: "In peace I will both lie down and sleep, for You alone, O LORD, make me to dwell in safety." (Notice this safety isn't dependent on what part of town you live in, or who your neighbors are.)

John 14:27: "Peace I leave with you; My peace I give to you; not as the world gives do I give to you. Do not let your heart be troubled, nor let it be fearful."

Romans 5:1: "Therefore, having been justified by faith, we have peace with God through our Lord Jesus Christ..."

Enjoy this peace of our Lord, our Rock eternal.

Eternal God,

Thank You for the blessing of Your peace, which is not dependent on what is happening around me. Even when my life and surroundings are chaotic, preserve me and fill me with Your perfect peace, which passes all human understanding. In Jesus' Name,
Amen.

October 5

"I am the LORD, that is my name..." (Isaiah 42:8)

Our names can represent the essence of who we are. Below are some Hebrew names for God that help reveal His nature:

El, Elohim	God
El Shaddai	God Almighty
Yahweh	The Great "I Am"
Adonai	The Sovereign Lord
Yahweh-Yireh	The Great God Who Provides
Yahweh-Rapha	The Great God Who Heals
Yahweh-Nissi	The Great God Our Banner
Yahweh-Shalom	The Great God Our Peace
Yahweh-Rohi	The Great God My Shepherd

Dear Lord,

You are Almighty God, You are my Sovereign Lord. You are the God of Abraham, Isaac, and Jacob. You are my Provider and my Shepherd. You are my Peace, You are my Lord. Praise to the Lord! In Jesus' Name,
Amen.

October 6

Are [angels] not all ministering spirits, sent out to render service for the sake of those who will inherit salvation? (Hebrews 1:14)

I don't know about you, but sometimes I wonder about angels. There are so many books and TV specials about angels. In such materials Christ is often not mentioned, so I have to wonder sometimes where people think the angels came from.

I also wonder if I've ever seen an angel without realizing it. I heard a story of a police officer waiting for backup before going in to arrest a gang. When he could see that the gang members were about to get away, he made the decision to go ahead and arrest them before backup arrived— a risky move, to say the least. To his surprise, they didn't give him any trouble, but went along with him peacefully. Afterwards, when he asked one of them why they hadn't resisted, one gang member told him, "You've got to be kidding! There was no way I was going to fight you; your guys were a lot bigger and stronger. I knew there was no way I could take them!" The officer was amazed, because he knew he had been the only one there. This officer was a man who prayed daily for God's protection, and from this experience, he knew God had sent angels to watch over him.

Have you ever had "unexplained" help, maybe that you weren't even aware of? It may have been God's angels caring for you.

God in Heaven,
Thank You for sending Your holy angels to earth to do Your will and come to the aid of Your children. Let them guard and keep me safe from all harm. In Jesus' Name,
Amen.

October 7

The good man out of the good treasure of his heart brings forth what is good; and the evil man out of the evil treasure brings forth what is evil; for his mouth speaks from that which fills his heart. (Luke 6:45)

According to this scripture, our speech and actions show our true beliefs and attitudes. Have you ever had the experience of being around someone when they're really angry? This can be very telling of what's in someone's heart. It can be shocking to hear a Christian person uttering obscenities and harsh, angry words.

Always think about what you are going to say before you speak. Our hearts should be overflowing with the love of Christ, and our speech needs to show it.

Holy Lord,

Judging from the things I think and say sometimes, the contents of my heart are poor indeed. But You have come into my heart. Cut all evil thoughts out from it, and let every word that comes from my mouth bring honor and glory to You. In Jesus' Name,
Amen.

October 8

I will not leave you as orphans; I will come to you. (John 14:18)

I know that some of you are lonely, and maybe even feel unloved. Perhaps you've lost one or both of your parents through death or divorce. Perhaps you feel abandoned, and the hurt runs deep. Or maybe you have parents at home, but things could be a whole lot better, and right now you feel like no one really cares.

Someone does care. This verse tells you that God will not leave you alone in this world, that He will come to you. Even if it seems like no one loves or cares for you right now, please know that God loves you very much. Remember, He already has come: He loved you enough to send His Son to die on the cross for you.

Take time today and tell God about your pain, and then ask Him to come to you. You will find that He is able to fill that void in your life and give you the strength to continue.

Faithful Lord,
You have promised that nothing can separate me from Your love in Christ Jesus, yet sometimes I still feel alone. Keep me from the temptation to forget Your loving and watchful presence when I am lonely. Teach me to come to You with my cares and sorrows, for in You I will find peace. In Jesus' Name,
Amen.

October 9

Sing praises to the LORD, who dwells in Zion; declare among the peoples His deeds. (Psalms 9:11)

Do you know that being a witness is not optional for Christians? We have been commanded to witness to others. As a matter of fact, we have been called to take God's Good News to the ends of the earth.

Many Christians feel shy or don't want to "offend" others by sharing their faith. But God isn't offering us a choice. Don't allow fear to keep you from talking with others. Pray and ask the Holy Spirit to use you, to give you the words and the boldness. Now, "boldness" doesn't mean getting in people's faces and yelling at them that they are going to hell; the Holy Spirit doesn't work through condemnation and making people feel like losers. Tell others of the joy, peace, and hope that is yours—and can be theirs—in Christ. Be obedient to God's will, and no matter where you are, ask God to help you share your faith.

Good Shepherd,

I ask that You use me as Your witness. Let my conduct reveal Your presence in my life, and let my every word bear witness to You and Your love. Open the eyes of those around me to see the joy, satisfaction, and blessed peace of life in You. In Jesus' Name,

Amen.

October 10

Why are you in despair, O my soul? and why have you become disturbed within me? Hope in God, for I shall again praise Him for the help of His presence. (Psalm 42:5-6)

Everyone feels depressed from time to time. I'm not talking about diagnosed clinical depression, which always needs to be treated, but about just feeling "down," maybe without even knowing why.

This feeling can be a signal to us that something isn't quite right in our lives. In Psalm 32:3, David felt anguished until he confessed his sins to God: "When I kept silent about my sin, my body wasted away through my groaning all day long." Cain's depression was due to guilt: "Then the LORD said to Cain, "Why are you angry? And why has your countenance fallen? If you do well, will not your countenance be lifted up? And if you do not do well, sin is crouching at the door; and its desire is for you, but you must master it."(Genesis 4:6-7).

We are told in Isaiah 61:3 that God bestows on us a "mantle of praise instead of a spirit of fainting." The next time you feel "the blues" coming on, begin to praise God. Tell Him you love Him, tell Him what a great God He is, and watch your depression vanish! The joy of the Lord is your strength—you can make it!

God, My Strength,

Help me to examine myself honestly, to see if something

in my life is separating me from You, and making me feel miserable. If I need help, let me find a caring and wise person to talk to. If the problem lies with me, let me be made aware of it and throw myself on Your mercy. You are my hope and my strength. In Jesus' Name,
Amen.

October 11

Let everything that has breath praise the LORD. Praise the LORD! (Psalm 150:6)

Praise plays a huge part in "spiritual warfare." When we are praising God, we are not fighting the battle; we are praising God because the battle has already been won! Did you know that when you praise God, it silences the enemy?

We should praise God even in adversity, and look for His salvation and deliverance. When Paul and Silas were in prison, they praised God: "[a]bout midnight Paul and Silas were praying and singing hymns of praise to God, and the prisoners were listening to them" (Acts 16:25). Notice it didn't say that they sat there and complained about their situation, nor did they sing quietly between themselves—the other prisoners listened to them.

Praising God brings Him into your situation. Look what happened to Paul and Silas: "suddenly there came a great earthquake, so that the foundations of the prison house were shaken; and immediately all the doors were opened and everyone's chains were unfastened." (Acts 16:26). God responds to our praise!

Almighty God,
You created the heavens and the earth and all that is in it; You have given me the promise of life everlasting. Let me begin and end each day by counting Your many blessings, and giving You thanks. In Jesus' Name,
Amen.

October 12

Through Him then, let us continually offer up a sacrifice of praise to God, that is, the fruit of lips that give thanks to His name. (Hebrews 13:15)

Here's another look at praise. Yesterday we talked about how praise silences the enemy. Today's scripture urges us to "continually offer up a sacrifice of praise."

Now, you can be sure that when Paul and Silas were in prison, they probably didn't "feel" like praising God, yet still they offered up a sacrifice of praise. How many times have you been in church, tired and grouchy, and just didn't "feel" like praising God? Or, after a long, tiring day, didn't "feel" like saying your prayers? Well, we need to do these things anyway. The fact that it's not always easy is why it's called a sacrifice of praise.

Dear Lord God,
Help me always to offer You thanksgiving and praise, even when I don't feel like it. Thank You for being with me at all times, good and bad. In the Name of Jesus, Who sacrificed Himself for me,
Amen.

October 13

It is the Spirit who gives life; the flesh profits nothing; the words that I have spoken to you are spirit and are life. (John 6:63)

Many Christians have no idea how much the Word of God has to offer. Here are just a few examples:

Faith: "So faith comes from hearing, and hearing by the word of Christ." (Romans 10:17).

Health: "My son, give attention to my words; incline your ear to my sayings. Do not let them depart from your sight; keep them in the midst of your heart. For they are life to those who find them and health to all their body." (Proverbs 4:20-22).

New Birth: "for you have been born again not of seed which is perishable but imperishable, that is, through the living and enduring word of God." (1 Peter 1:23).

Light: "The unfolding of Your words gives light; it gives understanding to the simple." (Psalm 119:130).

Cleansing: "You are already clean because of the word which I have spoken to you." (John 15:3)

Victory Over Sin: "Your word I have treasured in my heart, that I may not sin against You." (Psalm 119:11).

Living Lord,
All that I have is from Your hand: life, health, forgiveness of sins, and the saving faith. Let me never take these precious gifts for granted. Praise be to You forever! In Jesus' Name, ***Amen.***

October 14

Do not be eager in your heart to be angry, for anger resides in the bosom of fools. (Ecclesiastes 7:9)

Anger causes lots of problems. When angry, people can say things they don't mean, or even worse, do things like trying to get revenge or hurt someone physically. Sometimes such hateful words and actions arise over the most ridiculous things. I heard on the news one time that one brother shot another over who was getting the last pork chop at dinner time. Just imagine—a family destroyed over a pork chop.

The Bible warns us against associating with someone

with a hot temper: "Do not associate with a man given to anger; or go with a hot-tempered man, or you will learn his ways and find a snare for yourself." (Proverbs 22:24-25). We are also warned against revenge: "Never take your own revenge, beloved, but leave room for the wrath of God, for it is written, 'Veangeance is mine, I will repay,' says the Lord." (Romans 12:19). On the contrary, "If your enemy is hungry, give him food to eat; and if he is thirsty, give him water to drink; for you will heap burning coals on his head, and the LORD will reward you." (Proverbs 25:21). We all get angry from time to time, but think twice before acting on it. Keep your temper.

Gentle Lord,
When frustration and anger rise in my heart, forgive me. Help me to rise above petty problems and be strong in You. Teach me to bring my cares to Your feet and know the contentment that comes from You alone. In Jesus' Name,
Amen.

October 15

Your tongue devises destruction, like a sharp razor, O worker of deceit. (Psalm 52:2)

Gossip destroys the best of friends. It hurts feelings and betrays trust. We must be so careful to avoid gossip. Sometimes we rationalize what we're doing with excuses: "I'm only passing this on so you can keep so-and-so in your prayers..." Don't deceive yourself; if it were you being talked about, you would feel hurt and betrayed. Even if you're not the person who starts a rumor, you become responsible if you pass it on to others.

Before you open your mouth, think over how you'd feel about one of your friends saying about you what you're about to say. If you're the one hearing the gossip, let it stop with you.

Faithful Father,

Help me to know how to be a true friend. Let me be trustworthy, honest, compassionate, and responsible. Let me treasure and respect the confidences of others, and never betray anyone with careless or cruel gossip. In Jesus' Name,
Amen.

October 16

Now as to the love of the brethren, you have no need for anyone to write to you, for you yourselves are taught by God to love one another... (1 Thessalonians 4:9)

We've all heard this hundreds of times in one form or another: "Love your neighbor as yourself." But in all honesty, how many of us actually do it? Especially in school, where there are cliques who don't always behave toward one another with love. It's easy to love others, if they wear the right kind of clothes, or have a cool car, or maybe if they're cheerleaders, or in the band, or on the football team.

But what about those who don't fit into any of those categories? What about the person everyone else makes fun of because they wear old, out-of-style clothes, or don't belong to the "right" clubs, or are overweight? Do we still reach out to them and show God's unconditional love?

Christian love is for everyone—"Be devoted to one another in brotherly love; give preference to one another in honor" (Romans 12:10).

Dear Lord God,

You loved the unpopular people and the outcasts, even inviting them to eat with You. Please give me the courage to do the same, and to show Your love toward the "outsiders" in my life. Thank You for being my example of unconditional love. In Jesus' Name,
Amen.

October 17

But the day of the Lord will come like a thief, in which the heavens will pass away with a roar and the elements will be destroyed with intense heat, and the earth and its works will be burned up. (2 Peter 3:10)

Isn't it hard to imagine that one of these days Jesus is going to return "like a thief"? Even we who believe it can get so caught up in everyday things that we sometimes forget it really is going to happen. It certainly is difficult to picture, and more than a little scary. Knowing that the day is coming, we should put our efforts and confidence in what is lasting and eternal, and not be bound to earthly pursuits and things of this world that will not matter in the life to come.

We need to realize that time on this earth is short and we have a lot of work to do, so don't get caught up in collecting earthly things; we cannot take them with us when we go. Instead, use your time and energy loving and serving God, and spreading His Good News to others.

Almighty God,
Grant me the grace always to seek forgiveness for my sins. Fill my heart with faith, hope, and charity. Let me walk with You in righteousness and dwell in Your favor. And when it is time, let me die in Your peace and rise triumphantly with You to life everlasting. In Jesus' Name,
Amen.

October 18

For where jealousy and selfish ambition exist, there is disorder and every evil thing. But the wisdom from above is first pure, then peaceable, gentle, reasonable, full of mercy and good fruits, unwavering, without hypocrisy. (James 3:16-17)

If you're looking for wisdom, in need of answers, keep

this in mind when someone offers you counsel: wisdom from God never contradicts His Word. You will have peace about it, and it will be impartial and sincere. If someone is offering you advice that doesn't fit with God's Word, or it isn't pure or honest, then reject it.

All-Knowing Father,

I depend on You to lead me in Your way. Let my heart and mind be obedient to Your commands; help me to recognize what is from You, and reject what is not. Thank You for Your loving guidance. In Jesus' Name,
Amen.

October 19

Then David said to his son Solomon, "Be strong and courageous, and act; do not fear nor be dismayed, for the LORD God, my God, is with you. He will not fail you nor forsake you until all the work for the service of the house of the LORD is finished." (1 Chronicles 28:20)

This verse reminds us that God is with us, and that we don't have to be afraid or discouraged. Don't sit up all night, stressed out about relationships with your parents or friends; don't lie awake worrying about what's going to happen next year. Through King David's words to his son, God promises us that He will not fail us or forsake us. We can trust Him to meet the needs in our lives.

Whatever you are facing today that has you upset, give it to Him. Take time right now and pray. Tell God what you're going through, and ask Him to step in and help you. You can trust Him to walk through the tough times with you. The great thing about God is that He has a perfect track record. Are you willing to trust Him today?

Dear Father in Heaven,

Help me to go to You first when I am lonely or scared or

discouraged, for I know You are with me always and everywhere. You have graciously given me forgiveness of my sins and the promise of eternal life. Let me take courage from the hope that I may be strengthened for Your service. In Jesus' Name,

Amen.

October 20

Finally, brethren, whatever is true, whatever is honorable, whatever is right, whatever is pure, whatever is lovely, whatever is of good repute, if there is any excellence and if anything worthy of praise, dwell on these things. (Philippians 4:8)

What we feed into our minds comes out in our actions and speech. If you are being troubled by disturbing or un-Christian thoughts, or if you catch yourself speaking or acting in a way that makes you feel ashamed or uneasy, do a survey of what you have been reading or putting into your mind through television, video games, or movies. Replace anything that is not of God with wholesome things, and ask Him to help you keep your mind on the things that are true, noble, right, pure, lovely, admirable, excellent, and praiseworthy. It might be difficult at first, but you can do all things through Christ who strengthens you.

Lord,

Create in me a pure heart, and renew a right spirit within me. Let me reject pastimes that are not worthy of a child of God, things that would make me think or speak or act in a way that is inappropriate and a bad example. Instead, fill my mind and heart with whatever is true, admirable, and praiseworthy. In Jesus' Name,

Amen.

October 21

Therefore, if food causes my brother to stumble, I will never eat meat again, so that I will not cause my brother to stumble. (1 Corinthians 8:13)

Stumble—what does this mean? To struggle, make a mistake, or fall down, right? In this case it doesn't mean physically stumbling, but struggling, making mistakes, or falling down in our walk with Jesus—and we are warned very clearly against causing someone else to stumble.

In order to avoid this, here are a few questions to ask yourself that might help you in making decisions about what you say and do:

> Does it bring glory to God?
>
> Will it help you witness for Jesus?
>
> Does it go against scripture and cause you to sin?
>
> Will it be beneficial to others, or will it hurt someone else?
>
> Are you acting out of love or selfishness?
>
> Might it cause someone else to sin?

If we ask ourselves these questions beforehand, it will help us to think things through before we act.

Dear God,

Please help me to guard against causing anyone else to sin through my own thoughts, words, or actions. Please keep me from stumbling myself, and thank You for picking me up when I do. In Jesus' Name,
Amen.

October 22

Why do you spend money for what is not bread, and your wages for what does not satisfy? Listen carefully to me, and eat what is good, and delight yourself in abundance. (Isaiah 55:2)

It is easy to get caught up in the worldly way of thinking that we need to buy all the latest "stuff." That stuff on its own is not necessarily bad, unless we try to get our self-worth and satisfaction from it. We need to keep in mind that what really will make us happy in life is God. People fall into thinking that if we can just buy that car, go on that trip, or buy the right clothes, then we will be fulfilled. I don't know about you, but I know people who have all of that, and are still miserable. I even know Christians who have let their walk with God go sour, putting all their energy into trying to get their happiness from stuff.

If you are finding yourself unfulfilled, maybe it is time to do an inventory of your walk with Christ. Only He can truly satisfy you.

Dear Creator of All,

Help me to remember the difference between my needs and my wants, and not get caught up in selfish desires. Thank You for providing for me all that I really need, especially faith in You and the hope of eternal life. In Jesus' Name,
Amen.

October 23

"Lord, teach us to pray..." (Luke 11:1)

Most of us know Jesus' response to his disciples' plea, which was to teach them what we now know as the Lord's Prayer. Notice in that prayer how first He gives praise to God, and then makes His requests—He doesn't just jump in there and start telling God what He needs done for Him.

Do we praise God first, before starting our list of what we need and desire? Or do we go to God in prayer and then jump up when we're finished asking for things, without praising Him or taking the time to listen to Him? Sometimes we think God has not heard or answered our prayer, but maybe it's because we're just running in, giving Him a list of instructions, and never just being quiet and listening for Him. Or do we just rattle off a prayer and consider our duty done for the day?

Try listening when you pray: listen to yourself, think about it, and mean it—and then listen for Him.

Dear Lord God,
Hear us as we pray the prayer our Savior taught us:
Our Father, who art in heaven,
Hallowed be thy name,
Thy kingdom come,
Thy will be done on earth as it is in Heaven.
Give us this day our daily bread
And forgive us our trespasses as we forgive those who trespass against us;
And lead us not into temptation, but deliver us from evil.
For thine is the kingdom, and the power, and the glory,
Forever and ever.
Amen.

October 24

Through insolence comes nothing but strife... (Proverbs 13:10)

Being willing to say "I'm sorry" takes humility, and it is very hard to do sometimes. When there's an argument, if one person would just stop, think about the situation, and say "I'm sorry," that would almost always pretty much be the end of it. After all, what can the person say when the other one stops and sincerely apologizes? Are they still going to scream and yell? It's pretty hard to argue when there's only one person doing the arguing.

Pride is big during an argument; no one wants to be the one to back down. Pride brings about conflict, but remember, humility brings healing. Be the one who steps away and starts that healing.

Righteous God,

Let petty quarrels stop with me; let reconciliation start with me. Grant me the humility not to insist on proving that I'm "right." Instead, let me be even-tempered enough to walk away from an argument, and give me the courage to apologize when I am wrong. In Jesus' Name,
Amen.

October 25

All discipline for the moment seems not to be joyful, but sorrowful; yet to those who have been trained by it, afterwards it yields the peaceful fruit of righteousness. (Hebrews 12:11)

Have you ever overheard a parent say to his or her child, "If you do that again you are in trouble!" But when the child does it again—and again, and again—the parent still puts off doing anything about it. Most likely their failure to act is because they just want to give the child every opportunity to change his or her behavior. Also, disciplining a child can be more painful for the parent than for the child (it's true!).

God doesn't enjoy disciplining us. He gives us opportunity after opportunity to change our behavior. But discipline is for our own good, so that we learn when we do something that displeases God, and afterwards we will be stronger and more mature. God's discipline is different than what we receive from our parents. Obviously, He doesn't ground us or give us a lecture; sometimes it may be hard even to recognize what happens as His discipline. In any case, it's never punishment; it's a lesson, an opportunity to change our behavior, and it's what's best for us, even if we don't understand it at the time. "My son, do not reject the discipline of the LORD or loathe His reproof, for whom the LORD loves He reproves, even as a father corrects the son in whom he delights." (Proverbs 3:11-12).

Dear Heavenly Father,

Thank You for Your loving care, even for Your discipline when I need it. Please help me not to resent it, but to learn from it and use it as an opportunity to learn to serve You better. In Jesus' Name,
Amen.

October 26

Be on the alert, stand firm in the faith, act like men, be strong.
(1 Corinthians 16:13)

It can be easy to get sidetracked in our relationship with God because of outside pressure. We need to make sure that we are strong enough in our faith that we are not easily swayed by others to go in a different direction. Heed the warning of Matthew 7:15: "Beware of the false prophets, who come to you in sheep's clothing, but inwardly are ravenous wolves." This is just another reason why we must know the Word of God; so we can hold tight to what it says and not be led astray.

Heavenly Father,

I am sometimes confused by all the conflicting messages that I hear. Help me to discern what is true from what is false, what is right from what is wrong, through the study of Your word and the good advice of other Christians. Give me strength, faith, and courage to do Your will. In Jesus' Name,
Amen.

October 27

*The eternal God is a dwelling place, and underneath are the
everlasting arms... (Deuteronomy 33:27)*

Everybody is looking to "belong." When we feel we belong,
we feel secure, and we can share feelings and form relationships with others without fearing rejection.

The most awesome feeling of belonging comes from
becoming children of God. When you belong to God, there
is an instant, deep, and lasting connection with other
Christians. Belonging to God can set you apart in the eyes of
the world: "So all the peoples of the earth will see that you
are called by the name of the LORD, and they will be afraid
of you." (Deuteronomy 28:10).

If you're looking for a sense of belonging and security,
then look to God—that's the best feeling of security you can
ever get.

God, My Hiding Place,
I give you thanks for the joy and refuge of Christian
community, and the bonds of Your love that connect us.
Thank You for setting me apart as Your own, and giving me a
place where I truly belong. In Jesus' Name,
Amen.

October 28

*...and also the sons of Israel wept again and said, "Who will
give us meat to eat? "We remember the fish which we used to
eat free in Egypt, the cucumbers and the melons and the leeks
and the onions and the garlic, but now our appetite is gone.
There is nothing at all to look at except this manna." (Numbers
11:4-6)*

Have you ever known someone who did nothing but

complain? Take the Israelites: God had delivered them from bondage in Egypt, and when they were starving, He miraculously gave them manna to eat, which came down from heaven each night as they slept. But instead of being grateful that they were no longer starving to death, they got tired of manna and demanded something tastier!

We usually complain when we don't get what we want. If we would just stop and think on the things we do have instead of what we don't, our outlook would be different. The Bible compares complaining as to a dripping faucet—in other words, it gets old.

God of all Goodness,

You have given me much to be thankful for. Give me also a grateful heart; help me to focus on what I have instead of what I have not, and to distinguish what I need from what I want. I praise You, O God, not just for what You give me, but because You are worthy of praise. In Jesus' Name,
Amen.

October 29

You shall not take the name of the LORD your God in vain, for the LORD will not leave him unpunished who takes His name in vain. (Exodus 20:7)

Recognize this? It's the Second Commandment. Martin Luther explains this commandment in this way: "We are to fear and love God, so that we do not curse, swear, practice magic, lie, or deceive using God's name, but instead use that very name to call on, pray to, praise, and give thanks to God" (Martin Luther, *Luther's Small Catechism*).

Profanity and blasphemy should never be part of a Christian's vocabulary. Remember that what comes out of your mouth is a reflection of what's in your mind and heart.

Dear Lord God,

Let me never fall into the habit of using Your name in vain. Even though I hear Your name being invoked all around me, to express all manner of emotions, I know it should be used only in prayer and praise. Make my heart full of Your love, so that what comes out of my mouth may never offend. In Jesus' Name,

Amen.

October 30

Come and see the works of God, who is awesome in His deeds toward the sons of men. (Psalm 66:5)

Are you having difficulty being strong in your faith? I come from Florida where we have hurricanes. After having so many devastating storms come through and destroy homes, a building material was finally developed which was strong enough to withstand hurricane force winds.

That's the way our faith should be. The stronger we are in the Lord, the more we should be able to withstand the pressures of the world. One way to strengthen your faith is by reading God's Word. Another is to be open to His will. Another is through encouragement from other believers.

Build the strong foundation of your faith on these things, and watch to see the awesome works God does for us!

Lord God, My Strength,

Give my faith a strong foundation, so that it's not blown to pieces by every storm. Help me know where to turn for strength, and let me be ever grateful for Your works on my behalf. In Jesus' Name,

Amen.

October 31

There shall not be found among you anyone who makes his son or his daughter pass through the fire, one who uses divination, one who practices witchcraft, or one who interprets omens, or a sorcerer, or one who casts a spell, or a medium, or a spiritist, or one who calls up the dead. For whoever does these things is detestable to the LORD... (Deuteronomy 18:10-12)

Have you or someone you know ever had your fortune told "just for the fun of it?" Or used a Ouija board with a group of friends, or tried to have a seance, just to see if there was anything to it? Do you know, I even used to believe God spoke to me through my horoscope! I laugh about it now, but looking to these things for guidance isn't only silly, it's risky. So many Christians don't realize how this seemingly harmless, spooky fun can open up their lives for the devil to come in. Even attempting to contact spirits is asking for trouble.

This proves once again how important it is to know what God's Word says. Here He's clearly warning us away from any kind of spells, sorcery, or spiritism. So if you have been naive and gullible in allowing yourself to become involved in these things, or if you knew exactly what you were doing, repent and look only to God and His Word for answers.

Gracious Lord,

There are so many things to watch out for in life—many of them I don't even know can harm me. But You have chosen me in Your gracious love. Place Your angels above and beside me to protect me, and teach me from Your Word how I shall walk through life. In Jesus' Name,
Amen.

November 1

Remind them to be subject to rulers, to authorities, to be obedient, to be ready for every good deed... (Titus 3:1)

With election time coming up, it's very important that everyone old enough to vote gets out to the polls to let our leaders know how we feel about the issues. So many believe that one vote doesn't count, but it can and does make a difference! We also have to look further than television advertisements to find out who believes or stands for what. We need to be informed, and pray for guidance and wisdom in making our voting decisions.

It's equally important to pray for our leaders, no matter who they are, whether we agree with them or not. 1 Timothy 2:1 urges us that "prayers, petitions and thanksgivings, be made on behalf of all men, for kings and all who are in authority..." So keep yourself informed and active in the political process, and keep our leaders in your prayers.

Ruler of All,
I ask that You take into Your care our country's leaders. Fill them with knowledge and wisdom, and let them honor the responsibility of the service they have undertaken. Let me be a good citizen, giving my elected leaders the respect that is proper and supporting them with my prayers. Bless our government, our people, and our country. In Jesus' Name,
Amen.

November 2

But encourage one another day after day, as long as it is still called "Today," so that none of you will be hardened by the deceitfulness of sin. (Hebrews 3:13)

People often don't think of sin as really being sin. Instead, acts that we know are sinful and wrong are explained away as being the result of different "values," someone's unhappy childhood, or a host of other rationalizations.

Even if it seems everyone else is accepting sin like it's no big deal, we need to guard our hearts and never allow ourselves to get comfortable with it. Sin still exists; sin is still sin, and we need to make sure we're not hardened to it.

Merciful Father,

I know we live in a sinful world, and that I am a sinful being, made clean only through the blood of Your Son Jesus Christ. Let me never become complacent about sin, for if I stop believing that it exists, I have surely fallen into sin myself. Help me to avoid whatever separates me from You. In Jesus' Name,
Amen.

November 3

Keep watching and praying that you may not enter into temptation; the spirit is willing, but the flesh is weak. (Matthew 26:41)

This scripture tells us to "watch and pray"—in other words, be on guard—so that we will not be caught unaware by temptation.

Satan does his best by making something that is evil look "good" to us, even using people we think are our friends to entice us into sin. He knows our weak areas and is always trying to catch us off guard so that we will slip. He is just waiting for us to fall so he can use it to make us feel guilty and ashamed. Isn't it strange that the one who is tempting us is also the one standing ready to accuse us?

Whatever you're having trouble with, make sure you take it to God daily. He will give us the strength to resist.

Dear Lord,

Help me to recognize temptation for what it is, even when

it's disguised as something pleasurable or good. Give me the strength to turn away from it; when I fail, forgive me for the sake of Your Son. In Jesus' Name,
Amen.

November 4

For if you forgive men when they sin against you, your heavenly Father will also forgive you. But if you do not forgive men their sins, your Father will not forgive your sins. (Matthew 6:14)

It can be hard to forgive someone when you have been wronged. But forgiving the person who wronged you will keep you out of bondage. If you don't forgive them, then bitterness can take root, and your heart can become cold and hard. Worse, you yourself may not receive forgiveness.

We are commanded to forgive. It's not a matter of choice. This might seem difficult, especially if you've been hurt deeply, but God would not tell us to do something that we couldn't do. Ask Him to help you; tell Him that with His help, you can and will be obedient. You must choose to forgive even if you don't feel like it. Remember, we don't go by our feelings, because they can lead us astray. Instead, we need to be obedient to the Word of God. Making the choice to forgive is the first step to your own freedom.

O Lord God,

I do not find it easy to forgive. I have been wronged; those wrongs hurt me and make me angry. But Lord, You have forgiven me more times than I can count, for sins I have confessed to You and sins I don't even know I've committed. Because of Your compassion, make me willing and able to show forgiveness to others. In Jesus' Name,
Amen.

November 5

For the word of God is living and active and sharper than any two-edged sword, and piercing as far as the division of soul and spirit, of both joints and marrow, and able to judge the thoughts and intentions of the heart. (Hebrews 4:12)

Satan's goal is to get us bound and keep us bound. As we are children of God, he has no right to us, but Satan is a thief, so he doesn't care. We must enforce our rights as children of God and use the weapons God has supplied us, instead of trying to fight Satan with our own strength. Back in June, we looked at the following, which we can rely on in standing up against Satan:

The helmet of salvation (this protects our minds with the knowledge that we are children of God).

The breastplate of righteousness (this protects our heart and our emotions are so we don't have to doubt our self-worth).

The sword of the spirit (this is the Word of God).

The belt of truth (if you know God's Word, then it's difficult for Satan to trick you into believing his lies).

Feet filled with readiness to share God's Good News, anytime, anyplace!

Use these powerful weapons to fight sin and the devil.

God of All,

I can't rely on my own strength in my struggle against my own sinfulness. Let me rely on Your wisdom and power, that I may be safe from the power of the devil. In Jesus' Name,
Amen.

November 6

Teach me to do Your will, for You are my God; let Your good Spirit lead me on level ground. (Psalms 143:10)

Often we make a decision and choose a course of action, and then we ask God's blessing for it. What we should be doing is seeking God first, and finding out what He wants us to do. If we would do what this scripture tells us, we would really save ourselves a lot of time and trouble. We should be willing to do what He has chosen for us, instead of demanding that He bless whatever it is we have chosen for ourselves.

His ways are higher than our ways, and He knows best, even if it doesn't make sense to us at the time. "Trust in the LORD with all your heart and do not lean on your own understanding." (Proverbs 3:5) It's all about God's ways, and not our own.

Almighty and All-Wise God,
Your will is often beyond my understanding, but let me not use that as an excuse to doubt. Help me to remember that You will provide for me, Your beloved child, all that I truly need. With that knowledge, let me joyfully do Your will. In Jesus' Name,
Amen.

November 7

but God has chosen the foolish things of the world to shame the wise, and God has chosen the weak things of the world to shame the things which are strong... (1 Corinthians 1:27)

When God calls you to do something, don't allow feelings of inadequacy or unworthiness to stop you. God is looking for people who are willing to be used by Him, and you don't have to have a bunch of great "qualifications" to be chosen for His service. You can be sure that if God calls you to do something for Him, He will supply you all the necessary qualifications, and He will work things out.

It is precisely our unworthiness and lack of qualifications that makes our ability to do God's work so miraculous. For this we must give Him glory and praise. Remember, wherever He asks you to go, He will go with you and prepare the way.

Gracious God,

I confess that I have allowed discouragement and fear to hinder me in my work for Your kingdom. Lord, on my own, I'm not "qualified" to be in Your service, but I know that the blood of Your Son has made me worthy in Your sight. Give me the strength and courage to do Your will on earth. In Jesus' Name,
Amen.

November 8

Above all, keep fervent in your love for one another, because love covers a multitude of sins. Be hospitable to one another without complaint. As each one has received a special gift, employ it in serving one another as good stewards of the manifold grace of God. (1 Peter 4:8-10)

For most people, this time of year with the holidays approaching is a joyful time. It is full of love and anticipation of time spent with friends and family. For others, however, it can be a very difficult time, a reminder of broken relationships, hurts, conflicts, and angry words. Sometimes, these deep problems were caused by only trivial things. As Christians, we need to try extra hard to forgive and get past the problems, to try to make them right, because we have the love of God in our hearts. And if you love deeply, as we are told to do in this verse, you will be loved in return, and your own sins will be forgiven.

This holiday season, be a faithful administrator of God's grace. Love your neighbor, forgive old hurts, and use the gifts God gave you in His service, to His glory.

Father,

Forgive me for the hurts I have caused and the grudges I have held. Purify my soul with Your Holy Spirit, and come into my heart with Your pardoning grace. Bind together the hearts of my family and friends; help us to love one another and serve You in harmony. In Jesus' Name,
Amen.

November 9

Through indolence the rafters sag, and through slackness the house leaks. (Ecclesiastes 10:18)

There are a lot of things in life that we're never lazy about, like making sure we get enough to eat or drink, or spending time with friends. But how much do we tend to our spiritual "house"?

As this scripture suggests, it could start out small, like missing a devotion, but it can build to bigger things, like never going to church or praying, and soon the whole house of our faith is sagging and leaking. We would never intentionally say, "I'm going to stop praying and reading my Bible," but that's how it can end up if we aren't careful.

Don't be lazy with your faith. Take care of little leaks and problems from the beginning, and they won't turn into bigger problems later.

Heavenly Father,

Thank You for the gift of faith in You. Make me diligent in attending to that faith; let nothing be more important to me than a right relationship with You, attained through prayer, devotion, worship, and fellowship with brothers and sisters in Christ. In Jesus' Name,
Amen.

November 10

Are not two sparrows sold for a cent? And yet not one of them will fall to the ground apart from your Father. But the very hairs of your head are all numbered. So do not fear; you are more valuable than many sparrows. (Matthew 10:29-31)

A big problem for youth is uncertainty about their importance and self-worth. This can create difficulties in many areas of life, including the church. If we feel unimportant, we're not going to be as effective in reaching out to others with God's Word.

You are important to God, and God has wonderful plans for your life. If you are unsure of that, just read Jeremiah 29:11: "'For I know the plans that I have for you,' declares the LORD, 'plans for welfare and not for calamity to give you a future and a hope.'"

God, My Creator,

You know who I am, You know every action, thought, and feeling, and still You love me and want me as Your own. Help me never to doubt Your love; give me the self-confidence and assurance that is mine as a Child of God. Thank You for Your love, which is beyond my comprehension. In Jesus' Name,

Amen.

November 11

for you were formerly darkness, but now you are Light in the Lord; walk as children of Light (for the fruit of the Light consists in all goodness and righteousness and truth), trying to learn what is pleasing to the Lord. (Ephesians 5:8-10)

When you're not in church, can people tell you're a Christian? Do you live as a child of light, in goodness, righteousness and truth, as this scripture says? Or do you live with one foot in church and the other still in the world? Some people continue to live like they are in darkness even though they should live in God's example. God doesn't blaspheme, He's not selfish or rebellious, He treats His children with love—we should strive to do the same. Make every effort to let the light of Christ shine through you.

Dear Heavenly Father,
I walk in Your light; cleanse me of the desire to return to darkness and sin. Strengthen me in my faith, that Your light may shine through me and lead others to new life in You. In Jesus' Name,
Amen.

November 12

how much more will the blood of Christ, who through the eternal Spirit offered Himself without blemish to God, cleanse your conscience from dead works to serve the living God? (Hebrews 9:14)

A lot of people carry around guilt for things that they have done. Sometimes we allow this to happen because we feel we "deserve" it. But God doesn't want us to keep feeling guilty over things of the past, sins for which we have repented and been forgiven. As Paul says in Romans 8:1-2, "Therefore there is now no condemnation for those who are in Christ Jesus. For the law of the Spirit of life in Christ Jesus has set you free from the law of sin and of death."

Remind yourself of this; read it aloud if you have to when you feel burdened by your past sins, so that you can be free and better serve God.

Merciful God,
I give You thanks for the freedom from fear and death which is mine though the blood of Christ, shed for an unworthy world for the forgiveness of our sins. Let me not be

burdened by past sins for which I have repented. Alleluia, I am free! In Jesus' Name,
Amen.

November 13

How blessed are those who observe His testimonies, who seek Him with all their heart. (Psalm 119:2)

Some people think that happiness is having a lot of money, or being popular, or being successful on the job. But true happiness comes from God's Word, because He has our best interests in mind.

For example, God commands us not to have sex outside the bonds of holy matrimony. This is not only because it's against His commandments, but also because it can be destructive to us physically and emotionally. As another example, God knows that people fall into sin and despair when the desire for money goes rampant, so he tells us we cannot serve both God and money.

If you are looking for prosperity, contentment, peace, and blessings, then obey God's Word. Keeping His statutes, though it may be difficult at times, is ultimately to our great benefit, and it will bring us true happiness.

Holy God,

Help me to value the joy and peace of a life in Christ above the fleeting pleasures afforded by money, things, and "popularity." Thank You for the rules You set down for my benefit. In Jesus' Name,
Amen.

November 14

One who is gracious to a poor man lends to the Lord, and He will repay him for his good deed. (Proverbs 19:17)

Every year at about this time, I start to see the Salvation Army people standing patiently outside malls and department stores with their red buckets, collecting money for the poor, the hungry, and the homeless. It's easy to start seeing them as part of the holiday scene, and walk right by them without really noticing.

This year, make a conscious effort to help someone less fortunate than yourself. If you don't have money, give your time. Serve a meal at a homeless shelter, spend an afternoon helping out at your local food bank, bake and deliver cookies to homebound members of your church or community, go Christmas caroling at a convalescent home. Do these good works in the name of Him who has given us so much.

God of Mercy,

You have given me so much. I pray that You awaken me to the needs of those around me. Let me cheerfully give my time and money to help Your children who are less fortunate than I, and so celebrate this holiday season by bringing joy to others. In Jesus' Name,
Amen.

November 15

So do not worry about tomorrow; for tomorrow will care for itself. Each day has enough trouble of its own. (Matthew 6:34)

Worrying robs us of our joy, making us victims of fear and anxiety. Here we are told to take it one day at a time. Often we worry about things that haven't even happened yet, problems that are way down the road.

Did you know that worrying can also be prideful? If you're

worrying about something, it's like saying you have to handle the problem yourself, that God can't deal with it.

God wants us to take to Him every grief and concern we have, no matter how big or small. He has the answers.

Dear Heavenly Father,
I trust in You and Your providing for my daily well-being and my future hope. Don't let me get caught up in a web of anxieties that keep me from seeing Your loving, enfolding arms. In Jesus' Name,
Amen.

November 16

How blessed is he whose help is the God of Jacob, whose hope is in the LORD his God, Who made heaven and earth, the sea and all that is in them; Who keeps faith forever... (Psalm 146:5-6)

This verse can be a comfort for those times when we feel overwhelmed and alone. We have on our side the ever faithful Lord our God, who made the heavens, the earth, the sea, and everything in them (that includes us!) He is all-powerful, so He certainly has the answer to any problems that we go through. After all, He "is able to do far more abundantly beyond all that we ask or think, according to the power that works within us" (Ephesians 3:20), and "this hope we have as an anchor of the soul, a hope both sure and steadfast" (Hebrews 6:19).

If you're feeling down, go to the Rock of our salvation; there is no problem that has caught Him unaware. He is faithful and He will see you through.

Faithful God,
I give you thanks for Your creation; Your works are truly marvelous to behold. Lord, I believe that You, Who created the heavens, the earth, and me, can also create in me a

clean heart and give me new life. How can I fail to praise You? In Jesus' Name,
Amen.

November 17

And whoever in the name of a disciple gives to one of these little ones even a cup of cold water to drink, truly I say to you, he shall not lose his reward. (Matthew 10:42)

Sometimes we can share the Good News of Jesus with others through our deeds as well as our words. Helping out with such basic needs as food and shelter can really show Christ's love in action.

The youth group from my church recently went to Mexico to help build homes for the poor, and while they were there, they told the people they were helping all about Jesus Christ. Those people were much more receptive to hearing the youth group share their faith because they were being helped with a practical need in their life.

We need to do the same. If we wish people well but actually do nothing for them, how do we project our faith to them? The more good we do for others, the more God's light shines through us for them to see.

Compassionate God,
Please help me to be generous with the gifts You have bestowed on me, so that I may show Your love and help my brothers and sisters in need. In Jesus' Name,
Amen.

November 18

And if anyone's name was not found written in the book of life, he was thrown into the lake of fire. (Revelation 20:15)

Have you ever talked to a non-believer who thinks that

hell is where all the fun people go? I've been horrified to hear people say casually that they're going to "party" with the devil. It's really sad—and scary—to see how Satan has blinded people into thinking that hell is some kind of big, fun place. Mark 9:43 describes hell as a place of "unquenchable fire". In Luke 16:23, a man in hell is a man "in torment," and Matthew 13:42 describes a place where "there will be weeping and gnashing of teeth."

The wonderful news is that no one has to go to hell. Anyone can have eternal life. If you're not sure where you're spending eternity, make sure right now by praying this prayer:

Dear Lord,
Please forgive me of my sins; come into my heart and cleanse me and make me a brand new creation. I believe You died on the cross for me and that on the third day You rose again, and that You will return one day as Your Word declares. Be my Lord, Savior, and King. Thank you for redeeming me. In Jesus' Name,
Amen.

November 19

but just as it is written, "things which eye has not seen and ear has not heard, and which have not entered the heart of man, all that God has prepared for those who love him." (1 Corinthians 2:9)

Have you ever wondered what heaven will be like? Here are a few things the Bible says about it:

Revelation 21:4: He will wipe away every tear from their eyes; and there will no longer be any death; there will no longer be any mourning, or crying, or pain; the first things have passed away.

Revelation 22:5: And there will no longer be any night; and they will not have need of the light of a lamp nor the light of the sun, because the Lord God will illumine them; and they will reign forever and ever.

Revelation 21:18-19: The material of the wall was jasper; and the city was pure gold, like clear glass. The foundation stones of the city wall were adorned with every kind of precious stone.

1 Corinthians 15:44: [In heaven, we will be] raised a spiritual body.

All this can be ours through Christ: "I am the way, and the truth, and the life; no one comes to the Father but through me." (John 14:6).

Lord God of Hosts,
Heaven is hard to imagine from where I am, but I know it's real, and I know I will see You there one day. Let me be encouraged and my faith strengthened by this blessed hope. In Jesus' Name,
Amen.

November 20

Your adversary, the devil, prowls around like a roaring lion, seeking someone to devour. (1 Peter 5:8)

The devil is like a burglar who goes around looking for homes that aren't secure, checking to see if there's a window open or a door unlocked through which he can slip in. We are these homes. Satan can find a way to slip into our lives if we don't spend time with God through worship, Bible reading, and prayers. Failure to do these things can make us easy targets for Satan's lies and tricks. Being diligent makes us strong enough to see through them.

Satan even tried to tempt Jesus, but Jesus used the Word of God to defeat him. In Matthew 4:5-7, when Jesus was fasting in the desert, the devil took Him up to the top of a mountain and challenged Him to throw Himself off to prove that He really was the Son of God. But Jesus knew better: "On the other hand, it is written, 'You shall not put the Lord your God to the test.'" Notice that Satan even tried using the Word of God to tempt Jesus, but Jesus didn't fall for it.

Knowing God's Word will help us defeat Satan when he comes prowling around looking for victims.

Holy Father,

I have no fear of the devil as long as You are with me, for You are stronger than the Evil One. Help me not to become careless and open myself up to danger, but let me seek You daily through prayer and devotion. Thank You for Your love and protection. In Jesus' Name,
Amen.

November 21

For in Him all the fullness of Deity dwells in bodily form, and in Him you have been made complete, and He is the head over all rule and authority... (Colossians 2:9-10)

Read this verse several times so it will sink in. We have been given fullness in Christ. We don't need a boyfriend, girlfriend, popularity, a sports car, or anything else to make us complete. It is already done through Calvary. We need to remind ourselves of that daily, because it's all too easy to forget this glorious promise and fall into feeling insecure about ourselves. Remind yourself that Christ is in charge, the head over every power and authority. Colossians 2:8 warns, "See to it that no one takes you captive through philosophy and empty deception, according to the tradition of men, according to the elementary principles of the world, rather than according to Christ."

Lord God,

Let me not vainly seek fulfillment in worldly things or people. Instead, let me be thankful for all that You have given me: my life, and the hope of eternal life in the world to come. I rejoice daily in the fullness I have in You. In Jesus' Name,

Amen.

November 22

It is by his deeds that a lad distinguishes himself if his conduct is pure and right. (Proverbs 20:11)

I don't know about you, but one thing that really annoys me is when someone tells me they're going to do something (it can be as simple as returning a phone call) and then they don't. This applies both to friends and people in the business world, to Christians and non-Christians alike. It's frustrating to have to wonder whether you can depend on someone.

It shouldn't be that way with Christians. Our word needs to be something people can count on. Being people of integrity earns us a good reputation of honor and trustworthiness and makes us good witnesses. Be sure that the actions for which you're known are "pure and right."

Eternal God,

I don't have it in me to be "pure and right," but through Your Holy Spirit, I know I can be at least an imperfect example of Your perfect love. Help me to keep my promises, to be a trustworthy son, daughter, and friend, so that I may serve others for Your sake and to Your glory. In Jesus' Name,

Amen.

November 23

A wise man will hear and increase in learning, and a man of understanding will acquire wise counsel, to understand a proverb and a figure, the words of the wise and their riddles. (Proverbs 1:5-6)

Most Christians would say they want a deeper understanding of God and His will for our lives. But how much time do they actually spend studying and reading? It's impossible to understand all God has for us by spending only five or ten minutes reading God's Word and praying. The way to truly get to know someone is by spending quality time with that person. Our relationship with the Lord is no different. When we spend time with God, we will get to know His voice when He speaks to us. This scripture says that we will receive guidance by listening to the parables and adding to our learning. That doesn't sound like something that can be accomplished by skimming through the Bible.

Take the time to learn God's Word; it will add to your wisdom and enrich your life.

Almighty God,

Thank You for giving me the Bible, that I may better know You and Your will for my life. Forgive that I have sometimes shown indifference toward Your Word, and forgive me for the times when I view Your Word as just another obligation. Let me never forget that the Bible is the story of Your saving love for me and all believers. Thank You for this precious gift. In Jesus' Name,

Amen.

November 24

He came as a witness, to testify about the Light, so that all might believe through him. (John 1:7)

Recently a young man told me of a friend of his who was killed in a car accident. He had just heard the news, and naturally was grieving about it, not only for the loss of his friend, but also because she had died without his ever once telling her about Jesus Christ.

How many of us know someone that we've been meaning to sit down and talk with about Jesus, but where we have kept putting it off for one reason or another? Stop allowing fear and intimidation to get the best of you. You never know how long anyone is going to be on this earth. Make the most of every opportunity. Remember, we're not responsible for what people do with the Good News, but it is our responsibility to share it with them and give them the opportunity for eternal life.

My Lord and Creator,
I have missed too many opportunities to speak about You to my friends. Help me to recognize these opportunities, and give me the words to share Your Good News. Thank You for Your promise of eternal life, which I have through the death and glorious resurrection of Your Son. In Jesus' Name,
Amen.

November 25

In everything, therefore, treat people the same way you want them to treat you, for this is the Law and the Prophets. (Matthew 7:12)

If only we would remember this scripture at all times! It can be easy to fall into destructive habits like gossip, selfishness, and thoughtlessness toward others. We must keep in mind that everyone was created in God's image and, as our brothers and sisters in Christ, deserve our honor. Treating others with disrespect and cruelty doesn't say much about our maturity in Christ.

Dear Heavenly Father,

"Do unto others…" is easy to say but hard to do. Through my selfishness, I too often place my own feelings and needs above those of others. Lord, give me compassion, and the desire to see others not as strangers who are unimportant to me, but as Your children, just as I am Your child. In Jesus' Name,

Amen.

November 26

He who conceals his transgressions will not prosper, but he who confesses and forsakes them will find compassion. (Proverbs 28:13)

It can be difficult to believe that God can still make things turn out right after we've made a very wrong choice in our life. But nothing takes God by surprise, and He certainly is more than capable of fixing our mistakes.

When we realize we've made a wrong decision, we must confess it, and ask God to forgive us for acting in accordance with our own will instead of seeking His. His will may not always be very clear or understandable to us, but if we trust in Him, He will turn every situation around according to what He knows is best for us.

Lord God,

Forgive me for failing to put my trust in You when I get nervous. Help me to remember that You are all-knowing, with love and wisdom beyond my comprehension. Let me desire Your will, not mine, to be done in my life. In Jesus' Name,

Amen.

November 27

The one who guards his mouth preserves his life; the one who opens wide his lips comes to ruin. (Proverbs 13:3)

How many times have you lost your patience with someone and said something that you later regretted? I'm sure most of us have done that from time to time. It's easy to let little things get the better of you when you're tired, or have had a bad day. But think about how patient God is with us. In my case, He waited 19 years for me to come to faith, and yet He never gave up on me. He patiently kept drawing me to Him through the Holy Spirit.

Remember, patience is not a personality trait. It is evidence that the Holy Spirit is working in our hearts and minds, helping us to handle rough situations with grace and self-control.

Eternal God,
I know all too well how it feels to be spoken to in anger or impatience. Guard me against speaking the unkind and offensive words that so easily spring to my lips. Grant me patience and self-control through Your Holy Spirit, that I may not injure anyone else through rash words. In Jesus' Name, **Amen.**

November 28

But love your enemies, and do good, and lend, expecting nothing in return; and your reward will be great, and you will be sons of the Most High; for He Himself is kind to ungrateful and evil men. (Luke 6:35)

Seem impossible? Remember, God wouldn't tell us to do something if we weren't able to do it through Him. It's very easy always to love and care for the people who love us and care for us, but actually to love and do good to the people we can't stand, the people who are rude to us and treat us

271

like dirt? Well, it takes the Holy Spirit to do that.

I can't think of a better way to let your light shine than to love your enemies and to do good to them! Pray for God to work through you, and give you the strength to be obedient to Him in this way.

Father in Heaven,

I'm not good enough or strong enough to love my enemies or forgive those who hurt me. The light that shines before others is not mine, but Yours. Please give me the will to forgive, as You have graciously forgiven my innumerable offenses against You and those around me. In Jesus' Name,
Amen.

November 29

The desire of the sluggard puts him to death, for his hands refuse to work; All day long he is craving, while the righteous gives and does not hold back. (Proverbs 21:25)

People who are secure in God are satisfied, but sluggards, people full of greed for things they won't work for, are never satisfied. Greed is the result of emptiness and insecurity, a desire for "things" to fill the void—but that emptiness can only be filled with God and His love.

It's wonderful to know that as Christians, we can be free to give and share with others without being overly concerned for our own needs. God pays great "interest" on giving: "Give, and it will be given to you. They will pour into your lap a good measure—pressed down, shaken together, and running over. For by your standard of measure it will be measured to you in return." (Luke 6:38).

Gracious God,

Forgive my complacency, my unwillingness sometimes to see the needs of others. Grant that I may be generous with my time and possessions, to give to others what You have

272

given me. In Jesus' Name,
Amen.

November 30

Therefore I urge you, brethren, by the mercies of God, to present your bodies a living and holy sacrifice, acceptable to God, which is your spiritual service of worship. (Romans 12:1)

Do we actually treat our bodies like living sacrifices? Too often, we hurt our bodies by abusing them with drugs, alcohol, smoking, overeating, undereating. The list goes on. But our bodies belong to God, and we owe it to Him to keep them clean and healthy. As it says in 1 Corinthians 3:16, "Do you not know that you are a temple of God and that the Spirit of God dwells in you?" Don't defile God's dwelling place—your body—with things that bring only fleeting pleasure. Keep yourself clean.

O Lord God,
My body seems a poor sacrifice, but it and everything I have belongs to You. Fill my soul with the desire to serve only You, and grant me the strength to resist and overcome temptation, so that Your dwelling-place will be pleasing to you and strengthened for Your service. In Jesus' Name,
Amen.

December 1

Now faith is the assurance of things hoped for, the conviction of things not seen. (Hebrews 11:1)

I'm sure many of you have felt at one time or another that God had something special He wanted you to do. Maybe it was a career choice, or a call to the mission field, or to start your own ministry. And maybe as yet you haven't seen any evidence of this happening, and you are beginning to doubt your call.

Don't lose faith. He is preparing you to do His work, so don't be discouraged. When you have faith (being sure of what you hope for but can't see), you can't look at your "natural" circumstances, because when you get your eyes off God and start focusing on your situation, discouragement and doubt can start to take root. Stand firm in your faith!

Faithful God,
Thank You for the blessing of faith in You. Let me not be distracted by what's going on around me, but keep me focused on You. Strengthen my poor faith that I may joyfully follow Your call wherever it leads me. In Jesus' Name,
Amen.

December 2

I can do all things through Him who strengthens me. (Philippians 4:13)

Most of us have heard this verse a million times. Unfortunately, it seems the verses we've heard the most are the ones we really think about the least. We take them for granted and don't pay as much attention to them as we should. I can quote you this verse in my sleep, but I too often fail really to think about what I am saying when I quote this great verse.

It's amazing that I can do all things through Christ—and so can you! I've felt God's call to do things in the past that I just knew that I was unable to do, but after accepting what He had told me to do, I soon found out that I could do what it was he had called me to do, because He gave me the strength.

You may be facing things in your life that you feel you just can't handle. If you will ask God for the strength—and rely on Him and not yourself—you will see many things accomplished that you never thought possible. There are no limits on what we can do if we rely on God as our strength.

God of Might,
I know all things are possible through You, but sometimes I feel overcome by troubles. Forgive my fears and my lack of faith. Grant me the courage and the faith to face my problems with confidence in Your power and lovingkindness. In Jesus' Name,
Amen.

December 3

For by grace you have been saved through faith; and that not of yourselves, it is the gift of God; not as a result of works, so that no one may boast. (Ephesians 2:8-9)

Isn't it wonderful to know that there is nothing we can do to earn our salvation? That may sound odd, but it's actually quite a relief: nothing we do could ever be enough to earn our salvation, so nothing we do is required.

I spoke with someone once who said he felt he didn't "qualify" to be a Christian. But do you know what? No one does! I told him he fit right in with everyone else. There are a lot of people who feel they need to "clean up their act" first before they become a Christian. But look at it this way: if you were to have someone come in and clean your house for you, would you clean it up before they got there? Don't put the Lord off so that you can clean up your heart before He comes in—it will never work anyway; we can only be clean through Him.

Salvation is a free gift—the only thing you have to do is believe in Him.

Gracious God,
I know that the works of my hands can never make me deserving of my salvation, bought with the blood of Your Son. Thank You for the precious gift of faith, and let my good

275

works be a reflection of that faith, through Your love, and to Your glory. In Jesus' Name,
Amen.

December 4

*"Come now, and let us reason together," says the L*ORD*, "though your sins are as scarlet, they will be as white as snow; though they are red like crimson, they will be like wool." (Isaiah 1:18)*

It's so awesome that through God's forgiveness, we are actually cleansed of our sins. But how many times do we find it difficult to forgive ourselves for things we have done or failed to do? Once you have asked God for forgiveness of your sins, then that's it—He has forgiven you, and you need to let it go and forgive yourself. If you don't, then you're saying that what Jesus did on the cross wasn't good enough.

"Therefore let it be known to you, brethren, that through Him forgiveness of sins is proclaimed to you, and through Him everyone who believes is freed from all things, from which you could not be freed through the Law of Moses." (Acts 13:38-39).

It is more than good enough. Accept Christ's forgiveness, and move on.

Merciful Father,
I know I can have forgiveness of my sins because of the sacrifice of Your Son. Help me not to sin against You by refusing to accept that forgiveness, but instead to turn to You with a heart that is both truly repentant and entirely confident in Your love and mercy. In Jesus' Name,
Amen.

December 5

And Pilate pronounced sentence that their demand be granted.
And he released the man they were asking for who had been
thrown into prison for insurrection and murder, but he delivered
Jesus to their will. (Luke 23:24-25)

This is peer pressure at its worse and most tragic. Pilate
gave in to the pressure to release Barabbas, a murderer,
and sentenced Jesus to death. He probably feared losing
his position and being hated by the people, so he gave in to
the demands of the mob, even though he knew that Jesus
had done nothing wrong.

How about you? When the heat is on and everyone is
looking at you to see what you're going to do, how do you
handle the pressure? Do you give in, or do you stand up for
what is right, even if means being unpopular? Stay strong,
and do the right thing.

Dear Lord God,
Doing the right thing is hard sometimes—I'm afraid of being friendless and alone. Help me to remember that I am
never alone, for You are with me always, and give me the
courage to do what's right. In Jesus' Name,
Amen.

December 6

Therefore, prepare your minds for action, keep sober in spirit,
fix your hope completely on the grace to be brought to you at
the revelation of Jesus Christ. (1 Peter 1:13)

We need to realize that with the Holy Spirit in our lives,
we can have self-control. It doesn't matter what we are
being tempted with. It's a cop-out to try claiming that we just
have no control over sin in our lives.

Exercising self-control is walking in the light, saying no to all ungodliness. 2 Corinthians 10:5 tells us what to do: "We are destroying speculations and every lofty thing raised up against the knowledge of God, and we are taking every thought captive to the obedience of Christ". In other words, when an unclean thought pops into your mind, you demolish it by saying no to it and refusing to give in to it, because that would make your life inconsistent with the way God wants you to live it.

Mighty God,
I know that I am powerless alone, but You are the Victor over sin. Let me use the Holy Spirit's gift of self-control to resist sinful thoughts and actions, so that my speech and conduct may be a reflection of Your perfect love. In Jesus' Name,
Amen.

December 7

Let no unwholesome word proceed from your mouth, but only such a word as is good for edification according to the need of the moment, so that it will give grace to those who hear. (Ephesians 4:29)

Words can both build up and tear down. If you've ever had someone call you a name or say something hurtful to you, then you know what I'm talking about. People can feel either valued or worthless from what we say. We can lose valued friendships from our words if we're not careful.

"With it we bless our Lord and Father, and with it we curse men, who have been made in the likeness of God; from the same mouth come both blessing and cursing. My brethren, these things ought not to be this way." (James 3:9-10). When our speech is motivated by Satan, it's full of unspiritual thoughts and ideas, selfish ambition, and cruelty. When our speech is motivated by God, it's full of mercy, love, consideration for others, sincerity, peace, and righteousness.

Out of the abundance of the heart the mouth speaks—what's in your heart?

Lord God,
I know how it feels to be "torn down" with words. Help me to remember that before opening my mouth. Let my words be honest and caring, a reflection not of what's in my poor heart, but instead of Your love and mercy and goodness. In Jesus' Name,
Amen.

December 8

He will be great and will be called the Son of the Most High; and the Lord God will give Him the throne of His father David; and He will reign over the house of Jacob forever, and His kingdom will have no end. (Luke 1:32-33)

How has your holiday season been so far? Hectic? Are you going a million miles an hour and feel like you're still not getting enough done? Are you running around trying to get all of the gifts bought, the decorations up, the parties planned—all while trying not to run out of money?

If so, maybe you need to spend a little more time in prayer and reading God's Word to remember what this season is really all about. It can be very easy to get caught up in all the hustle and bustle, and get yourself worked up and worn out. The next thing you know, Christmas is over and you haven't really enjoyed the holiday.

Make sure you take the time to spend with the One who made this wonderful season possible: the Son of the Most High, Jesus.

Extra time in the Word: Luke 1-2: the story of Jesus' birth.

Father in Heaven,
I don't want to forget who this holiday season is all about.

Let me enjoy the gifts, the decorations, the parties—but always with a spirit of repentance and joyful anticipation, awaiting the birth of the Messiah. In Jesus' Name,
Amen.

December 9

The wind blows where it wishes and you hear the sound of it, but do not know where it comes from and where it is going; so is everyone who is born of the Spirit. (John 3:8)

If someone asked me to show God to him, describe what He looks like, well, I would have a hard time doing that, and so would you. If someone asked me to show him the wind, describe what it looks like, well, I would have a hard time doing that as well. That doesn't mean the wind doesn't exist, does it? We see the effects of the wind every day. I've felt a cool breeze on a hot summer day, heard it moving through the trees, even seen rooftops ripped off by strong winds. Even though we don't actually see the wind, we believe in it because we feel its presence and feel its effects.

God is the same way. I see the effect of God in my own life on a daily basis. I can't tell you what He looks like, but I can show you the effects of God in my life and the lives of others. Even though we don't see God with our eyes, never doubt His powerful presence in our lives.

Eternal God,

I know You are there, even when I feel most alone. Thank You for the blessed assurance of Your presence through all that I have and all that I am. In Jesus' Name,
Amen.

December 10

the weapons of our warfare are not of the flesh, but divinely powerful for the destruction of fortresses. (2 Corinthians 10:4)

All of us, at one time or another, have had to face one of Satan's "fortresses" in our life, an addiction sin that we just can't seem to get rid of. Well, good news can be found in this verse: We can demolish those strongholds!

I like that Paul uses the word "destruction" rather than "working at" or "chipping away." What a bummer it would be to know that we had to "chip away" at that fortress in our life—it sounds like such a slow, painful process. Instead, we can totally destroy the stronghold that has us trapped. But note that it's not with normal weapons that we demolish strongholds or fortresses, but with the spiritual weapons God has given us. We need to pray, renew our minds with God's Word daily, and find friends who will support us and hold us accountable.

Let this verse give you the hope and courage to demolish whatever strongholds you face, in Jesus' name. It *can* be done!

Almighty Father,

You demolished death and the devil through the sacrifice of Your Son. Let me lean on Your strength to resist sin and temptation in my daily life. Your might is wondrous to behold! In Jesus' Name,

Amen.

December 11

Do not call to mind the former things, or ponder things of the past. Behold, I will do something new... (Isaiah 43:18-19)

God has wonderful plans for all of us who love Him. Some people, however, can't get over hurts and problems of the past. They dwell on everything that's happened to them and harbor anger or resentment or hurt feelings. These people are being robbed of what God wants for them. On the other hand, there are people who have had some terrible things happen to them, and yet are living victorious lives for Christ. They simply refuse to allow feelings to control them.

When you feel trapped by the past, controlled by hurt or anger, do not yield to those feelings. Instead, say "I can do all things through Him who strengthens me" (Philippians 4:13), and move on, because God is doing new things in your life.

Dear Heavenly Father,

Wash away the pain of my old problems and sorrows. Let me not dwell on the past, and help me to deal with present challenges in a healthy way, so that I don't allow bitterness or self-pity to prevent me from living my life in Christ to the fullest. Thank You for giving me new life. In Jesus' Name, **Amen.**

December 12

If we confess our sins, He is faithful and righteous to forgive us our sins and to cleanse us from all unrighteousness. (John 1:9)

Confessing our sins is admitting to God that we realize our own selfish actions and attitudes are not His will for us. It is also showing our desire to be forgiven. When we confess our sins, it's making a conscious decision to turn our backs on those sins, and, most importantly, making a change in our attitude and behavior. "I acknowledged my sin to You, and my iniquity I did not hide; I said, 'I will confess my transgressions to the LORD'; and You forgave the guilt of my sin." (Psalm 32:5).

Remember, it's never too late to confess any sin. There is no sin too great for God to forgive.

Gracious God,

It's hard sometimes to admit my sins, even to You—even to myself. Give me the courage to own up to my mistakes and to turn away from them, so that I may receive Your forgiveness and start fresh. In Jesus' Name,
Amen.

December 13

If you love me, you will keep my commandments. (John 14:15)

Our parents have rules for us that they expect us to honor. For example, you probably have a rule that requires you to be home by a certain time. This is for your own good, as your parents care about your well-being and want you to be safe and secure.

Our Heavenly Father does the exact same thing. His commandments are not meant to be mean or hard; He doesn't make up strict rules just for fun, which we must then struggle to follow. His rules, like those of your parents, are for our own good.

Keep the fourth commandment and honor your parents by obeying their rules. Even if they don't all make sense to you now, you will eventually find that they were all for your benefit in making you a happy, safe, and secure person.

Heavenly Father,

You loved Your children enough to give us Your commandments through which we learn how we should live. Help me not to struggle against rules that are for my own good. Thank You for Your loving care. In Jesus' Name,
Amen.

December 14

Be on your guard! If your brother sins, rebuke him; and if he repents, forgive him. (Luke 17:3)

When we see friends living in what we know is rebellion to God's Word, we need to confront them. This is necessary sometimes, but it must be done with love and the proper attitude. Remember, it is always to help them repent and return to God, not to hurt them or show them that we're the better Christian.

Pray for strength and guidance in how to help bring your brother or sister back to the Lord, and be willing to accept such a rebuke yourself when you stray. "My brethren, if any among you strays from the truth and one turns him back, let him know that he who turns a sinner from the error of his way will save his soul from death and will cover a multitude of sins." (James 5:19-20).

Almighty God,
Thank You for giving me a community of Christian brothers and sisters in which I can grow and learn to love you better. When I see an erring fellow Christian, please give me the words to say to help bring this friend back to You. And when I am the one who has gone astray, please guide one of my brothers or sisters to do the same for me. In Jesus' Name,
Amen.

December 15

The voice of one crying in the wilderness, 'Make ready the way of the LORD, make his paths straight. Every ravine will be filled, and every mountain and hill will be brought low; the crooked will become straight, and the rough roads smooth; and all flesh will see the salvation of God.' (Luke 3:4-6)

Have you seen something, some sight or event, that

absolutely captured your imagination? Afterward, you can't stop thinking about it. I had a friend who went on a tour around Cape Canaveral, after which he got to be there to watch a Space Shuttle launch. He came back transformed and excited, thinking about nothing except what he should study in school so that one day he would become an astronaut-scientist who would be selected for a Shuttle mission.

When John the Baptist tells people that they should prepare to see the Salvation of God, he is telling them that they will get to witness something great, the greatest thing, something that will transform the universe. That thing is the Incarnation of God in Jesus Christ.

Dearest Lord,

During this Advent I wait to see something really great, because I am waiting to celebrate Your coming to earth to be one of us, born in a stable in Bethlehem one very cold and dark night. You were born a child and yet a king, and born to die for the sake of our salvation. In Jesus' Name, **Amen.**

December 16

The LORD will make you the head and not the tail, and you only will be above, and you will not be underneath, if you listen to the commandments of the LORD your God, which I charge you today, to observe them carefully... (Deuteronomy 28:13)

The world views success as having wealth, or lots of friends, or lots of "stuff." God views success differently.

In the book of Jeremiah, Jeremiah seemed totally unsuccessful. He had given up his money to serve God; he had no family; he was not popular, and no political or religious people would listen to his advice. But he was the one God chose to be a prophet to the nations.

Remember that God measures success by our obedience and faithfulness to Him and His Word, for which we are rewarded.

Sovereign Lord,
You make us Your children, Your disciples, Your chosen ones, though we are unworthy. Set me free from the vain desire for worldly success, and make me open to Your call, wherever it leads. In Jesus' Name,
Amen.

December 17

Let no one seek his own good, but that of his neighbor. (1 Corinthians 10:24)

If you really want to know people, look at their priorities and see what is important to them. Do they make time for friends, family, church, and community, or do they tend to their own needs first?

Putting God first in our lives is the most important priority we can have. When we don't have our priorities straight, we start focusing on ourselves and stop doing what is right in God's eyes. Remember to "trust in the LORD with all your heart and do not lean on your own understanding. In all your ways acknowledge Him, and He will make your paths straight." (Proverbs 3:5-6).

Holy Father,
You are above all things, whether we recognize it or not. Make my paths straight; help me not to be selfish or self-centered, but to love and serve You first, and then, through Your love, serve my neighbor. In Jesus' Name,
Amen.

December 18

I love the LORD, because He hears my voice and my supplications. Because He has inclined His ear to me, therefore I shall call upon Him as long as I live. (Psalm 116:1-2)

How many of us feel overwhelmed by problems, especially at this time of year? Probably quite a few. So isn't it great to know that God always hears us, that we can cry to Him, and He will never turn away?

Problems, fears, and grief don't vanish on the day we become Christians, nor can we realistically expect every moment of our holiday season to be jolly and festive. But when our holiday cheer breaks down and problems intrude into our lives, God will always help us. Call to Him as long as you live. He will not turn you away.

Merciful Father,

There is so much pressure to be "up" at this time of year, but because of the stress of the holiday season, I don't always feel that way. Grant that I may remain focused on the birth of Your Son; let me seek and find comfort and hope in the Advent of my Savior. In Jesus' Name,
Amen.

December 19

And He was saying to them all, "If anyone wishes to come after me, he must deny himself, and take up his cross daily and follow me. (Luke 9:23)

People can be very fickle, committed only to things that are convenient for them. This includes jobs, relationships, friendships, even marriage. It's so sad to hear of people getting tired of their commitment to their spouse for one reason or another—maybe using the excuse that they've "fallen out of love," like love is a hot air balloon that you can fall out of—

and deciding to throw in the towel and leave.

It requires much more strength and commitment than this to follow Christ. In this scripture, Jesus tells his listeners that they must be willing to deny themselves. In other words, be willing to give up everything to follow Him. Hard words, but this will show if the person is really ready to make that commitment to Him.

You probably will never be required to give up everything and everyone important to you, but take this opportunity to give some hard thought to your commitment to Christ and your loved ones. If you think the commitment is lacking, work on it.

Dear Lord God,

You give us our friends and loved ones for mutual support and encouragement, and You gave us Your Son for our salvation. Help me to treasure both, and to rededicate myself every day to be a faithful son, daughter, brother, sister, or friend to my loved ones, and most of all, a faithful servant to You. In Jesus' Name,

Amen.

December 20

Therefore we do not lose heart, but though our outer man is decaying, yet our inner man is being renewed day by day. For momentary, light affliction is producing for us an eternal weight of glory far beyond all comparison, while we look not at the things which are seen, but at the things which are not seen; for the things which are seen are temporal, but the things which are not seen are eternal. (2 Corinthians 4:16-18)

Do not lose heart! It probably doesn't take much convincing to tell you that this is the hardest time of year to feel happy. December is fraught with difficulties such as winter darkness, cold weather, and the sheer tyranny of the mad rush to buy presents for people. It can all seem very shallow and meaningless.

But apart from the way-overdone secular celebration of Christmas, there is a sure, eternal truth revealed finally at Christmas and Epiphany: the pure and simple message of Jesus. The heartwarming sentiment of the Christmas season can seem very fleeting, but there is an eternal glory that all of us should recognize when we listen to the carols and stories. Take heart in this! Celebrate Christmas with the wonderful knowledge that you know the true meaning of it all, in spite of everything within the season which can impose stress or mislead.

Glorious Lord,
The meaning of this holy season should be obvious to all, and yet I know that many people who say "Merry Christmas" don't even believe in You. Don't let me get sidetracked by everything else in this season. I want to see Your glory revealed in Bethlehem, just as the shepherds witnessed. In Jesus' Name,
Amen.

December 21

Martha then said to Jesus, "Lord, if You had been here, my brother would not have died. "Even now I know that whatever You ask of God, God will give You." (John 11:21-22)

Even though Martha's brother was already dead, she still believed he could be brought back to life. What faith! Can you imagine what she might have said if she had thought only about her feelings and by her circumstances? After all, things couldn't have looked any worse: Jesus had taken His time answering Mary and Martha's frantic message that their brother Lazarus was gravely ill. By the time He got there, Lazarus was dead. Martha could have yelled at Jesus, told him that if He would only have gotten there quicker, Lazarus wouldn't have died. But she was a woman of great faith. She looked past her circumstances and saw the situation through the eyes of faith. Follow Martha's example in your own life.

Dear Lord God,
You can and do perform miracles every day. Give me the faith of Martha; help me to see my own life through the eyes of faith, placing my hope completely in You, and trusting in Your will for me. In Jesus' Name,
Amen.

December 22

...work out your salvation with fear and trembling; for it is God who is at work in you, both to will and to work for His good pleasure. (Philippians 2:12-13)

This is to encourage anyone struggling with old "sin patterns" in their lives. A true Christian doesn't have to keep going back to the old ways and repeating old sins, for God makes change possible. If it weren't possible, He wouldn't talk about doing it in His Word. In order not to fall back into our old ways, we must remember to submit ourselves to God and to resist the devil so he will flee from us. We must also put on the "armor of God" described in Ephesians 6:10-17 and mentioned elsewhere in this devotional. You *can* break free of sinful habits.

My Lord,
I know that I am a new creation in You. Please help me to avoid situations that tempt me into sin and separate me from Your love. Thank You for the true freedom I have found in You. In Jesus' Name,
Amen.

December 23

Philip said to Him, 'Lord, show us the Father, and it is enough for us.' Jesus said to him, 'Have I been so long with you, and yet you have not come to know me, Philip? He who has seen me has seen the Father...' (John 14:8-9)

Philip thought that Jesus was simply some sort of sage revealer of God, not God Himself. He didn't realize quite what he was asking, even though he knew that no one could "see God's face and live." But Jesus sets him straight when he tells Philip directly who and what he really is: "He who has seen me has seen the Father." It is hard to understand, but the Incarnate Son of God is a person of the Trinity, co-equal with the Father and the Spirit in power, glory, eternity and divinity. The incident with Philip shows us another reason why Jesus came. In Him we can finally see God, because God has finally come to present the face of His divine presence and identity, and the face that we see is the face of Jesus Christ.

We don't need to look in any other place for the fullest revelation of God, because in Jesus we see God and are shown God's inestimable love.

Almighty God,

I don't always understand how Jesus can be both fully God and fully human, and I sure don't always understand a concept about Your identity such as the Trinity. But I believe in You, and I trust that I will one day understand, even as You fully understand me, and have created me out of Your divine mercy and goodness. Teach me to seek Your divine presence each morning when I awake to pray and read the holy words of Your Scripture. In Jesus' Name,
Amen.

December 24

And an angel of the Lord suddenly stood before them, and the glory of the Lord shone around them; and they were terribly frightened. But the angel said to them, "Do not be afraid; for behold, I bring you good news of great joy which will be for all the people; for today in the city of David there has been born for you a Savior, who is Christ the Lord. This will be a sign for you: you will find a baby wrapped in cloths and lying in a manger." And suddenly there appeared with the angel a multitude of the heavenly host praising God and saying, "Glory to God in the highest, and on earth peace among men with whom He is pleased." (Luke 2:9-14)

The shepherds had to have been the simplest people possible in this wondrous story. They lived in the fields with their flocks, a very lonely and undervalued job. But they were the ones who first heard the tremendous, majestic chorus reporting the Good News. They were the ones who were given the sudden glimpse into the divine, eternal realm and heavenly, angelic court.

As a believer, don't ever think of yourself as being so simple that you are of no value. In Christ's holy name you have an eternal inheritance stored up in heaven. The life you now live is an eternal life lived with God in Christ. Your life, from the perspective of eternity, is now no longer or ever again an ordinary life. You are now one of the heavenly host who praise God, and who will live with him in eternal righteousness, innocence and blessedness.

Great and Glorious Lord,
I give You thanks during this beginning of Christmas that You have chosen someone as undeserving as I am to hear the Good News given to us from the heavenly realm. Thank you for conforming us to the image of Your beloved Son Jesus Christ, who is born in our hearts this season, to the glory of Your name and kingdom. In Jesus' Name,
Amen.

December 25

For a child will be born to us, a son will be given to us; and the government will rest on His shoulders; and His name will be called Wonderful Counselor, Mighty God, Eternal Father, Prince of Peace. (Isaiah 9:6)

Merry Christmas!

This is what Christmas is all about. Jesus, who came to the earth as a baby; who took all our sins upon Himself and was crucified on a cross; and who rose on the third day. He will return again to earth, not as a baby but as the King of Kings and Lord of Lords, to whom every knee will bow and every tongue will confess that He is Lord.

This is why we celebrate this season. So don't get upset if you don't get everything you wanted for Christmas, because you have received the greatest gift of all, eternal life. If you're feeling empty inside and are longing for peace this holiday season, it can be yours. Ask God to forgive your sins, cleanse you, and come into your heart.

Let our Mighty God, the Everlasting Father, the Prince of Peace, make this a truly joyous holiday for you.

God of Bountiful Providence,

All that I need this season I now have found in You. I have stood at the manger and found the greatest treasure possible in the face of a little baby, who is Your divine Son and the Savior of a fallen and needful world. Thank You for the greatest gift and the greatest love anyone could ever receive! In Jesus' Name,

Amen.

December 26

"Now Lord, You are releasing Your bond-servant to depart in peace, according to Your word; for my eyes have seen Your salvation, which You have prepared in the presence of all peoples, a light of revelation to the Gentiles, and the glory of Your people Israel." (Luke 2:29-32)

Many people had seen the baby Jesus so far, but most had not understood or appreciated what they were seeing. An old man, Simeon, somehow knew, finally, that this was Israel's consolation, and the goal of his lifelong quest to see God face-to-face. In the Old Covenant, Moses had been told rather oddly that "No one may see my face and live!" But now, in the New Covenant, there would be direct access to God through a loving, gracious Savior who was God Incarnate — God in human flesh. The disciple Philip had once said to Jesus, "Lord, show us the Father and that will be enough." But Jesus simply told him the truth: "Philip, if you've seen me you've seen the Father"!

The same thing happened with Simeon that day, except that Simeon knew immediately what and whom he was holding when he held the baby Jesus: the eternal, invisible, almighty God had appeared and finally shown His face, and the face looking back at Simeon was the innocent face of a baby.

Eternal Lord,

Now that I know about Your Son born in Bethlehem, strengthen my faith to believe the Greatest Story ever told. Inspire and guide my life as it is lived out as Your beloved child. Show me the right paths, and teach me what I should do for my vocation. Thank You for such an incredible joy in knowing You! In Jesus' Name,

Amen.

December 27

And you have said, 'I am a god, I sit in the seat of gods in the heart of the seas'; yet you are a man and not God, although you make your heart like the heart of God... (Ezekiel 28:2)

Pride—there it is again. I'm not referring to "good" pride, that is, self-confidence and feeling good about ourselves or something we've accomplished. No, what the above verse describes is vanity, arrogance, placing ourselves above others because of an exaggerated sense of our own importance. That kind of pride always brings trouble.

Pride separates us from God, when we can't admit even to Him that we've made a mistake or we need some help. What good does it do to try fooling God? Pride separates us from our friends, too. It makes us value ourselves more than those around us—and how can we love our neighbor as ourselves if we think we're the most important person around?

Separation from God, separation from our friends; it's just not worth it. Make "humility" one of the things you ask God for in your prayer time, so you won't suffer the effects of pride.

Almighty God,
I am indeed proud of who I am in You, but give me a humble heart, so that I may not, through vanity and arrogance, hurt my friends and family or separate myself from Your love. In Jesus' Name,
Amen.

December 28

For the commandment is a lamp and the teaching is light; And reproofs for discipline are the way of life... (Proverbs 6:23)

If only people took reading the Bible more seriously, they would realize what it can do for them. Reading the Word of

God is vital to our good relationship with God; it's the most convenient means of communication from Him to us. Also, it helps us handle situations, instructing us in matters of relationships and marriage, parenting, morality, money, our duty to the poor, how to handle conflict, pride, gossip, and on and on.

In our search for answers on all of these issues, let's not forget that God has already given us all the answers through His Word, the Bible.

Author of all Goodness,

Thank You for Your Word. When I feel confused, alone, or frightened, help me to remember to turn to the Bible first, through which You speak directly to me and answer all my questions. Reading Your Word keeps me right where I want to be: close to You. In Jesus' Name,
Amen.

December 29

Finally, be strong in the Lord and in the strength of His might. (Ephesians 6:10)

A notion of the human individual that does not acknowledge God as Creator, Redeemer and Sanctifier assumes that deep within all of us exists everything, every resource and strength, that we would ever need to stay and guide us. Christians recognize, however, that we are sinful, fallen and imperfect beings who must look outside ourselves, beyond our own egos and selfish striving, to the divine source of all life, God Almighty, who created "the heavens and the earth," as well as each of us.

Throughout the Bible we read of God's mighty acts of redemption with His chosen people Israel, and how much He cares for each and every one of us. God is the ultimate power and authority, and God's nature has even been revealed to us in His own essential Power, Jesus Christ.

When you need power for living your life, power to be strong, and power for guidance amidst all of life's challenges, be strong in the Power of God, Jesus Christ, who is our blessing for everything we need in our life.

God of All Power, Majesty and Glory!

I give You thanks that even the hairs of my head are numbered, and known by You. You have created the greatest things in the universe, things beyond human comprehension, and yet You also created me and all humanity. Help me to remember Your many past blessings, and to be aware of Your present, daily care for each of us. In Jesus' Name, **Amen.**

December 30

"Therefore, come out from their midst and be separate," says the Lord. "And do not touch what is unclean; And I will welcome you." (2 Corinthians 6:17)

As Christians, we must work extra hard at being good examples, so that people will see we're different, so they'll "see your good works, and glorify your Father who is in heaven." (Matthew 5:16). Too many of us carry on with wordly or sinful habits, whether it's getting drunk, smoking, or using drugs; reading horoscopes or consulting psychics; sexual activity outside of marriage; or obscene or blasphemous language. This is really disturbing: we are supposed to be different.

Being "separate" from the world doesn't mean we have to live in a commune made up only of Christians, or that we can't have any friends who don't go to our church, or that we can't read anything but the Bible. It does mean that we are different because we are God's, and our actions and lives must show it.

Dear Heavenly Father,

Help me to be an example of Your love through my words and actions, not for my own sake, but to glorify You before others. Thank You for setting me apart as Your own. In Jesus' Name,

Amen.

December 31

Now to Him who is able to do far more abundantly beyond all that we ask or think, according to the power that works within us, to Him be the glory in the church and in Christ Jesus to all generations forever and ever. Amen. (Ephesians 3:20-21)

This verse is full of glorious hope. Look at this scripture and let it sink deep into your spirit, because it affirms once again that, no matter what you are facing, with God all things are possible. With all the darkness in the world, we need to know that this power of God is available to all of us, and we need to keep our spiritual batteries charged to the fullest, by praying daily and having devotions.

Let us, His people, who have received so much through Him and in Him, never fail to give Him the glory, for ever and ever. And let all God's people say: Amen!

Lord God,

I give You great thanks for this past year, and I look forward to the glories yet to be revealed in the coming year. May Your will be done, including in my life, and may I always look to the glory and majesty and power of Your holy name! In Jesus' Name,

Amen.